An Entry in the Train Register

J.D. Francis

First Published 2007

ISBN 978-0-9514636-1-1

Published by: J.D. Francis

Front Cover:
The Down Main Home Gantry at Newton Abbot East frames the signal box. The higher pair of signals refer to the Down Through line, the centre pair to the Down Relief and the right hand pair to the Down Main. These latter two are at the same height, giving no distinction of importance or speed between the two routes. The stop arms directing to the Through and Main lines are wooden and attached to Great Western kidney shaped spectacles whilst the Relief line signal has a later Western Region spectacle and enamel arm. The West box intermediate distant for the Relief line (centre) is fixed whilst the other two intermediates are both of the Westinghouse type pivoted on the signal motor. All are wooden. The three foot arm on the left routes to the shed and carriage sidings. Although applying to the Down Main, which is to the right, the gantry straddles the Down Siding leading out of Hackney Yard.

(Author)

DEDICATION

To the generations of Signalmen who undertook their duties as company servants.

ACKNOWLEDGEMENTS

In completing this book I would like to acknowledge the special assistance received from Chris Chapman who ran a critical eye over the text, provided some of his and his late father Tom's excellent photographs and jogged my memory on a few matters. Likewise Ian Wannell who kindly commented on the draft text, suggested improvements and reminded me of a few things I might otherwise have omitted. Thanks also to former colleague, now renowned author, Adrian Vaughan who was pleased to let me include some of his photographs. Most of all I must thank my wife Rachel for her encouragement and for her assistance in preparing the manuscript.

Diagrams of the signalling layouts throughout the West of England are available from the Signalling Record Society. Details regarding diagrams, publications and membership are available from the society's website at www.s-r-s.org.uk.

CONTENTS

FOREWORD

Fortune can manifest itself in many ways; it may be monetary, the result of a windfall; it may be receipt of a legacy or perhaps the outcome of a chance meeting. Sometimes fortune may smile upon us when achieving a result by design. Often the less tangible forms are like beauty, seen only in the eye of the beholder.

Fortune has bestowed itself on me in various ways and at various times. This book attempts to explain one fortune, an experience over a period of years which can never be repeated, for the environment in which it took place has altered irrevocably. These pages recall part of my life as a railway signalman. Had I known that I would one day write this book then perhaps I would have recorded notes or kept an extensive diary during that time. Sadly I did not and therefore I shall not know how many memories I have mislaid in the remoter corners of my mind. Life as a railway signalman was not a simple existence, there were good and bad times, highs and lows, but the overall experience I am most fortunate to have enjoyed. I was proud to do the job.

I first started to write this book whilst on holiday in Perth, Western Australia, a long way in distance and time from the Western Region of British Railways in the 1970s. Its production came from a desire to record the unique environment and life experienced in and around the signal box. It has taken many years of spare moments, in many countries, to compile but on each occasion that I have taken the time to stop and record my memories or to research some facts, I have been transported back to times and places that gave me immense satisfaction. I hope you enjoy sharing just some of my experiences, resurrected from a store cupboard of memories about the best time of my working career.

Leaving home at the tender age of four and travelling with my aunt to the Warwickshire village of Dorridge to stay with her and my uncle for the summer undoubtedly set the future course of my life. The suburban train journey from Kent into London was just the start. A dash across the capital from Charing Cross to Paddington in a black taxi heightened the adventure. I can vividly recall the black pannier tanks resting by the stop blocks, steam drifting roofwards from cylinders and pipes, not knowing then that these brought in the empty coaching stock from Old Oak Common. We hurried onto a platform, my aunt checking with the fireman of the pannier, who was leaning from his footplate, that the train was bound for Birmingham Snow Hill. Then, barely settled in a compartment, I experienced my first main line journey. We travelled out via High Wycombe, Princes Risborough, Banbury and Leamington to Knowle and Dorridge.

We walked Angus, the Highland terrier everyday to the footpath that crossed the railway on a narrow bridge just south of the station. Lasting memories were formed of steam hauled expresses on the main lines, local trains and long heavy freights dragging along the relief lines. At night, the freight and parcel trains could be heard labouring through the stillness and, between parted bedroom curtains, the red glow of a firebox and the outline of a locomotive could be seen across the rooftops.

Six summers later I visited again. This time diesels were beginning to usurp steam, but more detail sticks in the mind. There was the "Pines Express" heading for Bournemouth, local diesel multiple units, the dashing "Blue Pullman" on its way to Birmingham and a nearby signal box controlling a mixture of upper and lower quadrant signals. I watched the activity and listened to the sounds coming from the box and even spoke to the signalman on one occasion. The crashing levers and staccato ringing of the bells heightened the mystery of what went on inside.

With these new images firmly recorded in my mind, I began my first term at Maidstone Grammar School. The school had an extensive library with a fair range of railway books to whet the appetite of enthusiastic pupils. Amongst them was Norman Marlow's *Footplate and Signal Cabin*. Written in 1956, there had never before been a book which described so well the rudiments of signalling couched together with life in the box. Expertly written, the combination was captivating for me. The school copy had never previously been off the shelf as often as it was during my terms there. Many books are now available today telling reminiscences of railway life, some of them about signalling. Other books contained pictures of signal boxes, occasionally an interior shot with the signalman stood before his levers, block instruments and bells. But Marlow's book was not a reminiscence, rather a factual record that opened a window on a place and time in railway signalling which he told with both feeling and understanding.

Years later I was lucky enough to obtain a near mint copy of *Footplate and Signal Cabin* which still sits on my bookshelf. It was an inspiration to me then and it still inspires me today. Wanting to learn more about signalling I acquainted myself with Eddie Twitchen, one of the signalmen at our nearby station of Aylesford. Entering that box to find brightly coloured levers with burnished steel handles, polished linoleum and shining brass convinced me that here was an interest of which I would never tire. This was where the railway was controlled from. I met other signalmen in due course like Charlie Salter at Cuxton, Ken Gerrish at Gillingham B, Tony at Rainham and reliefmen like Jim Jelly enabling me to visit signal boxes further along the line and beyond. Under the encouraging tuition of Don Tippett, I was able to enjoy many occasions working the 115 lever signal box at Maidstone West.

During a summer holiday to Devon I sat on the platform at Totnes, watching and listening, fascinated by the variety of trains that passed. The signalman went about his business ringing bells and crashing levers. The motorail train called to unload holidaymakers' cars and the "Cornish Riviera" sailed through on its way west. I looked enviously across at the signal box on the opposite platform thinking what a wonderful place to be. A few days later, standing on the road bridge

The view from the footpath bridge just south of Knowle and Dorridge station with the signal box in the foreground between the main and relief lines. A Paddington bound express, hauled by a Brush type '4' passes, unusually, on the Up Relief line.

just west of Newton Abbot station I marvelled at the expansive scene of station, sidings, shed and semaphore signals. West box sat amidst the railway it controlled and I said to myself: "One day".

The West of England main line has always been one of the most enjoyable to ride over. For me it also holds memories invisible to any other observer. Today it is no longer controlled by mechanical signalling throughout its length and so for me has lost one of its main attractions; but there remain particular highlights in the journey that always stand out and which act as milestones in anticipation both for the journey and for the memories they trigger.

Running alongside the Kennet and Avon canal is enjoyable as both canal and railway climb towards Crofton. Passing down through Savernake the canal switches to the other side of the line and then, dropping out of the Vale of Pewsey beyond Patney, the vista down towards Westbury comes into view with the cement works chimney in the distance. Beyond the White Horse and through rural Somerset the line crosses over the River Parrett by a steel girder bridge and onto the ancient Levels. Having climbed Wellington Bank, under the watch of the nearby tower, the route bursts into Devon upon leaving Whiteball Tunnel. Departure from Exeter is followed by twisting around the Exe Estuary at Starcross alongside bobbing boats, the spit of sand at the Warren reaching across almost to Exmouth and then running around the ledge between sea and cliffs, an indelible impression of green, blue and red - all stark, bright and in contrast, before diving through tunnels and heading safely inland again alongside the Teign Estuary.

Like Devon, Cornwall is reached with the help of a man made structure but the view above the Tamar is savoured at a slow speed. Finally, after passing clay tips and derelict engine houses there is the short dash before journey's end from Cornwall's north coast to its south coast where the panorama of Mount's Bay opens up and the railway skirts the beach to its destination at Penzance. If I was to be a signalman anywhere, then it would have to be on this line.

The highlight of passing from Somerset into Devon took on even more significance once I had become a signalman at Whiteball. Living and working in the countryside here, and then at other country boxes, brought the beauty and the harshness of the seasons alive reminding me of the vivid accuracy of John Clare's opus poem *The Shepherd's Calendar*.

This book is dedicated to those Signalmen who were born to the job. They know who they are and I have received pleasure in knowing just a few of them.

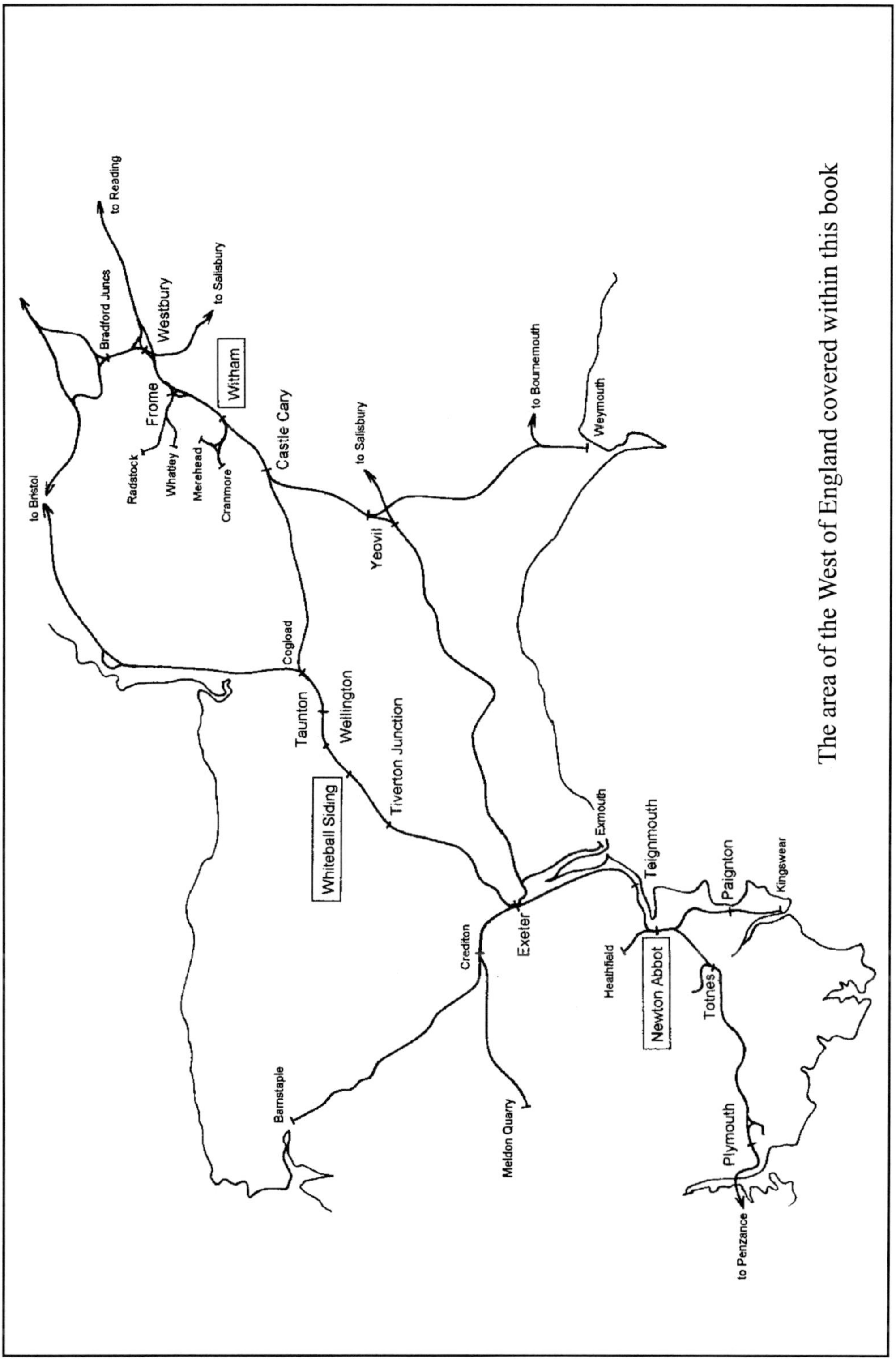

The area of the West of England covered within this book

CHAPTER ONE

RED, WHITE AND BLUE

A few miles to the west of Wellington, where the county of Somerset borders with its Devon neighbour, is White Ball Hill. The name Ball was used hereabouts to describe a knoll, or rounded hill. The main A38 trunk road climbs White Ball Hill on its way westwards towards Cullompton and part way up, on the Somerset side, is the village of White Ball whilst, a short way down the other side, in Devon, is the settlement of Red Ball.

Not far off the A38 between the two there is a small locality called, more simply, Redhill. This consists of no more than a couple of farms, halfway along the lane from the main road to the village of Burlescombe, just before it crosses the West of England main railway line on a steel overbridge known locally as Black Bridge. The A38 itself crosses the railway twice, firstly at Beam Bridge, part way up Wellington bank and then again over the top of Whiteball tunnel. The first location allowed the railway to establish a temporary terminus awaiting completion of the tunnel before extending the line through to Exeter in May 1844. Stagecoaches connected with the trains at this point for the leg to and from Exeter. In the latter case the road traveller is unaware of the line underneath. The tunnel is 1,092 yards long and marks the end of the long drag up Wellington bank from Taunton for down trains and the beginning of a speedy downhill sprint for up trains after the continual climb from Exeter. Unlike the Grand Western Canal, which took a westerly detour around the hill to follow the easier route of the river Tone, the Bristol and Exeter railway excavated a more direct line on its way west.

Down trains enter the eastern portal of the tunnel in Somerset and emerge from the western end in Devon, for the county boundary passes across the top of the hill. There is even a house above the tunnel reputed to be sat astride the boundary line. The 1 in 80 gradient of Wellington bank is just a taster for the West of England trains heading for the more gruelling South Devon banks of Dainton and Rattery but is nevertheless a formidable ascent to climb in its own right. Most people with an interest in railways and more especially Great Western devotees know it as the place where No. 3440 "City of Truro" reached 102.3 mph working an Up Ocean Mail train on 9th May 1904.

With the summit of the bank came Whiteball Siding Signal Box. The box was implanted into the deep cutting side forming the western approaches to the Tunnel and in the shadow of a narrow stone accommodation overbridge linking a farmer's fields split by the line. My first recollection of Whiteball box was on a late summer's evening when passing by on a Paddington bound express. The sun had set and in the twilight a glimpse of the brightly lit cabin penetrated my compartment. It left an impression of an oasis against the labouring sound of the diesel hydraulic locomotive just surmounting the grade before being swallowed by the super blackness of the tunnel. I did not know it at the time but that imprint was eventually to lead me to the box four years later and the start of my life as a signalman.

Why did I choose Whiteball? The answer is simple. It fulfilled my idea of what constituted a good starter box on the West of England main line with a bit of interest and fortunately it had a vacancy at just the right time. There was also a vacancy available at Cogload to the east of Taunton where the Berks and Hants line 'cut off' from Athelney joined in alongside the original route from Bristol, but that initial twilight memory of Whiteball tipped the balance.

I was looking forward very much to being a Signalman now that I had finally admitted it was my true vocation. Don Tippett at Maidstone West was right all along and if he had not told me to stop pretending and go and do it, perhaps I might never have done so. Thanks Don. Although I had been brought up in former South Eastern and Chatham country, visits to the West of England and books on the GWR had drawn my attention that way. Moving from the Southern Region to the Western whilst maintaining continuity of service and, at the same time transferring between the Signal and Telecommunications department and the Traffic department, proved an interesting challenge for the bureaucracy of British Railways.

The first morning, before 8am when finally entering the box, has happy memories for me only eclipsed by those a few weeks later once alone and in sole charge. I arrived a little late that day having missed the Redhill turning and become lost around the lanes of Westleigh and Burlescombe looking for Black Bridge. I eventually realised my mistake in navigation and found the white painted wicket gate adjacent to the bridge that crossed the line. The gate had a letter box attached. This was provided for the delivery of post to the signal box by the Royal Mail, such was its remoteness now from the nearest station. The lane, barely wide enough for cars, had a lay-by gouged into the hedge at this point so that the signalmen who came by car could park there. I had a motorbike and this I took through the gate to a path, down the bank and under the bridge out of sight from the road for safety. From here it was a quarter mile walk alongside the down loop line to the box which could be seen jutting forward under the arch of the stone bridge linking the fields. This was a walk performed by others many times before and to be repeated almost daily by myself for a time in all weathers.

The autumn mist was lifting and the watery sunshine declaring its reluctant presence as I walked up the line. Entering the box I found Glenn Merchant, a Taunton special class relief signalman with whom I had spoken before over the telephone. He proved himself to be even more pleasant a person in reality. A lifelong railwayman, including National Service at Longmoor, Glenn, like most signalmen, held a fascinating store of memories and tales. He was in his fifties and, as a special class relief signalman, had reached the top grade of his profession. Although many signal boxes had been shut he and his other Taunton based colleagues covered from Whiteball Siding through to Somerton, including the two remaining big boxes in Taunton itself - West Station and East Junction. After a cup of tea and a chat the working of the box was passed over to me under his watchful eye. I was now a "Strapper", as many a young learner had become known when starting out in their first box and I was now on the "Broad Gauge" railway.

I had learnt the rudiments of the signalman's job whilst still a schoolboy in my spare time and then latterly whilst working on the Southern Region in the Signal and Telecommunications department around various suburban boxes. Here though was a main line and the personal requirement to be perfectly familiar with the rules and regulations as well as local instructions and special bell codes which had to be learnt. That was not all: I found there were new railway words and phrases peculiar to the Western like "Groundman", "Backboard" and "Runner" and I had to learn West Country phraseology and understand the local dialect too, in order to converse and make sense; especially over the telephone which always managed to emphasise the slow drawl of the brogue with its lengthened vowels, its rolling r's, the letter s pronounced z as in Zummerzet and the letter f as v like in varmer for farmer. Sounds like "Ooh aar", terms of endearment like "Me Dear" and "My Lover" and phrases like "Ow be?" and "Where be too?" were all new to me, as was the use of "You'm" for "You are" and "They" for "Those" or "Them". Conversely, I must have sounded wildly out of place with my Kentish accent. With encouragement from Glenn as my tutor I soon grew in confidence, the working of the box becoming second nature.

While learning I was able to visit the adjacent boxes at Wellington and Tiverton Junction and even obtain some overtime shifts as a "Groundman" during single line working on Saturday nights, including a shift as a hand signalman at Wellington when the crossover and loop points there were renewed. Single line

AT WELLINGTON.–The Main lines trailing crossover with slip Connection to No.1 Siding and the trailing connection from Down Main to No.1 Siding together with all the associated Disc Signals have been taken out of use. The Disc in the Down Loop reading to Down Main has also been taken out of use.

SUNDAY 1 DECEMBER – AT WELLINGTON.–A new trailing Main lines crossover with associated Disc signals will be brought into use as shown in heavy type on the diagram. The Up Main Starting signal will be recovered and the existing Up Main Advanced Starting signal will be renamed Up Main Starting. Track circuits will be adjusted accordingly.

(1)

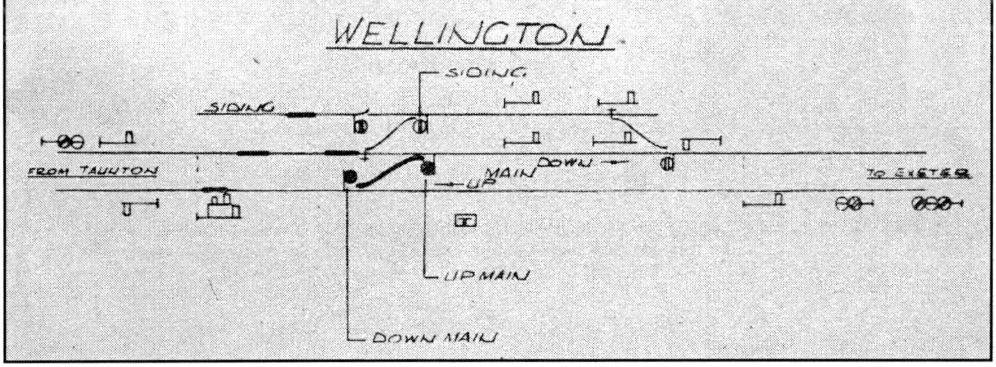

An extract from Section C of the K2 Weekly Notice showing the entry for the point renewals at Wellington.

3. COGLOAD TO PENZANCE

UNTIL FURTHER NOTICE

84–Cogload and Taunton East Jn.	All lines	07 30 to 18 30 (Daily). Bridgeworks. 161 and 161¼ mp. Machinery in use. Contractor's men at site.
85–Exeter City Basin and Exminster	Down and Up	07 30 to 19 00 (Daily). Contractors pile driving 197¾ and 198 mp. Machinery in use. Materials lying about.
86–Teignmouth	Side of Down	07 30 to 16 30 (Daily). Roadworks. 208¾ and 209 mp.
87–Teignmouth and Newton Abbot East	Down and Up	07 00 to 17 00 (Daily). Bridgeworks. At 213m. 1ch. Contractor's machinery at site. Materials lying about.
88–Saltash and St. Germans	Down and Up	07 00 to 17 00 (Daily). Viaduct repairs. 255m. 75chs. Machinery in use. Contractors men at site.

SATURDAY, 30 NOVEMBER TO SUNDAY, 1 DECEMBER

89–Silkmill Crossing and Whiteball Tunnel	Down Main Down Main BLOCKED	22 45 (Sat.) to 04 45 (Sun.) 04 45 to 15 30 (Sun.) SLW OVER UP MAIN FROM 10 45 (SUN.)
ALSO 90–Wellington	Down Loop BLOCKED	04 45 to 15 30 (Sun.)
	Down Main BLOCKED	15 30 to 17 00 (Sun.) DOWN TRAINS VIA DOWN LOOP.
ALSO 91–Whiteball Tunnel and Wellington	Up Main BLOCKED	22 45 (Sat.) to 10 45 (Sun.) SLW OVER DOWN MAIN. Track renewals. 170 and 170¼ mp. Crane and Traxcavator in use. Signal box open. **Victory and Bradford Crossing Barriers manned.**

See next page

Part of the page from Section B of the same K2 detailing the possessions and single line working associated with the renewals at Wellington . Ivor Herridge has written "See next page" at the bottom to refer to the arrangements for the next day, Sunday.

working was in force from Silk Mill Crossing through to Whiteball. I was positioned out at Wellington's Down Home signal, working under the directions of the signalman to display either a red or green lamp to down trains depending on whether it was safe for them to pass the signal and proceed past the worksite, where a crane was working, towards the signal box. Later I took the opportunity to see inside other boxes in the area during time off and to meet colleagues in order to put faces to voices. The two big Taunton boxes were impressive with their long lever frames, acres of floor area, dozens of windows and arrays of instruments. Amazingly everything shone from constant care. East Junction was the busier of the two and this is where the local National Union of Railwaymen (NUR) rep' resided in the guise of Ron Squires.

At 14 feet by 12 feet there was little room inside Whiteball box; you could not swing the proverbial cat. The space was dominated by the 27 lever frame and block shelf above, both at the front of the box. The diagram was fixed above the block shelf in a wooden frame that was too big for it which meant the painted linen depiction sat at the bottom with space around it to the sides and top. An assortment of instruments adorned the shelf, including four track circuit indicators, all for the down line, there being no track circuits on the up line. The block instrument to Tiverton Junction had an associated bell with a dome shape whilst that to Wellington was provided with a cow bell. The block shelf was suspended from the ceiling by two X shaped brackets. The bracket nearest the door had three detonators clipped to it ready for use in case of an emergency. As well as being used as fog signals, detonators were used to protect the line in the event of an accident, a failed train or other mishap. Like most boxes on the Western there were also levers in the frame which, when pulled, placed a pair of detonators on the rail. One lever, painted with alternate black and white chevrons pointing upwards, operated a placer for the up line, another, with the chevrons pointing downwards, a placer for the down line. With a shelf life of five years, every detonator was embossed with its date of manufacture and each year the newly manufactured "dets" were coated with a different colour paint on a seven year cycle of yellow, blue, white, orange, red, green and grey to leave twenty four months before an out of date colour appeared again. The colours rotated in this order. Hanging by string from a hook above the front windows was a card gradient diagram covering the line between Taunton and Exeter. This highlighted the severity of the approaches to Whiteball which occupied the highest spot on the seemingly mountainous depiction.

Unusually for a signal box, but again due to lack of space, there was no armchair. This was a distinct deficiency in comfort terms compared to most signal boxes, especially during the quieter periods. There was only a wooden chair and small table, plus the usual low stool found in every Great Western box, upon which I perched whilst learning. A couple of sheets of newspaper, changed each day for fresh, sufficed for a tablecloth. But the place was mine, my first box, and it was cosy.

Three wooden lockers set against the back wall provided storage space for the chattels of each of the three resident men. The Train Register book sat on the top of the lockers as there was no room for a separate Train Register desk. Above the telephones a fading black and white photograph of a steam hauled express passing the box was pinned to the wall near where notices, arranged in groups to cover special trains, engineering works and job vacancies, hung from bulldog clips hooked over nails. Above these was the roundhead clock, its face painted with roman numerals and the corporate GWR roundel symbol, its tick soporific. The coal stove was positioned in the back corner furthest from the door alongside which was a bucket of coal, small shovel and a brush. Coal was delivered by special train from Taunton every few months, being shovelled off the wagon onto a pile alongside the down siding a few yards from the bottom of the box steps. Sitting on a shelf screwed to the wall was a "Baby Belling" electric cooker that had a ring on the top for boiling the

Whiteball Siding signal box viewed from the Down Main line. The porchway at the top of the stairs is visible. *(Author)*

toilet facilities comprised a chemical (Elsan) lavatory in a small hut perched on the side of the cutting above the box. I found this too disgusting to use. Despite the mains connection, the electricity supply was insufficient to operate the motor points at the end of the goods loop so a hand generator, colloquially known as a "hurdy-gurdy", sat on a metal frame near the door.

Outside, the railway scene of tracks and signals was completed by the marching row of telegraph poles that followed the line westwards but to the east passed behind the box along the top of the cutting and took a route overland above the tunnel to the Somerset side. Opposite the box was milepost 174 signifying the distance from Paddington (via Bath), although via the newer and more direct Berks and Hants route, Whiteball Siding was a little under 154 miles from London. At this distance it was just over halfway, in mileage terms, between Paddington and Penzance. The cast iron nameplate on the front of the box confirmed its name yet the working timetable and notices always called the place Whiteball Tunnel, misleading many to use the wrong name. Even the Special Instructions for the box, or Footnotes as they were known, were headed by the incorrect name. This document was pinned to the wall and contained the additional local rules appertaining to Whiteball.

To "take on" in the job meant satisfying the local District Inspector (DI), Tom Earlam, at Exeter that I was competent. This involved a theory test

kettle or heating a saucepan and a small oven inside which doubled as a grill that could toast a slice of bread in thirty seconds flat. I learnt this from bitter experience because I had to scrape the carbon off the bread on more than one occasion. Just the distraction of a block bell ringing could mean all the difference between a slice of attractive golden toast and a piece of flaming black charcoal.

The luxury of mains electricity, an amenity some other boxes still lacked, meant that electric lighting was installed but there was no running water. An enamel bowl for washing usually sat upright on the window ledge, straddling the corners of two windows. Waste water was thrown out onto the ballast, as were any remnants of tea from the tea pot. A bucket of cold water and churns containing fresh water were kept in the porchway at the top of the stairs. The of the rules and regulations on a one to one basis across the DI's desk in his office at Exeter St Davids station, followed by a practical session in the signal box before being sent to Bristol to be further examined by Chief Inspector John Forrester. I caught the 06.30 Bristol, one of the few trains that called at Tiverton Junction, to go down to Exeter. A two hour grilling by the DI ended with advice that he would be up to watch me work the box during the following morning and, subject to his satisfaction, I should go to Bristol on the Friday. "Now" said Tom "I'll call Eddie Guerin in Middle box so that you can go across there until your next train back to Tiverton Junction". So, for the next hour or so I was able to enjoy watching the working at Exeter Middle in the company of Eddie and his booking boy until the 11.55 Paignton was belled up from West box. When I picked up my helmet and gloves to leave I found the gloves rather heavy, a cast iron lever collar had been placed by Eddie inside each as a prank.

The Chief Inspector's office in Bristol was located in the elegant B&E building outside Temple Meads station that had once been the headquarters of the Bristol and Exeter Railway. With trepidation I entered this befitting building to be welcomed by the words "Alright my lad" which was Mr Forrester's well known greeting whenever he met one of his signalmen. I left a couple of hours later elated - fully qualified. My first visit to Bristol had been nerve wracking but successful and I had the pleasure of signing the competence slip for Whiteball box. My wage would now be £29 per week as a class 'A' signalman. I had graduated from the stool to the chair.

I was to go to Bristol a number of times over subsequent years for rules exams upon promotion around the Region but remembered from that first encounter that Mr Forrester retained true practical railway experience from his many years of service that enabled him to always ask questions that could not be answered straight out of the book. He had, for example queried me over the intricacies of Regulation 25 (Failure of Block Signalling Apparatus) and what I would do to keep traffic moving under such circumstances. In particular he was keen to know what time intervals I would allow for different types of train when complete loss of communication between the boxes was experienced. The factors governing these time intervals were written in the regulation but nowhere, not even in the box footnotes, were any actual times written for guidance at each box. His probing therefore tested me to ensure that I had thought beyond the written words and that I knew how the rules and regulations were to be applied in real practical terms.

My new uniform, when it finally arrived, reflected the days of the glorious steam railway. Unlike the modern "continental" style uniforms issued to train crew and station staff in the 70s, signalmen and shunters continued to receive a black serge uniform with hat, neither of which had been modernised apart from the silver buttons and cap badge which all bore the BR double arrow symbol. This was the only recognition of change, confirming a growing opinion amongst signalmen that they were a forgotten, dying grade. However, I was much happier to wear this "traditional" uniform, proud to be a career railwayman, better still a signalman.

I met a lot of signalmen and learnt much about them in those early days. This was very much a world of older colleagues, each with a wealth of personal experience. I learnt of their hardships in previous years and their bitterness over the demise of Taunton as an important junction, following the closures of the Chard, Yeovil, Barnstaple and Minehead branches with the attendant loss of many boxes. This retrenchment was still fresh in their minds as they considered the inevitable approach of resignalling to the main line that would eventually see the abolition of all their boxes and their livelihoods. Some of the Taunton reliefmen that came to Whiteball, all special characters, were Tom Thresher, Ron Jenkins, Ken Marney, Ken Murray, Derek Lock, Ron Lockyer and Dennis Davey. Whiteball was at the western limit of their district which extended to Somerton in the other direction. The reliefmen coming to Whiteball were not covering the vacancy I was to fill but that of Bert Tooze who was away long term sick having been knocked off his motorbike by a car on the A38 on his way home from work. He never returned to the box, forced to contemplate early retirement through his injuries. Thc man I had come to replace was John Wyatt and once I had "taken on" he was able to assume his move to Stoke Canon, further down the line towards Exeter. John had started his career as a booking boy in Taunton East Junction before he was old enough for his own box at Taunton East Loop. Many lads had started out as booking boys in the large, busy boxes. It was an excellent form of "apprenticeship" preparing many a youngster for a career as a signalman. John had since been at Durston before transferring to Whiteball, and after Stoke Canon became a reliefman at Exeter, then moved to Cornwall when the Exeter area was eventually resignalled to work at Penzance and St Erth.

The other regular signalman at Whiteball was Ivor Herridge. Ivor had been coming to Whiteball for 32 years, first whilst at Burlescombe when the signalmen there shared the Whiteball weekend work and latterly full time after Burlescombe station and box had been abolished. A widower now, he lived in one of the railway cottages above the cutting at Burlescombe and would walk the mile or so up the track to relieve me each day. At twenty minutes before changeover time he would appear around the bend beyond Black Bridge as a small dark figure of a daytime with his haversack across his shoulder and cloth cap upon his head, or just a bobbing hand lamp of a night-time or winter morning. He needed that cloth cap for his haircut was always regimental to say the least, what nowadays would be called a number one. He would disappear for a moment at the bridge to climb the bank and check the mail box, then ten minutes later he would be in the warmth of the box exchanging a friendly greeting and preparing to let me depart.

My departure was back the way he had come, at least as far as the bridge, then up the muddy bank, first to open and pin back the gate with a rock kept for the purpose whilst the motorbike engine warmed and then to power up the slope and burst forth into the narrow lane. This was a hazardous exercise, especially the bursting forth, but fortunately no-one ever coincided in the lane with this action. The bank was too steep and slippery to wheel the bike up. Home was a rented house on a farm in Sampford Moor, three miles back across the border in Somerset. Sampford Moor was a quiet collection of farms and houses on the western edge of the Blackdown Hills just a couple of miles beneath the stone obelisk of the

Wellington Monument. Built to commemorate the victory of the Duke of Wellington over Napoleon, the three sided monument commanded a superb vantage point with views for miles around, being visible itself from the railway for much of the journey between Taunton and Whiteball.

Luckily, I had happened across this rental accommodation at Cordwents Farm advertised in the Exchange and Mart, a magazine more associated with the sale of goods but with a useful property section too. On the farm, owned by the Hayes family, I learnt to chop my own firewood and survive with the minimum of help. The Hayes were broad Somerset folk, he carried a ruddy outdoor complexion and would spread cream, not butter, on his bread and she would let me keep frozen food in her refrigerator. They worked the farm between them with part-time help from Jack who lived down in nearby Sampford Arundel. He drove a purple three-wheeler Reliant car and I would pass his house on the way to the box each day. Alongside their tractor in one of the barns I would keep my bike. Blackie, the sheepdog, would be there to see me off to work or to greet me back whatever time of day or night. Sampford Moor boasted a village pub, the Blue Ball, a Free House which sold a good selection of beverages, outside which was a telephone box giving connection to family and the rest of the world. In neighbouring Sampford Arundel there was a Post Office and a village hall. A barn dancing club met every other Wednesday night in the hall at 8pm, giving me the opportunity to join in with community activity.

Living on the farm brought many new experiences, from seeing and helping with the milking of the dairy herd to watching newborn lambs. Outside the house was an apple orchard where the trees displayed beautiful pink blossom in spring. In the autumn the falling apples were collected and placed between layers of straw in a giant hand press at the back of the barn to create home made scrumpy cider decanted into a variety of old bottles recycled for the purpose. Before spring had barely begun to show signs of arriving the same orchard played host to the lambing ewes, their new born kicking and jumping as they gambolled at play between the trees.

Wellington was the nearest town, four miles away. The closest bus route was from Rockwell Green, itself three miles distant. From here the bus went via Wellington to Taunton. It was a fair old walk to Rockwell Green so sometimes I would go on the bike, leaving it at the garage there where I normally filled up with petrol. Not that I could ever be a big spender on fuel of course, the tank only took a gallon at a time and that would last well over 100 miles.

The journey to work was mainly along some of those notorious single width lanes with ten foot high hedges on either side, apart from a short stretch on the A38 main road. My means of transport was a ubiquitous Honda 70. It was not a scooter nor could it be described truly as a motorbike, but it served a useful purpose. When I had originally left home in Aylesford, I did not possess a full driving licence, so a Honda 70 with 'L' plates affixed was a cheap method of instant transport. I packed the belongings I would most need into it's two panniers and more into a rucksack carried on my back before bidding farewell to my parents then wheeling it across the road to the railway station and into the van of a 2-HAP electric unit for the first leg of my journey west. The van happened to be at the front end so I sat up with the driver and guard for the five stops to the junction at Strood chatting about my new venture to which they offered much support. Driving across London from Charing Cross to Paddington proved rather hair raising in the traffic, dodging between big red buses and being cut-up by black cabs but the rest of the journey that Sunday was straightforward, including the navigation out of Taunton onto the A38, past Wellington and on to Sampford Moor and the farm before dusk.

Shift patterns comprised the standard three week rotation of 6am to 2pm (early turn), 10pm to 6am (night turn) and 2pm to 10pm (late turn). A week of early turn would be followed by a week of nights which would then be followed by a week of late turn. To save the railway money Whiteball was normally switched out from 1pm on Saturday until a quarter to midnight on Sunday during the winter and from 9pm Saturday during the summer when traffic was lighter. The late turn signalman therefore normally only worked Saturday afternoons during the summer timetable period. The early turn man on a Saturday would either switch-out or be relieved and then take rest until ten o'clock on Monday night. Meanwhile the night man would have Saturday night off as a rest night and return at 15 minutes to midnight on Sunday when he would open the box again. By booking on duty before midnight the shift registered as a Sunday turn, thus attracting an enhanced rate of overtime. Besides, the same man would be working a Monday shift anyway when he returned the following afternoon at 2pm after "doubling back" with just eight hours rest. The switch, which allowed the box to close, provided through electrical connection between the boxes on either side, the signals being left at clear to effectively extend the block section. Whiteball had been fitted with a switch since 21st March 1965. When the box was open on a Saturday afternoon, changeover took place at 1pm in common with virtually every other box in the country. This was a widely adopted mutual courtesy designed to favour the early turn man by providing him with a longer Saturday afternoon as part of his weekend off.

The box was, however, often open on many Saturday nights and Sundays for engineering work. Indeed my first turn of duty after "passing out" was on a Saturday night requiring the granting of an engineer's absolute possession on one line and single line working by Pilotman over the other. Talk about baptism of fire! Even in winter the box might remain open on a Saturday afternoon to shorten the section if additional trains were running such as when an important football match was being played at Torquay United or Plymouth Argyle. Football excursions would run under the code word "Footex", bringing the away team supporters during the late morning and early afternoon. The return trains would head back during the evening, full of happy or disappointed fans, depending on the score line from Plainmoor or Homepark. The Saturday shifts usually meant having to work Rest Days as it was not always possible to roster a reliefman to travel all the way out to Whiteball, nor was it cost effective. When one man was off, either through holiday or sickness and there were no reliefmen available then 12 hour working would be introduced. In this way two men kept the box open between them by each working from 6.00 to 6.00, one on days the other on nights.

I looked forward to going to work, regardless of the day of the week or the time of day. That "Monday morning" feeling, the curse of many a worker, just did not exist. Then, as since, the job brought a special enjoyment I was eager not to miss. Earlies, Lates or Nights it was always a pleasure, although rising early in the morning was never easy. So much so that I must admit the other two shifts proved more attractive. I have always found it difficult to be an early riser, thus the need to be awake before 5am in order to reach the signal box for early turn was a chore. Years later I am no better. But, once awake and out, the joy of a new morning is nevertheless unrivalled. There is something very special about the freshness and peaceful silence of a new day, as yet unspoilt by the rest of mankind going about his business.

This first winter through which I was at Whiteball served to emphasise my inadequacy at being able to wake before the crack of dawn. To ensure that I would not oversleep I invested in a new alarm clock from the jewellers in Wellington. It was one of those models with a pair of enormous bells on top that, when activated, could wake an entire household. The clock served its purpose, never failing to wrest me from slumber but the loudness of its tick prevented me from falling asleep in the first place. The answer, I found, was to place the clock on a chair across the other side of the huge bedroom thereby reducing the volume of its tick. This ploy worked and had the added advantage of putting the clock out of direct reach so that I was unable to turn it off when its alarm sounded and so drop back to sleep. One occasion, a year or two later, when I did oversleep was an incident I would never be allowed to forget - but that comes later on in my story.

The farmhouse was a cold building during the winter with just me living there alone and only a fireplace in the living room for heat. I tried all three bedrooms in an attempt to find the warmest but found none preferable. I would look forward to the cosy warmth of the box but after the bike ride often arrived with hands so cold I was unable to sign on duty in the Train Register for some minutes. The Train Register Book was used to record the exchange of all bell codes, the passing of trains, opening and closing, signing on and off duty, messages regarding train running and any occurrences. The left hand side pages of the book were dedicated to the Down Line whilst the right hand pages were reserved for the Up Line. Having been schooled to use a fountain pen I always used one to make the entries in the Train Register although many signalmen preferred a BR supplied biro. In the Taunton area train descriptions were recorded using the reporting number (headcode) listed in the timetable rather than the train's originating point and time. Thus the 07.38 Plymouth to Edinburgh was recorded in the Train Register as 1S27 and the 18.55 Avonmouth to Ponsandane as 7B30 for example. The regular exchange of bells were logged in their correct column as the time whilst all other entries were either written in the remarks column or across the page with the time appended at the end. As a signalman one was therefore constantly aware of time. Indeed it was measured to the nearest half minute and always precise in the form of the hour and minutes. There was no such time as half past or quarter to.

The distance of the box from the road meant that visitors were a rarity. The permanent-way patrolman would walk the length from Wellington on Monday,

Wednesday and Friday mornings, fishplate spanner slung across his shoulder and a knapsack on the other containing flask and sandwiches. The lampman from Taunton would call on Friday to trim the wicks and replenish the paraffin in the signal lamps, making use of the corrugated iron lamp hut next to the box. This housed a drum of paraffin on a wooden trestle and a shelf on which to work, together with spare lamps and wicks. On Thursdays the Area Manager, Mr Ross, or his assistant, Mr Walkey, would bring the pay and stores out from Taunton and collect the timesheets. Other than that the occasional visit from the Wellington signal lineman, Ivor Brewer, or the District Inspector (DI), Tom Earlam, from Exeter or his assistant, Clem Chapman, were the only ones to be expected. A good ten minutes grace ensued between spotting a visitor adjacent to the bridge and their arrival at the cabin. Time aplenty to warn the boxes on either side of the approach of an official.

It is interesting to remember that all over the country local railway managers spent Thursday mornings delivering cash filled pay packets to the outlying boxes under their charge. At the outset of the day they carried a not inconsiderable sum of money on them with a pay packet for each resident man and many of the reliefmen. In addition to receiving his own pay, the early turn signalman would sign for custody of the late and night turn men's pay packets and for any reliefman's should one be rostered over the next two shifts. These would be safely secreted away ready for when these men came on duty later in the day.

Most Great Western boxes were fitted with discrete telephones to adjacent boxes in addition to the omnibus and selector circuits, of which more later. These discrete lines allowed the men at each end of a block section to carry on a conversation or exchange messages safe in the knowledge that no-one else was listening in. These instruments were known as Box to Box or Boxer telephones, or in other parts of the country as block 'phones.

On the approach of officialdom a quick "6 beats" (normally "obstruction danger" on the block bell) on the ringing key of each Boxer telephone ensured that the signalmen on either side were made instantly aware that any "slack-working" should cease for the moment, for there was a "Black Mac" or "Brass Hat" about to quote a couple of expressions describing the DI or a manager. "Slack-working" is the term Inspectors employ to define the corner cutting signalmen would use to simplify their work. The habits which signalmen dropped into varied around the country but would include such simplification as not using the "Call Attention" bell signal before offering a train to the next box or before sending the "Train out of Section" signal to the box in rear. Until harmonisation of the Rules and Regulations by British Railways the Western Region had never required the "Call Attention" to be used before sending "Train out of Section" nor the "Train out of Section" to be acknowledged by the receiving signalman. Continuation of such old ways was stubbornly adhered to as being "Great Western" unless an Inspector was present. Whenever an Inspector visited they would sign their name across the next line in the train register book using a red biro, then scrutinise recent entries for correctness, marking any errors or gaps in red pen.

There was contact of course with train crews occasionally and with those of a particular train regularly. The 05.55

Plymouth to Old Oak Common empty newspaper vans, headcode 5A06, was booked in the working timetable to stop at Whiteball at 07.59 "as required" to set down water, it being conveyed by galvanised milk churn on the footplate of the empty vans engine. In earlier times the Wellington banking engines had delivered the water, carrying the containers on their buffer beams. So, on a few mornings of the week the vans would briefly stop and the fireman would hand down a full churn of water, taking in return an empty one. We had three churns to rotate and would leave the Up Distant at caution as a sign to the crew if we had an empty one to put on. When the train crew had a full one on board they would stop anyway - if they remembered. The empties were dropped at Taunton, where a porter would transfer them to the brake compartment of a down passenger train so they could reach Exeter St Davids. Here another porter would fill the empty churn from a platform tap and convey it over to the up side ready for the Old Oak vans next morning.

The handing up of an empty churn to the fireman presented little problem, but receiving the full one needed care. The open doorway of the locomotive, always a 1000 class "Western", was at around head height when one was stood in the "six-foot" between the running lines. The fireman would "walk" the churn to the edge of his door and pass it down by both handles. Taking hold at this point was fine but lowering it to the ground involved a manoeuvre in likeness to a weightlifter performing the lift and jerk but in the opposite direction. I have always been average in stature so invariably found this task a little difficult. Nevertheless time has proven that enjoyment is born from not only the simple things but those that are difficult too. Whiteball was one of many boxes that still had no running water but plumbing would have somehow detracted from the place. As mentioned we kept the churns out in the porch at the top of the stairs on a wooden trestle. Beneath the trestle sat a bucket of cold water for hand washing, changed daily, and on the end of the trestle was a bar of soap.

The bar of soap provided us with a regular visitor of a different sort. This came in the form of a white field mouse. Shortly after midnight the 19.30 St Blazey to Temple Mills partially fitted goods would clear Wellington and the bells and levers would remain silent for perhaps forty minutes. This was the quietest spell of the night at Whiteball. The next train on the down would be 6B31 the 20.50 Paddington Goods to Plymouth Friary NCL ("National Carriers Limited") train at about 01.45 through Taunton and normally there was nothing on the up until the 21.10 Plymouth Friary to Severn Tunnel Junction, usually asked clear by Tiverton Junction around 00.50. So, unless something was running late or there was an extra train, then stillness would pervade until the Friary passed Hele and Bradninch and was asked up by Tiverton. With only the sounds of nature beyond the box, soft ticking from the clock and just the light on in the porchway, an air of tranquillity crept over the place.

For our friend the field mouse, which must have lodged nearby, now was the midnight feast time. The bar of soap resting on the end of the trestle in the porchway was a delicacy never missed between midnight and 1am. Once sounds had ceased for five or so minutes, he, or maybe it was a she, would clamber up onto the trestle and enjoy a twenty minute gorge, nibbling away at the end of the cake with ferocious front teeth, whilst keeping a firm grip upon it with both front claws. This was a fascinating spectacle to watch at such close quarters. The celebrated naturalist David Attenborough could not have got closer. Twenty minutes was always the maximum unless disturbed by sudden movement or the piercing sound of a bell. The mouse would then disappear from whence it came and into the shadows, leaving the notch ended remains of its supper, no doubt to be sick somewhere and recover ready for the next night. Meanwhile the cake of soap would be fashioned to resume a smooth rounded finish at the hands of the signalmen whenever they washed over the next twenty four hours.

Another of nature's regular visitors was the crow, in fact these were visitors to most country boxes as they inhabited the trees adjacent to many a railway line. Crows were said to be the ghosts of old gangers for the way they would strut along the rail, top wings tucked in and heads pointing forward just like a ganger clad in a black greatcoat with arms folded behind his back inspecting the track. These birds would scavenge from the line and surrounding area always accepting a crust or bacon rind thrown from the box. There was other wildlife too in the form of owls, kestrels, rabbits and stoats. These could all be viewed from the comfort of the box. Like many country boxes, Whiteball was a box for wildlife lovers. Although not far from habitation, with Redhill Farm, Higher Eastbrook Farm and Eastbrook House nearby it felt like the box was miles from any neighbour. It was like living amongst nature but within the protection of four walls and a roof - a working hide. A quiet moment between trains during the daytime might be punctuated by the excruciating sound of a terrified rabbit being dragged away by a stoat. At night the stillness could be hauntingly accentuated by the nearby hooting of an owl.

The down side of the cutting never really saw much sun, especially during the winter months and so the signal box remained in shadow, not helped by the nearby bridge. Frost could last all day, keeping the sleepers white and snow would stubbornly resist melting on the down side of the line whilst on the up side it would capitulate to the sun's rays. In spring the sides of the cutting were covered in primroses. The tunnel, just 340 yards away was dark and eerie, always dripping with water. Indeed, in winter icicles of stalactite proportions could form from its roof given a long enough spell between trains. Trains heading east disappeared as they were swallowed up into the mass of the hill, their red tail lamps fading into the darkness but those coming west burst out into Devon to take up the next leg of their journey. The Up Starting signal sat at the mouth of the tunnel guarding both it and the section ahead. Beyond the signal an area of brickwork on the tunnel portal was whitewashed to help drivers sight the signal arm against the otherwise dark background.

Whiteball Siding Signal Box boasted an interesting history. It was built around 1874 to the design of signalling contractor Saxby & Farmer with the characteristic rounded end toplights above the main windows that were a hallmark of that company. One night towards the end of 1955 the box was subject to a fire caused by the over zealous charging of a "Tilley" lamp. I was to meet the culprit, Gordon (Willy) Vowden, a few years later on moving to Newton Abbot as a relief signalman. Willy espoused that his setting fire to Whiteball had most definitely been an accident but that the rebuilt box was an improvement for which he was proud to take the credit. One thing was for certain, the saga of the Whiteball fire was just one colourful story that Willy could recall from a repertoire of lifelong incidents and embellished happenings on the railway. The fire resulted in the top half of the box being rebuilt in the Western Region style of the time with a wooden structure housing windows that came to within a few inches of the operating floor. The brick base remained, largely unchanged from its original construction. Perhaps the provision of electricity had been sought to prevent a repetition of this incident.

Fires caused by tilley lamps or coal stoves were not uncommon in fact. Even in the seventies Tilleys were kept for emergency lighting and used by staff working trackside at night. John Wyatt related how he nearly achieved similar notoriety to Willy one day at Durston but managed to throw the spurting lamp out of the window saving the box from certain destruction. A spot of paint and a patch of new lino were the only repairs required in that instance.

Whiteball was fitted with a 27 lever frame of the GWR Vertical Tappet 3-bar type. This was a different type of frame to that which I had become familiar on the Southern, but like other Great Western frames I was to use later, easy to operate. It had been altered at various times to accommodate layout changes. The most recent had been in 1964 when the Down Relief line to Burlescombe, laid in 1927, had been shortened to a Down Goods Loop and the new motorised exit points controlled by lever 22 at Whiteball. Burlescombe box subsequently then closed on 26th July 1964. Similarly there had been an Intermediate Block signal on the up line towards Wellington at Beam Bridge. When this was abolished lever 5 became spare, as did levers 9 and 10 when the Up Siding was removed. Now, apart from the Down Goods Loop, there remained the Down Refuge Siding, which trailed eastwards from the box towards the tunnel mouth, and a trailing crossover between the up and down lines. The loop continued to be used to regulate slower trains from the path of expresses whilst the refuge siding saw occasional use for putting off a vehicle with a hot axle box or for the stabling of a tamping machine

The signalman's view looking back towards the tunnel. The Down Homes bracket is visible as is the whitewashed area on the portal brickwork. Note the long shadows in the cutting. *(Author)*

between jobs. We usually referred to these machines as Plassers after the company which built them, although they were not the only make which ran around, Matisa being another.

In addition to mechanical locking, some levers were fitted with electric locks released by a track circuit or "Line Clear" indication from the next signal box. To economise on power consumption these were only energised when requiring to move the associated lever. The Great Western and later the Western Region did not usually provide any form of automatically operated economiser contact to these electric lock circuits. Instead, a plunger would be provided on the block shelf above the lever for which electric lock it operated, the plunger having a neat ivorine label on which was engraved the lever's number. With facing point lock levers, which normally stood reverse in the frame, the lock plunger operated a timed stick circuit which would pick the electric lock for between five to seven seconds, giving ample time to move the lever away from the reverse position before the lock dropped back. In the case of signal levers fitted with electric locks, no stick circuit was provided requiring co-ordinated action by the signalman to press the plunger whilst moving the lever away from the normal position, after which the plunger could be released. When pressing a plunger the electric circuit would complete and the signalman would listen to hear the lock "pick" in the locking room below before attempting to first move the lever.

To keep the brass plungers as well as the lever tops shiny, required both to be protected from the hand by the lever cloth. I soon learnt the technique of taking one corner of the cloth, which measured 21½" x 22½", in my left hand to operate the lock plunger whilst allowing the opposite corner to fall towards the lever so that the right hand could clasp the lever and its catch handle then edge the lever from the normal position. The left hand would then leave the lock plunger bringing the lever cloth with it to the top of the lever allowing both hands to pull the lever over.

The Red, White and Blue chequered lever cloth was both part of the signalman's equipment and part of his dress, it was his "badge of office". The life of the lever cloth was never long, constantly being impaled upon lever and catch handle. Besides being used as part of the art of lever pulling they were also useful as dusters and cloths, usually being relegated to these tasks once worn or torn. The cloth had another use although unofficial. By waving it vigorously from an open window at the driver of an approaching train that had been "checked" by the distant signal being at caution, it conveyed the message that all the "boards" were now off and that the driver had right of way into the advance section. By night the box hand lamp took the place of the lever cloth in passing on this information. A white light waved up and down from within the dimly lit box would be all that was needed to assure the driver that he could open the throttle. These signals became so universally adopted on the Western that even where a driver could see the section signal drop to clear beyond the box he would often still wait for the tell tale indication from the signalman as confirmation that all was clear. Later I was to find the odd box, such as Teignmouth, where switching the interior electric light on and off in quick succession was known at that location by footplatemen as the all clear ahead. On recognising the signal, a driver would respond with a short toot on the horn, followed by the tell tale shafts of exhaust fumes and the sound of an unleashed diesel engine. Often at night the recognition would be by the returned flash of the drivers bardic lamp from behind the windscreen or the rapid switching on and off a few times of the cab interior light. No doubt this widely recognised but unofficial hand signal was derived from the raised hand which, in rule 51(c), denoted "right-away".

When not in action the lever cloth could often be found draped across a suitably located facing point lock lever, but many men preferred to carry it about their person, either hanging from a trouser pocket or draped across a shoulder, as if it represented their status. This was more for the reason that it was easier to find when wanted and spared walking should it have been left at the wrong end of the box. Whether it was the left or right side pocket or shoulder was dictated by which hand the signalman normally used to press the lock plungers. In my travels I have noticed that the quietly confident signalman would keep the cloth hanging from a corner tucked in his pocket, whilst the more cocky of the profession would parade with it over his shoulder. With myself, I found the cloth spent most of its time protruding from the left pocket interspersed with the occasional right shoulder drape. The pattern on the cloth changed subtly over the years. From having originally been GWR, the initials BR(W) woven across the middle were dropped in favour of just BR and later ceased altogether.

CHAPTER TWO

REGULATING

One of the tasks which the signalmen at Whiteball box had undertaken since its first construction was the detaching of pilot and bank engines. In steam days up trains had often been assisted by pilot locomotives attached to the front at Exeter. On the down, overweight passenger and most goods trains were given a banker or two at the back from Wellington. Even in these diesel days it was pleasing to find that the odd freight still needed a push up the bank from Wellington. So Whiteball continued to discharge the age old duty of detaching bankers. Detaching is not really the correct word as, although coupled to the rear of trains on leaving Taunton, each train would stop at Wellington so that the coupling could be dropped, allowing the bankers to loose push from there to the summit. By this means the train could be pushed over the top and then continue on without having to stop at Whiteball.

The presence of a bank engine on the rear of a train was heralded by the addition of the bell signal 2 pause 2 "Engine Assisting in Rear of Train" from Wellington once the "Train Entering Section" signal had been acknowledged. The 2-2 was sent for each engine so that in addition to checking the train was complete with tail lamp, the signalman at Whiteball could ensure all of the banking engines arrived too before sending the "Train out of Section" signal.

The bank engines would come to a stand outside the signal box as the train began to gather speed and disappear away towards Tiverton Junction. I say bank engines, as invariably a pair of type '2' or type '3' locomotives in multiple were used. These engines normally resided at Taunton, being employed during the day time on local trip and ballast workings. Occasionally they would be pressed into service to come to the rescue of a failed train. At night they would perform banking duties as required. As well as banking some of the regular goods trains like 7V61, the 09.50 Bescot to Exeter Riverside, when tonnage was too great for the train engine they had a particularly busy time in the autumn when sugar beet trains ran to Exeter and St Blazey from various parts of East Anglia. These overweight trains formed of 50 or more box vans originated from the likes of Ipswich, Cantley and Ely with reporting numbers 6V59, 6V51, 6V49 and 6V42, having taken all day to traverse the country and then needing a push from Somerset into Devon under the cover of night. The empties from these trains always worked back to Whitemoor Yard in Cambridgeshire, usually running as 6E41, 6E42 and 6E44.

The daytime ballast trip workings were used to drop ballast where it was needed for remedial work by the local gang or in readiness for a mechanised machine. They would also drop other materials such as rail or sleepers for spot renewal jobs or pick up scrap. With the co-operation of the signalmen these trains would work between the other trains, refuging in loops or sidings such as those at Whiteball to avoid causing delay. Belled using the 2-3-3 code it was essential for the signalman to ensure the guard knew how long he was allowed before being expected to get clear at the next box. These trains were accepted under the Warning Arrangement (Regulation 5) so that a clearing point was not required and thus other movements could be permitted within the protection of the home signal regardless of where the train might be in the section and how long it would be before it arrived.

These were still firmly the days of the diesel hydraulics on the Western Region. The "Warships" had not long been withdrawn and the "Hymeks" were on the way out leaving the "Westerns" in charge of many of the express services. The "Westerns" were the first diesels to attract a following amongst the enthusiast fraternity. There were 74 of them in the class, each with a name prefixed by "Western". Numbered from D1000 to D1073 they were also known as "Thousands". Many of the inter-regional trains to and from the Midland, Eastern and Scottish Regions were worked by "Peaks" whilst Brush type '4s' and type '2s' covered some of the duties, together with the occasional type '3'. All of the loco's sported BR blue livery with yellow end panels and the white "arrows of indecision" on the cab side. A few of the Brush locomotives carried names, as did many of the "Peaks", the latter being named after army regiments. At this time no regular diesel multiple unit workings operated between Taunton and Exeter so the only units to pass Whiteball were the occasional empty workings to or from Laira depot at Plymouth for maintenance or a drivers' route learning trip. Units were ideal for route learning as the staff could sit in the front saloon observing the line ahead through the glass partition behind the driver. With their leisurely pace, these route learners usually managed to get in the way of a following express, so the trainee crews were invariably treated to a sojourn in Whiteball loop.

A diverse assortment of traffic was timetabled to pass with extras and special trains adding to the variety. Most of the more interesting trains ran at night or early in the morning, largely unseen by the general population and missed entirely by the railway enthusiast fraternity. Signalmen were, however, able to see and control them all from the "comfort" of their boxes. Compared with previous decades however, the railway infrastructure, the variety of traffic and the intricacies of the working were now shadows of a once greater era. Older signalmen had lived through a far more fascinating railway. Extra train workings were notified via Weekly or Special Notices mailed to the box or brought out on Thursdays with the pay. The notices were marked up prominently in biro by the receiving signalman to highlight additional trains or amended timings before being hung prominently on a nail on the wall in the grip of a bulldog clip. Passenger and freight workings were hung on separate clips. Another bulldog clip held the fortnightly vacancy lists which advertised jobs on the region for station, yard and signal box staff. Expired and superseded notices were torn in half and held together by another bulldog clip to form a scrap pad for jotting down messages and reminders. Last minute extras, the details of which had not been published, were advised by Control over the telephone or by message passed on from box to box.

From my earlier teenage days spent with experienced signalmen I had learnt that the ability to make rapid decisions at any time is a key attribute for a good signalman. Whether it be a decision to run a freight ahead of a passenger or to throw the signals back in front of a train in an emergency there is little opportunity for deliberation. Staying on top of the job, minute by minute, and retaining a sound knowledge of the rules and regulations are paramount to supporting instant reactions. Unlike most other jobs there is no opportunity for discussion over a course of action or the luxury of a practice or dry run to see if an idea or plan works. Decision made, the die is cast.

At Whiteball I learnt how to put the rules and regulations into practice, not just for the routine operations but when dealing with incidents that occurred from time to time. Failed locomotives or trains becoming stuck on the bank were not uncommon. Nor were hot axle boxes or sticking brakes on the variety of freight wagons that passed. A hot box rarely caught fire before being spotted but might be seen glowing at night. They certainly let off an acrid smell, accompanied by a high pitched squeal which was usually the way to detect them. Dragging brakes could be a spectacular sight at night sending out sparks like a catherine wheel firework whilst the rim of the wheel glowed red. During my time at Whiteball and subsequently at many other boxes I became exposed to dealing with these and a variety of other emergencies. Missing or unlit tail lamps, doors open on passenger trains or door handles not turned, and on occasion doors open on freight trains too, shifted loads, fires, broken rails, obstructions on the line, trespassers and vandals, suicides, stray animals (especially lambs in the spring), these all presented themselves for instant response. Equipment failure and even a derailment were to arise at one time or another during my career. Even though the rules and regulations were explicit, real life events often necessitated interpretation and in some instances the turning of a blind eye to keep the railway running. No wonder when unions called for a "work to rule" the job could come to a standstill.

The blind eye would be turned for those situations that, between them, the signalmen could manage without having to cause unnecessary delay. So what might such a situation be? If a red light had been left switched on at the rear of a locomotive, shining between it and its train or perhaps a locomotive door left open then, strictly speaking, the train should be stopped and the light extinguished or the door closed and it ascertained that no staff had fallen out. Likewise in the case of an inward swinging door on an empty van. Rather than cause delay by sending the "Stop and Examine" signal the train would be allowed to continue to the next station at which it was booked to call, the misdemeanour being rectified there by a judicious phone call or two. Similarly, if a headlamp was out or a red light illuminated on the front of a locomotive then it might be possible to draw the driver's attention to the error by pointing at the front of the loco' with one hand whilst tapping one's forehead with the other. Invariably this alerted the driver to the problem such that it was quickly remedied. But if ever a true safety issue arose, signalmen would never hesitate to act in accordance with the rules and regulations to protect life and property.

If a signalman flouted the rules or made a mistake he would be put on a charge, being issued with a Form 1, also known as a "Please Explain". If found guilty of a serious misdemeanour he would then receive a Form 2, alongwith a few days suspension and a note on his record. I'm pleased to say that my signalling career passed without ever receiving an official charge. The Inspector and his Assistant would supervise the signalmen under their control by visiting the boxes in their area from time to time and by watching the working. In the case of remote boxes like Whiteball this was no simple routine and hence each individual signalman only received a visit on an infrequent basis. We were thus largely trusted to work unsupervised. Occasionally the Train Registers would be withdrawn from a series of consecutive boxes so that a correspondence check could be made for a particular day's entries in what was effectively an audit procedure, although it was never termed as such at the time.

Whenever the Inspectors were out and about on the railway their role meant they were ever vigilant as to the execution of the rules and regulations. One afternoon I had been leaning on the handrail of the open window, watching the passing of a down passenger train, when I glimpsed Clem Chapman, the Assistant DI from Exeter, lounging in a first class compartment. I thought no more of it until, twenty minutes later, the telephone rang and his voice issued from the earpiece. "Glad to see you properly observing trains" he said "but I did notice your distant lever was still reverse in the frame as I went by". "Don't forget rule C.4.5.1 that says the signalman must replace a distant signal to caution immediately he can ascertain the train has passed the signal."

I had not long been working the box on my own when my first locomotive failure occurred. The train concerned was the 07.04 Derby to Plymouth which expired just as it came out of the tunnel, the loco' unable to drag itself and its train the last few yards to the top of the bank. Having stopped short of my home signal, the last few coaches were still in the tunnel, but at least the crossover was free to be used once the signal was replaced to danger. Rescue was provided by a pair of Brush type '3s' sent up from Exeter. I think they might have been the Taunton trip engines that had earlier taken a rake of empty 'Dogfish' wagons from Fairwater down to Riverside. I was able to cross the engines over and back them onto the front of the failed train, the ensemble getting underway after a 40 minute delay. The 09.30 Paddington to Penzance had been waiting at Wellington to follow but this was the only other delay before traffic returned to normal.

Whiteball worked with Wellington signal box three miles and 1,331 yards to the east (3m 61ch) and Tiverton Junction five miles and 226 yards to the west although in the section to Tiverton Junction there was a level crossing on a minor road, halfway between Burlescombe and Sampford Peverell known as Pugham Crossing. The lane formed a short cut between Westleigh and the A38 trunk road. Manned by a resident crossing keeper with a cottage, this was provided with hand gates protected by colour light home and distant signals in each direction but was not a Block Post. A set of repeater block indicators and a bell sat above the 3 lever frame in the outdoor hut so that the crossing keeper could see the status of both lines and eavesdrop on the exchange of bells between Whiteball and Tiverton Junction. Towards the end of 1974 the road was truncated, the crossing being abolished and the signals removed, despite a new bridge having been built to carry the lane across the M5 motorway which opened not long afterwards. The motorway of course soon set about challenging the railway for traffic, both passenger and freight. The block section between Wellington and Whiteball had once been the longest between Taunton and Newton Abbot. At one time there had been 33 signal boxes open on this stretch of railway, giving an average block length of 1.6 miles. Now the Wellington - Whiteball section was one of the shorter blocks, apart from those at the larger stations. Since the loss of local and slower traffic the intermediate boxes had been thinned out.

Regulation of the traffic to ensure that priority was given to class 1 trains formed part of the signalman's job. When a down goods train passed Wellington it would take around twelve minutes to climb the bank and run down the other side to Tiverton Junction. If the signalman there had to loop the train, so that it could be passed by a faster train, then this time could be extended to 15 minutes, or even longer for a fully fitted freight. Why should the fitted train, with its higher speed and better braking have taken longer? The reason is that the signal box at Tiverton Junction sat halfway along the up platform, right in the middle of the layout it controlled. A freight train arriving in either of the platform loop lines did not therefore fully pass the box before coming to a stand. A partly fitted or loose coupled goods always had a brake van, in which the guard rode, as the rearmost vehicle thus once in clear inside the loop, the signalman could not only see the brake van but the guard would raise his arm, or a white light at night to signal that the train was complete in accordance with rule 147 (or H.4.12.1 as it had become in the new rule book of 1972). Hence the "Train out of Section" signal could be sent immediately.

With a fully fitted freight there was no brake van bringing up the rear and thus the guard rode in the back cab of the locomotive to observe his train. On arriving in the loop, therefore, the guard would have to climb down and walk back to the rear of the train to check that the tail lamp was present before giving the signal that the train was complete. Alternatively the driver would stop the train as it entered the loop to allow the guard to step down there. Upon the train being drawn forward the guard would then be able to give the "in-clear" signal. The latter method saved a little time but either way letting a fitted train down to Tiverton loop was guaranteed to take some time.

At Whiteball the down loop started just beyond the box, enabling the signalman to observe the entire train as it entered, so ascertaining its completeness regardless of its class. Thus it was usually preferable to loop freights at Whiteball, both for this reason, and because it was over the top of the bank, unlike at Wellington where the line quickly steepened on leaving the loop. Drivers of heavy trains did not appreciate having to tackle the bank from a dead stand out of Wellington loop. So the Wellington signalmen always tried to keep freights running up to Whiteball and the Whiteball signalmen usually took no chances with letting them run on to Tiverton Junction.

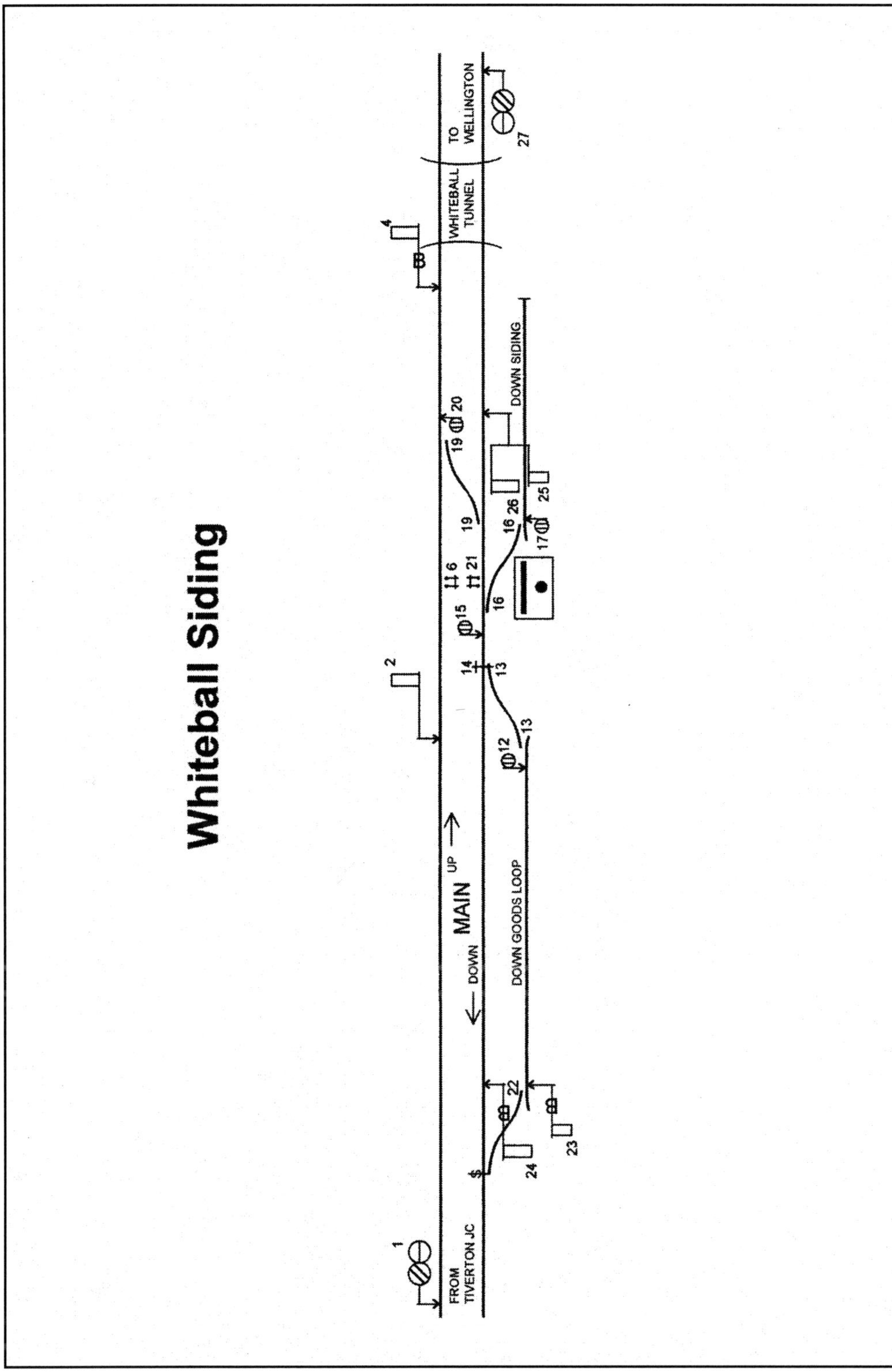
Whiteball Siding
FROM TIVERTON JC
TO WELLINGTON
WHITEBALL TUNNEL
DOWN MAIN UP
DOWN GOODS LOOP
DOWN SIDING

If a signalman let a goods run on a tight margin it was known as "purging" and he would be called a "purger" by his mates but if he was known not to take a chance when there was ample margin he would be taunted as being "windy".

When a class 7 or 8 partly fitted freight or an unfitted class 9 entered the loop the guard would come out onto the veranda of the brake van to carry out rule 121 (H.7.4.1 in the 1972 rule book) which required removal of the red filter from the side lamp nearest the main line so that it would show a white light. The other two lamps would be left to show red. By doing so any following train, either on the down line or entering the loop would know that the goods was stood on the loop line rather than the main line. The loop was permissive which meant that, provided there was room, more than one train could be allowed into it at a time. I can only remember doing this once, when putting a light engine inside behind a freight. The side lamps were mounted on brackets so that they normally shone a white light forward on each side of the train, as well as red to the rear. The driver and secondman could then periodically check during the journey, by looking back from time to time, that the whole train was still complete, with their guard bouncing along behind.

A typical set of events comprising the looping of a train at Whiteball would go something like the following. The time is edging towards half past one with the end of another early turn in sight. The broom will need to be put round soon, the kettle filled, the fire stoked up and the coal bucket restocked before Ivor arrives at ten to two to relieve me. A fitted goods, the 04.27 Stoke-on-Trent to St Blazey empty clay 6V53, is on its way up the bank from Wellington and I have 'phoned back to the signalman at Athelney, eight miles on the other side of Taunton, to see how the "Limited" is doing. The 11.30 Paddington to Penzance, headcode 1B45, runs non-stop from Paddington to Exeter. Known to the public as the "Cornish Riviera", to railwaymen it is the "Limited" due to the restricted number of coaches and hence load it carries. Dating from Great Western days, when it had been multi-portioned and ran non-stop between Paddington and Plymouth it is still one of the crack trains on the Western Region and is therefore given special attention by all staff. 1B45 was due through Taunton at 13.29 and would take only 8½ minutes to then pass Whiteball.

It was often early due to the allowances of recovery and pathing time in the working timetable shown with a circle around the number, known therefore as circle time. If the train had had a clear run down from London and there were no speed restrictions en route following engineering work then the circle time, aided by spirited running, often saw a ten minute early arrival into Exeter commensurate with the prestige of the train. This meant the possibility of a seven or eight minute early passing at Whiteball. A check of the K2 Weekly Notice would reveal what speed restrictions or not were imposed. "Passed me five early", John Cornelius at Athelney had said. No choice then, the goods would have to polish up the rails in the down loop.

There is a clunk from the track repeat relay downstairs followed by the red bar in the shelf mounted indicator for the tunnel track circuit tipping from clear to occupied, making a metallic "tink" sound as it falls against the stop pin, signifying that the empty clay has passed the down distant at caution. The driver will be using the uphill gradient to bring

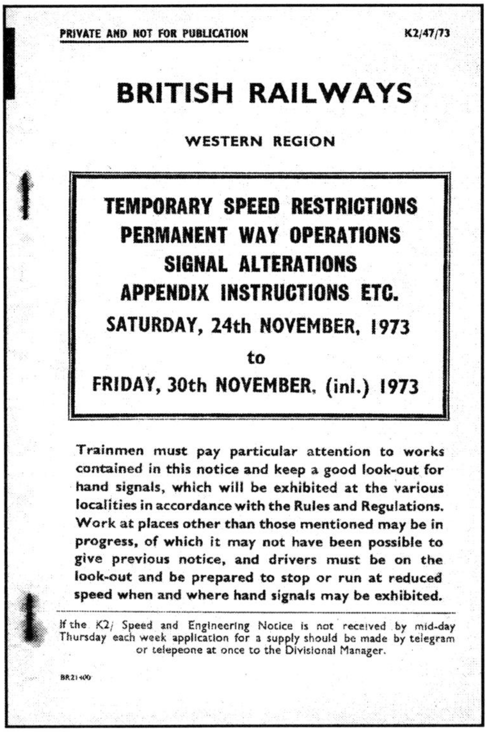

PRIVATE AND NOT FOR PUBLICATION K2/47/73

BRITISH RAILWAYS

WESTERN REGION

TEMPORARY SPEED RESTRICTIONS
PERMANENT WAY OPERATIONS
SIGNAL ALTERATIONS
APPENDIX INSTRUCTIONS ETC.
SATURDAY, 24th NOVEMBER, 1973
to
FRIDAY, 30th NOVEMBER, (inl.) 1973

Trainmen must pay particular attention to works contained in this notice and keep a good look-out for hand signals, which will be exhibited at the various localities in accordance with the Rules and Regulations. Work at places other than those mentioned may be in progress, of which it may not have been possible to give previous notice, and drivers must be on the look-out and be prepared to stop or run at reduced speed when and where hand signals may be exhibited.

If the K2/ Speed and Engineering Notice is not received by mid-day Thursday each week application for a supply should be made by telegram or telepeone at once to the Divisional Manager.

BR21400

The front cover of a K2 Weekly Notice which contained details of temporary speed restrictions, engineering works, signalling and permanent way alterations and general instructions and notices.

the train's speed under control. The box to box 'phone from Wellington buzzes out a quick four "rings" (zing-zing-zing-zing) signifying that the "Limited" has now passed Silk Mill and the Wellington signalman is eagerly waiting to clear his signals for it. The use of the box to box 'phone for this purpose provided a useful unofficial means of communication.

As the empty clay train toils uphill through the black hole of the tunnel I can see the white lights of the locomotive's headcode growing larger and brighter but also visibly rising from the climb until, all of a sudden, the train breaks out into the early afternoon sunshine which is now finding its way into the cutting. As usual a "Peak" is at the head of the train, the driver responding with a toot on the horn as I lower the 3 foot arm of the Down Main to Down Loop Home (No. 25) signifying that he is being "put inside" for the following express. Not being due by until 14.15 and having run non stop from Bristol where he took over the train, the driver is probably not surprised to find that he will be spending a few minutes sidelined at Whiteball.

The sun casts a shadow of the train onto the up line and, with half the train now over the summit, the weight of the formation is keeping the vehicles moving as the locomotive passes the box and turns in over the facing points to the loop. A friendly wave from the driver receives a similar response from me, likewise to and from the guard in the back cab. The dusty 5-plank clay wagons follow, squealing like troublesome trucks from a Reverend Awdry story, over the points and into the loop beyond. There are 42 in all, with an oil tail lamp hanging from the bracket on the last one. The clock is ticking as the rear of the train edges in clear of the trap points. I restore the home signal to danger then quickly unbolt the points with facing point lock lever No. 14, normalise the points with lever No. 13 and rebolt them again. Then its turn the commutator of the down main block from "Train on Line" straight round to "Line Clear" and tap out 2 pause 1 pause 4 on the block bell to Wellington signifying "Train out of Section" for the clay and acceptance of the "Limited" at the same time.

Back down the hill, three and three quarter miles away in Wellington Signal Box, Eric Jeans has been waiting by his levers, cloth in hand, urgently watching the minute hand of the box clock edging forward in its wooden case knowing that the "Limited" is fast approaching his distant signal. As the block indicator flips over to "Line Clear" and the 2-1-4 rattles out on the bell he is quickly "pulling off". There are five stop signals to clear and then finally the colour light distant. As the distant changes from yellow to green, the needle in the electric repeater on the block shelf flicks from "on" to "off" and the warning bell rings out for a split second.

Eric is confident that the driver will have seen a green signal. This is reinforced less than a minute later when the down "Limited" streaks past at 90 mph, the "Western" class diesel sending up its twin exhaust from the two Maybach engines under full throttle in an effort to attack the steepening grades ahead with every single horse power of the 2,700 available. Two beats on the bell from Wellington and I get the road ahead to Leo Morris at Tiverton Junction and pull off (that's levers 26, 24 and 27). Sitting in the loop, the driver on the clay empties sees the Down Main Starter alongside him drop to clear and realises that it must have been tight to let him run up the hill to Whiteball.

Two minutes later the indicator for the track circuit in the tunnel again tips to occupied but its not many seconds before the "Limited" roars out of the tunnel, its speed now reduced to 70 mph by the long climb, but still higher than many expresses due to its limited load of just eight coaches and significantly faster than in steam days when passenger trains would rarely breast the summit at more than 30 mph. This time the driver sounds a few short notes on the horn in recognition that the clay has been looped for him to take preference. I raise my arm in response. The blue and grey of the coaches stream by, hammering over the points, six minutes early, as the long hand of the clock passes 31. There's every chance of a nine or ten early arrival at Exeter St. Davids. The train is well patronised with many passengers enjoying coffee at the end of their lunch in the restaurant car. Do any of them notice me running my eyes along the train to ensure all is in order or do any of them spot the clay empties sidelined for their express passage? There is nothing untoward to be seen. The tail lamp on the rear signifies that the train is complete. I send "Train Entering Section" to Tiverton Junction, replacing the signals behind to protect the train then send "Train out of Section" to Wellington, normalising the block at the same time.

Then it's time to bring the Train Register up to date with the appropriate entries before setting the loop exit points ready to let the clay follow out behind the "Limited". The next class 1 train is not due to pass before 14.03 so there is plenty of time for the freight to reach Exeter Riverside where it is booked for examination and a change of crew. The loop points are fitted with an electric motor at the facing trap end but are sprung at the trailing end in the down main. Power for the motor is provided by turning the handle of the "hurdy gurdy" hand generator. The normal and reverse point directions are selected by placing the point lever (No. 22) in either the 'B' or 'D' positions as they are known, part way through the lever stroke. Full normal or reverse of the lever can only be achieved once the points have been electrically detected in the correct corresponding position.

On winding the generator, the weight of the points can be felt by the resistance of the handle to turn. The electric indicator drops from normal as the points begin to move and then flicks to reverse as soon as they are detected in their new position. At the same moment the drive circuit is disconnected and the generator handle spins freely, released from the load. The knack, is to stop turning just before this and let the points complete their movement having exerted the least human effort.

Seeing the trap points now set across to the main line, the driver of the clay empties knows that his sojourn will be short and that he will soon be on his way. Four minutes later and the "Limited" has raced through Tiverton Junction. The bell rings out 2 pause 1 and the block indicator drops to "Normal". I send a single beat to "Call Attention" which, when answered by Leo at Tiverton, is followed by 4 pause 1, "Is Line Clear for a fully fitted express freight". The needle deflects to "Line Clear" and I quickly pull the loop starter "off" with lever 23 as 4 pause 1 is returned. To save Leo from walking away from his block and having to return I put the clay straight "on line" with 2 beats. He answers and pegs the block needle over to "Train on Line" recognising that the clay will have been in the loop for the "Limited".

An acknowledgement from the locomotive horn drifts back on the breeze as the train drops otherwise silently out of the loop barely eight minutes after it arrived and disappears out of sight on its journey westwards. With 107 miles to go before reaching St Blazey how many more passenger trains will overtake it?

A freight or locomotive might be looped once or twice a shift at Whiteball in order to give preference to a more important train such as an express passenger, the sleepers, the postal or a parcel train. The timetable showed three freight trains each day booked to be held in the loop at Whiteball when I first went there. Invariably goods traffic ran early, usually improving on booked timings to the extent that the working timetable meant little to such trains. Hence signalmen dealt with freights in the most efficient manner, slotting them between the time critical passenger and other faster trains as and when there was a path. During the course of each 24 hours the actual movements turned into the loop depended on how individual services were running and whether delay would be caused to a passenger train or not. Sometimes, having looped a goods, it could be difficult to let it away before a more important train, if the margin was insufficient. Indeed one night the driver of the late running 00.55 Westbury to Exeter Riverside cement telephoned me from the Loop Starter to ask if he was in for the Sleepers. Having confirmed this, he then expressed his surprise when I went on to tell him that, due to more late running, he would be there not only for the Sleepers but for both parts of the Papers too which had still to come.

I remember one Wednesday evening around 8pm when Riverside Yard at Exeter was full and no more goods trains could be accepted until room was made. The 09.50 Bescot - Riverside (7V61) was held back in the loop at Hele, Tiverton kept his platform loop clear for the 14.45 Leeds which was booked to call and I sidelined the 08.05 Wednesday's only Stoke-on-Trent to St. Blazey back at Whiteball. The down loop could hold 60 SLUs (Single Length Units) plus engine and brake van. An SLU was measured as 21 feet long, equivalent to a four wheeled wagon such as a coal truck or covered van measured from buffer end to buffer end. Longer vehicles were measured as multiples of SLUs. It was important to check on the length of any goods train that was proposed to "go inside" to make sure it would fit. Signalmen would generally count the vehicles as they went by in case a problem was spotted and thus they could advise which vehicle was at fault. From the total count and an assessment of the various wagons in the consist a fairly good guess of overall SLU length could be made. So, more often than not, the signalman at Silk Mill or Wellington could advise Whiteball whether the train would fit in the loop or not. If in doubt, Control could be telephoned. They would know the length exactly, based on the paper record of the consist recorded at its last pick up or set down point.

Wellington down loop was of similar length, being able to hold 61 plus engine and van but Tiverton Junction could only hold 50. Thus any train with a length greater than 50 would need more careful regulation, perhaps being held back at Whiteball if it could not reach Hele and Bradninch before being overhauled by an express. Hele could hold 86 and thus act as a lay-by for anything. As well as the down loop, Whiteball also retained a down siding. This could recess 39 plus engine and van but was usually only used to hold bank engines or crippled wagons. Both up and down loop lines at Tiverton Junction also served respective station platforms whilst one of the sidings fed an oil distribution terminal which attracted rail traffic from Fawley refinery. Although the Tiverton branch had closed, the Culm Valley branch to Hemyock remained open for a daily trip to the dairy to exchange one or two milk tanks. When the return trip to Riverside Yard was ready to leave Tiverton Junction mid afternoon Leo would call on the 'phone to check there was no train asked to me by Wellington to make sure there was a margin for the trip.

Leo was a long standing railwayman who cycled the six miles from his home in Tiverton out to the Junction. He spoke with a high pitched voice which earned him the nickname of "Squeaker". It was known that he liked his cider, so the signalmen either side had to "keep an eye" on him so that he didn't get himself or us into trouble. I never had any problems in this regard but Leo's liking for drink brought his railway career to an ignominious end some years later. One night, having come on duty after celebrating his 53rd birthday, he fell sound asleep, causing serious delay to trains. The driver of one train went forward to the box to find Leo asleep and "under the influence". Despite 35 years of service he lost his job and even received a two month custodial sentence from the Magistrates at Cullompton. A sad end to a lifetime on the railway.

The most difficult movement to regulate was that of a diesel shunter. These locomotives rarely left the station or yard where they were employed but, from time to time, would travel to a major depot like Bath Road or Laira for a heavy overhaul or repair. With a top speed of just 15mph there was little opportunity to run them during the daytime between trains and so they would usually travel at night. Even then they would spend time in nearly every loop or siding waiting a margin to reach the next. As an alternative they were sometimes marshalled within a loose coupled freight train with their gears disconnected so that they could be hauled at 45mph. This was of course more preferable as far as us signalmen were concerned.

The Great Western Railway had introduced a range of special bell codes to identify certain trains more precisely and to assist signalmen with their routing.

Many of these applied in the vicinity of their principal stations like Plymouth, Newton Abbot, Exeter and Taunton and continued in use throughout the BR era until the end of mechanical signalling. The signalman at Tiverton Junction was responsible for advising Whiteball of the routing of all up express trains at Taunton. The Sectional Appendix called for drivers to assist the signalman by whistling as they passed. The following three whistle codes were used:

Via Durston, not stopping at Taunton 1 long 1 short;

Via Somerton, not stopping at Taunton 1 long 2 short;

Via Somerton, stopping at Taunton 1 long 3 short.

BRITISH RAILWAYS (WESTERN REGION).

THE STANDARD REGULATIONS FOR BLOCK WORKING ARE SHEWN IN THE BOOK OF REGULATIONS FOR TRAIN SIGNALLING ON DOUBLE AND SINGLE LINES.

Additional Instructions for Whiteball Tunnel Signal Box, Burlescombe Station.

Regulation 4.

When Wellington Signal Box is in circuit the "Is Line Clear?" signal must be sent for Down Trains as soon as the "Train Approaching" signal is received.

When Burlescombe Signal Box is in circuit the "Is Line Clear?" signal must be sent for Up Trains as soon as the "Is Line Clear?" signal is received.

Regulation 4 (c).

After "Line Clear" has been given for a Down Freight Train with the points set for a line of rail which is clear for a quarter of a mile in advance of the Home Signal, the Signalman, if the "Train Entering Section" signal has not been received for the train for which "Line Clear" has been given and no signals have been lowered for it, may reverse the facing points and lower the Home Signal without first stopping the train at it.

This working is prohibited during fog or falling snow.

Regulation 5.

The "Warning" signal may be sent for Up Trains not conveying passengers, provided there is not a train conveying passengers to the rear of the Clearing Point.

ROUTING OF UP EXPRESS PASSENGER TRAINS.

The undermentioned routing signals must be sent, for Up Express Passenger Trains not booked to stop at Taunton, to the Signal Box in advance as soon as the "Train Entering Section" signal has been acknowledged from that Signal Box:—

Trains travelling via Durston ... ... 3—3—1
Trains travelling via Somerton ... ... 3—3—3

To assist the Signalman at this Signal Box in ascertaining the route of Up Express Passenger Trains not stopping at Taunton the enginemen will give the following whistles on passing this Signal Box:—

Trains travelling via Durston ... ... 1 long, 1 short
Trains travelling via Somerton ... ... 1 long, 2 short

The sounding of the engine whistle will not relieve the Signalman from satisfying himself as to the route of all Up Express Passenger Trains not stopping at Taunton, and signalling them forward by the correct code as shewn above.

WORKING DURING FOG OR FALLING SNOW.

When no Fogsignalman is on duty, a Down Train may be accepted in accordance with Double Line Block Regulation 4 (e) paragraph 1.

20th November 1956

District Operating Superintendent.

The signal box footnotes for Whiteball from November 1956. The box is incorrectly named as Whiteball Tunnel. There is no reference to the 3-3-3-4 bell signal or its associated whistle code, leading to the conclusion that these must have been introduced at a later date.

If no whistle code was sounded then this signified the train was travelling via Bristol and was booked to call at Taunton. The train headcode, displayed on the front of the locomotive and matching that printed in the working timetable, would also assist the signalman in recognising the train and hence its routing. For example, 1A19 was the up "Cornish Riviera Limited", routed via Somerton and not booked to call at Taunton. The whistle codes were rarely sounded by drivers in later years and even the display of headcodes on the locomotive indicator blinds was discontinued during the summer of 1975 so that signalmen then had to rely on the timetable, the look of the consist, and advice to each other on the order of running.

For the Taunton area a number of special bell still codes existed. Three of these were used at Whiteball, being started by the signalman at Tiverton Junction as up trains entered the section. They applied to class 1 passenger trains and corresponded to the three categories mentioned previously. The normal 4 beats was used by Tiverton Junction to offer an express passenger up to Whiteball. If travelling via Bristol and stopping at Taunton it would be offered on as a 4 beats right through Taunton. If however the train conformed to one of the other three categories then Tiverton Junction would additionally send the appropriate routing code once the "Train Entering Section" bell signal had been acknowledged. The Whiteball signalman would then offer the train forward to Wellington using this special code rather than the standard 4 beats. The code would be used right through Taunton as far as Cogload box before reverting back to 4 beats. The special codes were:

Via Durston, not stopping at Taunton 3 pause 3 pause 1;
Via Somerton, not stopping at Taunton 3 pause 3 pause 3;
Via Somerton, stopping at Taunton 3 pause 3 pause 3 pause 4.

These codes were rung very fast, each signalman employing his own unique style. The latter code could often be heard as 9-1-1-1-1, the three three's being rung as 9 and the 4 having distinct spaces between each beat. Having been first entered in the train register as a 4 bells, the special code was recorded in the remarks column at the right hand side of the page.

The use of a transistor radio for personal entertainment in the box was strictly forbidden, as were portable televisions. Most signalmen broke rule A.1.2.6 and kept a small radio secreted away at the back of their locker which they brought out at quiet times for company or on a Saturday afternoon to listen to the sporting fixtures and to get the football results. A few had portable televisions but these could easily be too much of a distraction from working the box. I bought my transistor radio from the first floor of Smith's in Fore Street, Taunton; a stylish Benkson Continental that could be powered from batteries or the mains. What a saviour it was on long winter evenings when it would bring me quiz shows into the box to exercise the mind, comedy programmes to make me laugh or the tea time magazine entertainment of the *John Dunn Show*. Likewise on night shift, when it brought the company of easy listening programmes from the BBC like *Night Ride* and *Music Thru' Midnight*. An hour or two of listening would be just enough to break the shift up, especially when the eight or twelve hours usually passed without any direct contact with fellow human beings. The radio was also important for keeping in touch with what was happening in the world at large as back at the farm I had no television. I still have my Benkson Continental all these years later and today when I switch it on I am instantly transported back to the dark winter nights in the signal box.

CHAPTER THREE

THE AMBER MESSAGE

Handling the lever frame was not about using brute force but about applying body weight and movement, not unlike the techniques employed in judo. Each lever had a unique pull and push which was mastered with practise. That for a nearby signal might be light and easy to pull but would need help when being returned to the normal position. In contrast a signal many yards away, whilst demanding a hefty pull, would provide sufficient weight in its apparatus and length of wire to return its lever to normal entirely of its own accord, as soon as the catch was released.

Point levers often required as much or more action behind the push as the pull, in order to move the heavy switch blades across their slide chairs. The further from the box, generally the heavier they were to work, due to the weight of the rodding and the losses in travel at the various cranks and compensators. Double ended switches, such as a crossover, were obviously heavier than a single ended point. Good maintenance by the signal lineman and the permanent way gang, with regular oiling too, helped for smooth operation. The practised signalman expended minimal effort in moving the levers to and fro, using only a single hand where one would do or launching just sufficient movement to achieve the desired response - not too much and never too little.

Both distant signals at Whiteball were of the two-aspect colour light type. These showed amber for caution and green for all-clear. The Up Distant was 1,688 yards away and the Down Distant 1,599 yards away on the other side of the tunnel. Being electrically operated the relevant levers, 1 and 27, in the frame had their handles cut short as a reminder that little physical effort was required to operate them. The Western Region had embarked on a steady programme of distant signal renewal in the 1950s and 60s under which wire worked semaphore distants were replaced with colour light versions on its main lines. These were often placed further out to give greater braking distances for the higher speed trains and were welcomed by drivers for their increased visibility, especially during fog. Whereas semaphore distant signals required "fogging" it was not necessary to provide fog signalmen at colour light distants during periods of fog or falling snow.

To repeat the aspect of each distant back in the box, a three position indicator was provided above each of levers 1 and 27. The indicator would show "ON", "LIGHT OUT" or "OFF" according to what the actual signal displayed and at the "LIGHT OUT" position a bell would ring to attract attention to this fault. There was also a second indicator associated with the power supply to the signal.

This had two positions, either "NORMAL WORKING" when the mains was on and "STANDBY IN USE" when only the battery was connected. The "STANDBY" indication also operated the audible alert. The bell could be silenced by the operation of a switch. For the short space of time that the signal aspect changed from amber to green or back again the bell would ring. The duration of the ring was perhaps a few hundred milliseconds and this sound, when reversing or normalising a distant signal lever, was expected by the signalman and accompanied the movement of the indicator needle.

It was of course the signalman's desire to always keep trains moving at their full speed when possible, despite what many drivers thought, and so a green distant or "backboard" as it was known was the best thing to give a driver upon his approach. An amber distant would convey the warning message to a driver that he may not have a clear run past the next signal box. When the progress of a passenger train was stopped, or "checked" for whatever reason, curiosity was invariably aroused. Heads would appear from door windows in an effort to ascertain the likely cause whilst seated passengers distracted from their reading or conversation might spot the signal box and point towards it for the benefit of a travelling companion. No doubt speculation abounded, especially if the train was brought to a stand at the box because there was some problem with it or in order for its driver and guard to be informed of an incident ahead.

The variety of traffic signalled along the West of England main line added to the enjoyment of being a railwayman at a place like Whiteball. I have mentioned a few of the trains like the "Limited", the Old Oak vans and the Stoke clay empties. There were many more. Other named passenger trains were the "Cornishman" which ran between Leeds and Penzance, the "Devonian" between Leeds and Paignton, and the "Golden Hind" between Paddington and Penzance. Somehow the down trains carried more prestige, attracting more interest and romance than their counterparts in the up direction. Most of the trains did not have official names but they were nevertheless impressive, many loading up to 12 or 13 coaches. On Friday's extra timetabled trains ran and before and after Bank Holidays additional relief trains supplemented the booked service such was the volume of passengers. At night the sleepers, postal and newspaper trains were the class 1 movements, alongwith the overnight sit-ups nicknamed the "Owl" and the "Waker" plus the Penzance - Sheffield known to many as "The Northern". The various parcel trains, not just from London but from Curzon Street and Bradford, also commanded special attention, as did the 14.45 Penzance to Paddington "Perishables" so named as it conveyed West Country produce to the London Markets. The 20.20 Paddington to Penzance parcels was nicknamed the "Brute" on account of its load comprising parcels stacked in BRUTE trolleys. These trolleys were a common site on the platforms and concourses of main stations where they were towed around behind battery tractor units. The name stood for British Rail Universal Trolley Equipment.

Some of the goods trains had aliases too. The NCL (National Carriers Ltd) was known as the "Blue Spot" as it was made up of four-wheeled ex-refrigerator vans that carried a blue spot designation mark painted on the side to signify they were fitted with roller bearings. Having been built originally to convey fish, two rakes of these vans operated a nightly parcels train between Paddington Goods and Plymouth Friary on behalf of NCL. Many of the night time trains gave the impression of travelling at greater speeds than their daytime counterparts. The "Blue Spot" was no exception, the four-wheel vans bouncing along enthusiastically behind the engine like a long streamer, appearing to have little contact with the rails. Certain trains were known as "untouchables" reflecting the importance of their timekeeping and prestige. The "Hind" and the "Limited" were sometimes referred to by this name as was the "Postal" at night.

The night time trains drew special interest all of their own as they were passed on from box to box along the line in the otherwise quietness of the night. The "Postal", or West of England Travelling Post Office (TPO), conveyed mystique and romance as it flashed by in the early hours with its red letter boxes in the side of the sorting vans into which a letter could be posted during its brief stops at stations on the journey. Each van bore the Royal Mail crest comprising the letters ER beneath a Crown and through the narrow windows could be seen the rows of wooden pigeon holes into which the postmen were busily sorting the mail for individual rounds on the move before bagging ready to offload at Exeter, Plymouth and stations in Cornwall. There were sorters too on the paper trains, organising batches for each of the wholesalers enroute, dexterously tying these up with string and stacking them ready by the van doors.

The class 7 and 8 general freights brought a variety of traffic in all manner of vehicles from coal wagons, through box vans, to flat wagons. These largely ran to and from the yards at Exeter Riverside, Plymouth Friary and St Blazey although Tavistock Junction (near Plymouth), Truro, Drump Lane (at Redruth) and Ponsandane (outside Penzance) were also served. The up country originating or destination points were Carlisle, Washwood Heath, Warrington, Bescot and particularly Severn Tunnel Junction which was the Western Region's main marshalling yard. These trains carried their telltale triple red lamps on the rear of the brake van as they disappeared into the distance, smoke curling away from the chimney of the brake van's fire that kept the guard warm within his bumpy, spartan environment. Often the guard would venture onto the veranda as they passed to exchange a wave. At other times they might flash a white hand lamp from within to advise their presence rather than venture out into the cold.

One particular nightly Severn Tunnel service (the 20.20 to Exeter Riverside) always conveyed a flat wagon marshalled behind the loco' carrying three brand new Morris automobiles, usually a Mini and two Marinas, for a west country distributor. The splash of light from the signal box would momentarily bring the vivid colours of the bodywork alive and reflect off the chrome bumpers as they passed the window - a tantalising spectacle as few of the signalmen that watched them pass would ever earn enough money to afford a brand new car. Fish specials ran to east coast canneries, the light reflecting back from a mobile sea of silver skinned mackerel deposited in open wagons. China clay for paper making ran to The Potteries and to Sheerness in fitted trains. Company block services ran conveying oil, bitumen, fertiliser, cement and milk. There were timetabled ballast movements from Meldon Quarry in North Devon and the high speed parcel and perishable traffic. Other special freights ran from time to time such as long welded rail trains and the Chipman's weed spraying train made an annual visit. There were tamper movements, the Neptune track recording vehicle from time to time and then there was the track recording train, known as the "Whitewash Train" which dropped various colour paint onto the track to highlight deficiencies in the permanent way as it sped along at line speed. The local gang could then find these streaks of paint deposited on the sleepers and ballast and set about fixing the problem. Drivers could see the paint too and know to expect a lurch or dip but also know the problem had been identified. The railway played a key role in moving fresh milk from the farmers of the West to the doorsteps of London and the Home Counties. The milk trains were known to run in multiple portions to serve demand, picking up tanks, or "Miltas" as they were coded, from a variety of West Country Creameries such as St. Erth, Dolcoath, Lostwithiel and Totnes. Then, calling at Riverside the tanks tripped from Torrington, Chard and Hemyock would be collected. The 28 ton loaded tanks were glass lined, like giant vacuum flasks on wheels and with six equally spaced wheels each they sent out a unique up tempo beat as they rattled over the rail joints.

The passenger trains to and from Paddington were always known as Londons unless they had a specific name like "The Limited" or "The Hind". They were referred to as Up Londons and Down Londons in conversation or when making enquiries. The Londons regularly loaded to twelve coaches, usually with a van (either a BG or GUV) at the country end for luggage and parcels. At the London end would be the buffet portion comprising either a buffet or restaurant car, a first class carriage and two or three second class vehicles. For trains running to or from Cornwall, the buffet portion was detached/attached at Plymouth North Road.

But who was on those expresses as they hurtled by; TV personalities, film stars, writers, politicians, criminals or just ordinary folk such as businessmen and families? Whilst the daytime passenger trains carried all manner of discernible people, many reading, some dozing, some in conversation or just watching the countryside flash by, children with their sticky fingers pressed against the windows, people playing cards, or grannies knitting, the night time trains were different. The sleepers did not reveal their human cargo whereas the "Owl" and the "Waker" showed the occupants stretched out on the cushions, if the blinds were left up in a compartment, or sat up in a seat with their coats pulled tightly over them for warmth. The glimpse was momentary as each window passed, the dim light from the interior being lost as it hit the darkness outside. Wisps of steam would swirl around the coaches as it escaped from leaks and joints in the heating pipework.

Night time was special. Between trains you could contemplate that every few miles along the line there was a fellow signalman alert and safely passing traffic, their box an oasis of warmth and habitation, even in the small hours. Every driver would search the darkness, not only for the signals but for each dimly lit box as a landmark, safe in the knowledge that they had come through one block section and would be protected going into the next. There was something isolated and unique about being in such a solitary place in the middle of the night. There was the stillness, the dark and the sounds from nocturnal creatures. On a clear, warm summer's night the view from the doorway could be of a blanket of a million bright stars then on a cold winter's night the flame of the warm fire could mesmerise as it danced its infinite variation.

With the night shift at Whiteball being busier than early turn I soon learnt how exhausting it could be to stay awake all night, as sleeping during the daytime was never as sound or as long as a normal night's sleep. It was preferable for the shift to be steadily busy rather than have long gaps of inaction that might allow the body to succumb towards sleep. For once this happened it would bring on a listless feeling that could be hard to break from and so the night would be spoilt. The night shift week usually turned out to be the most tiring, acting as it did against nature's body clock. Lethargic movement, loss of appetite and scratchy eyes were some of the symptoms. Going home in the morning my body experienced a kind of exhaustion beyond normal tiredness. To fall into bed was a welcome necessity, made all the more sweet by the knowledge that alarm clocks were sounding all over the country for the majority of the population. Then, by the end of the week, just as acclimatisation had taken place, it was time to double-back for late turn but at least from Tuesday morning onwards a lay in was possible.

During night time signalmen alone at isolated boxes would dread the sound of footsteps. Whiteball was about as isolated as they came. Between the box and the loop a few cables ran in a short stretch of concrete troughing through the bridge hole. The troughing formed part of the walking route to and from the box, the lids making a distinctive clip clopping sound underfoot. During the small hours of one pitch dark night, the silence was suddenly punctuated by that tell-tale clip clopping sound. I was not expecting anyone and I had seen no lamp light approach. Alone and now nervous I slipped the bolt across on the door and called from the window but received no response, except for the sound of movement on the ballast. I shone the bardic lamp out onto the track, relieved to pick out a large dog which hesitated for a moment before loping off back down the line. It had probably strayed onto the line from Eastbrook House or one of the farms during a nocturnal exploration. I was happy for it to find its own way home.

An old school chum came to stay for a couple of days during a week when I was on nights. He showed enthusiasm to accompany me out to the box, riding pillion on the bike through the lanes in the dark. Unfortunately he lacked the stamina necessary to stay awake, so by the small hours was curled up on the floor in front of the lockers, trying to blot out the sound of the ringing bells, the crashing of the levers and the passing trains whilst I stepped around him.

A strange ritual that took place twice a year during the night shift was the adjustment of time between Greenwich Mean Time and British Summer Time. For most of the population this involved moving the clocks forwards or backwards by an hour prior to going to bed on the relevant Saturday night. For railwaymen who found themselves on duty on these particular nights there was a specific time at which the clocks were altered so that everyone remained co-ordinated. Thus at 2am on the given Sunday morning in

March, time would be advanced by 60 minutes to 3am such that a whole hour vanished. At 3am on the equivalent Sunday morning in October time was put back to 2am, the 60 minutes from 2am to 3am having to be relived. Signalmen adjusted their box clocks at the given hour, making an appropriate entry in their train registers. Those lucky enough to be on duty on the Saturday night in March only had to work a 7 or 11 hour shift whilst those on duty in October had their's extended to 9 or 13 hours with the bonus of an additional hour's overtime being paid.

As for the overnight trains, well they all ended up running an hour late on the Sunday in March. In October, those that could be allowed to continue early did so but the "Sleepers", "Owl" and "Waker" were all held at their first calling point after 3am to wait for the time to catch up, effectively extending their journey time but adhering to the published timetable.

Signal boxes were usually well looked after by their resident men. Whiteball was no exception. There was personal pride in the cleanliness and presentation. The linoleum on the floor was washed and polished, the windows were cleaned, the brass was polished and the steel lever tops were burnished. The ashes were removed from the fire, the coal bucket filled and the broom was put round before every shift change. This was a ritual that had been performed up and down the country at every box since boxes had existed. It was an act of courtesy, leaving the box clean and tidy for the colleague who would be spending the next shift in a "home away from home". Indeed, it is a sobering thought to realise that, when working six or seven days a week, signalmen would spend more waken hours in their box than they ever would at home.

If one man in a box did not pull his weight in respect of keeping it spick and span his mates would soon let him know by one means or another. I recall one disgruntled chap sweeping up at the beginning of his shift, placing all the dirt and dust in an envelope addressed to his colleague together with the words "you left this behind", before pinning the envelope to the wall in a prominent place above the train register.

Day and Martin's wax floor polish was provided from the railway stores, as was Day and Martin's metal polish. The latter doubled as an excellent window cleaner when applied and removed with newspaper whilst the wax floor polish was not only good for the lino'; it made an ideal lubricant for the brass runners of the sliding windows. To brighten the lever tops every box had a burnisher made from chain-mail sewn to a square of leather. Then, for cleaning the wash basin and paintwork there was Glitto scouring powder which came in a cardboard tube. The cleaning materials and stores were kept in a single locker or left on a shelf above the side windows.

For many, the comfort was extended by keeping a pair of old shoes or even a pair of slippers in their locker. These could then be worn throughout the shift to relax the feet and save wear and tear on the travelling shoes. I took an old pair of plimsolls, or dapps as they were known locally, to wear at Whiteball which served this purpose and lasted me a number of years.

One of the reminder appliances provided in the signal box was the lever collar. This was a weighty round casting, painted red, that could be dropped over the handle of a lever thereby preventing

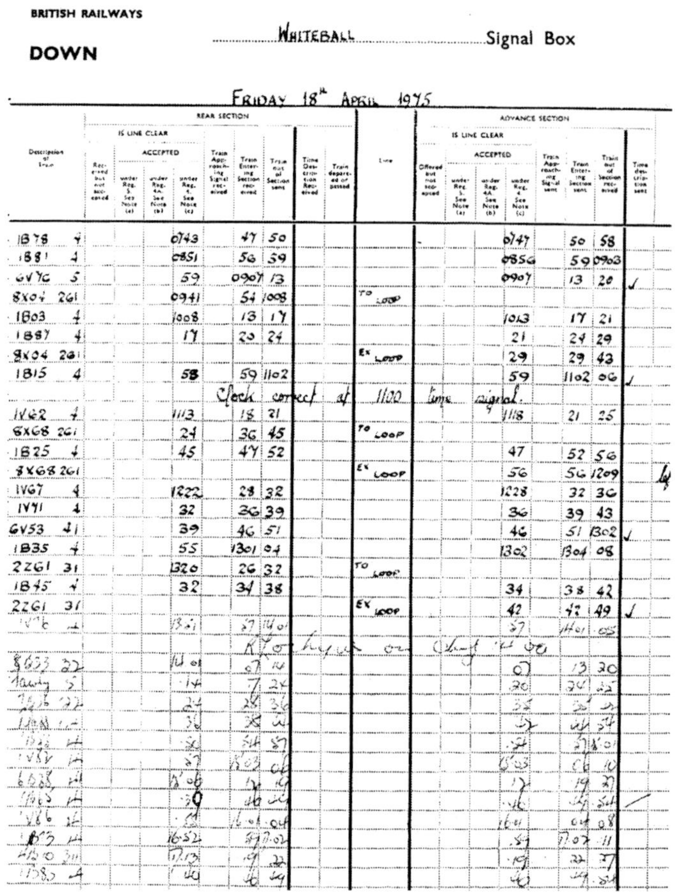

BRITISH RAILWAYS

DOWN Whiteball Signal Box

Friday 18th April 1975

Description of Train	REAR SECTION – IS LINE CLEAR – Received but not accepted	Accepted under Reg. 5. See Note (a)	Accepted under Reg. 4A. See Note (b)	Accepted under Reg. 4. See Note (c)	Train Approaching Signal received	Train Entering Section received	Train out of Section sent	Time Description Received	Train departed or passed	Line	ADVANCE SECTION – IS LINE CLEAR – Offered but not accepted	Accepted under Reg. 5. See Note (a)	Accepted under Reg. 4A. See Note (b)	Accepted under Reg. 4. See Note (c)	Train Approaching Signal sent	Train Entering Section sent	Train out of Section received	Time description sent
1B78 4				0743		47	50							0747		50	58	
1B81 4				0851		56	59							0856		59	0903	
6V76 5				59		0907	13							0907		13	20	✓
8X04 261				0941		54	1008			To Loop								
1B03 4				1008		13	17							1013		17	21	
1B87 4				17		20	24							21		24	29	
8X04 261										Ex Loop				29		29	43	
1B15 4				58		59	1102							59		1102	06	✓
Clock correct at 1100 time signal.																		
1V62 4				1113		18	21							1118		21	25	
8X68 261				24		36	45			To Loop								
1B25 4				45		47	52							47		52	56	
8X68 261										Ex Loop				56		56	1209	
1V67 4				1222		28	32							1228		32	36	
1V71 4				32		36	39							36		39	43	
6V53 41				39		46	51							46		51	1302	✓
1B35 4				55		1301	04							1302		1304	08	
2Z61 31				1320		26	32			To Loop								
1B45 4				32		34	38							34		38	42	
2Z61 31										Ex Loop				42		42	49	✓
[illegible] 4				[illegible]		57	14.01							57		14.01	05	
R. Lockyer on [illegible] 14 00																		
[illegible] 22				14 01		07	14							07		13	20	
Tamper 5				14		17	24							20		24	25	
[illegible] 22				24		28	36							32		[illegible]	[illegible]	
[illegible] 4				30		38	[illegible]							[illegible]		44	54	
[illegible] 4				50		54	57							54		57	15.01	
[illegible] 4				57		15.03	06							15.03		06	10	
[illegible] 4				15.06		14	19							17		19	27	
[illegible] 4				39		46	[illegible]							46		[illegible]	54	
[illegible] 4				[illegible]		16.01	04							16.01		04	08	
[illegible] 4				16.52		57	17.02							57		17.07	11	
[illegible] 31				17.13		19	22							19		22	27	
[illegible] 4				40		46	49							40		49	54	

The down line page from the train register book starting part way into a typical early turn at Whiteball on Friday 18th April 1975. Apart from the regular services, a couple of long welded rail trains (8X04 and 8X68) on their way to a weekend relaying job further west are looped for expresses to pass, whilst the "route learner" unit (2Z61) has ten minutes in the loop to allow passage of 1B45, the "Limited" which is on time. From the timings it looks like 8X68 may have "tickled" the 09.30 Paddington to Penzance (1B25) at Wellington, knocking the London back to right time passing Whiteball. Both rail trains are classified as 8X and signalled 2-6-1 to signify they are slow moving out-of-gauge loads.

The Stoke clay (6V53) has taken 11 minutes to clear the section to Tiverton Junction having been "put inside" there to let the 10.30 Paddington to Penzance (1B35) run by - and it only just made it. Taunton reliefman Ron Lockyer has relieved me just before 2pm. Following the 09.20 Liverpool Lime Street which passed two minutes early at 14.01 there are no less than three freights and a tamper before the next passenger at 14.57; the 12.30 from Paddington running eight minutes late. The first of the freights is the 10.43 Severn Tunnel Junction to Exeter Riverside, the second is the 09.48 Fawley to Tiverton Junction oil tanks and the third is the 12.25 Avonmouth to Exeter City Basin tanks.

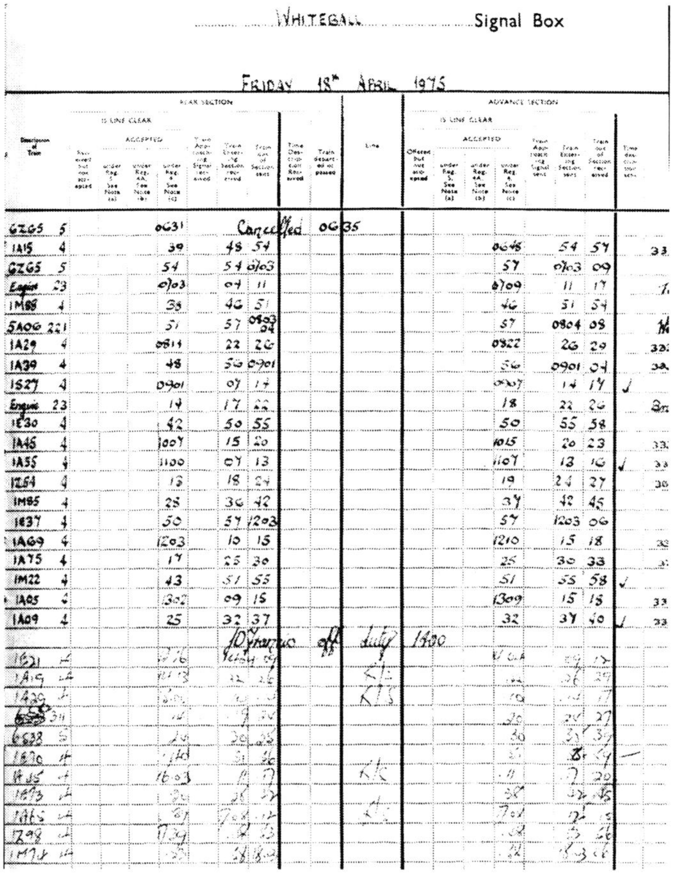

WHITEGALL Signal Box

FRIDAY 18th APRIL 1975

Description of Train		Rear Section: Accepted	Train Entering Section	Train out of Section	Line	Advance Section: Accepted	Train Entering Section	Train out of Section		Time
6Z65	5	0631	Cancelled 0635							
1A15	4	39	48	54		0648	54	57		33
6Z65	5	54	54	0703		57	0703	09		
Engine	23	0703	04	11		0709	11	17		7.
1M88	4	38	46	51		46	51	54		
5A06	221	51	57	0803 04		57	0804	08		[illegible]
1A29	4	0814	22	26		0822	26	29		33
1A39	4	48	56	0901		56	0901	04		3a
1S27	4	0901	07	14		0907	14	17	✓	
Engine	23	14	17	22		18	22	26		Br
1E30	4	42	50	55		50	55	58		
1A45	4	1007	15	20		1015	20	23		33
1A55	4	1100	07	13		1107	13	16	✓	33
1Z54	4	13	18	24		19	24	27		30
1M85	4	28	36	42		37	42	45		
1E37	4	50	57	1203		57	1203	06		
1A69	4	1203	10	15		1210	15	18		33
1A75	4	17	25	30		25	30	33		3
1M22	4	43	51	55		51	55	58	✓	
1A05	4	1302	09	15		1309	15	18		33
1A09	4	25	32	37		32	37	40	✓	33

[Signature] off duty 1400

The up line page from the same day. The first entry shows how the signalman at Tiverton Junction has thought better of letting extra freight 6Z65 continue in front of 1A15, the 05.10 Plymouth to Paddington. He cancels the train, runs the London past it and then lets it follow at 06.54. Two light engines travel up during the morning, one bound for Taunton, the other for Bristol. The 05.55 Plymouth to Old Oak vans stop at 08.03 to exchange water cans and there is an additional up express for the north (1Z54) running as a relief to 1M85 the 07.40 Penzance to Liverpool Lime Street which is belled forward as a 3-3-1 signifying that it would not call at Taunton.

The tick marks show when times had been rung through to Control at Bristol. Note how Ron uses the "R/S" in the line column to record that a routing signal was sent rather than writing the actual code in the remarks column.

the movement of the catch and so reminding the signalman that the lever should not be operated. A number of collars were provided in every box. They would be used to hold a signal lever at danger to protect a standing train, or to hold the section signal lever until such time as the signalman had conversed with the driver over some problem in the block ahead, or for any number of purposes that might occur in the working of the box.

They had other, less official uses too: A few of them dropped over the handle of a broom, around the head of which an old jumper, or the like had been tied, gave sufficient weight to help create a very effective floor polisher; A collar placed in the slot of the section signal lever would allow the signal to be placed to danger without letting the lever return fully to normal in the frame, thus avoiding it becoming locked again necessitating the asking of another "Line Clear". This was useful if a train had to be stopped for some reason after the signals had been cleared or the signal wire needed adjustment to obtain a good "off" indication and hence a second pull.

The size and shape of the collars provided on the Western also meant they doubled as very good egg cups. I used them myself for this purpose, often enjoying a couple of boiled eggs for breakfast on early turn or sometimes for tea on late turn alongwith some previously prepared bread and butter. This was long before the introduction of standard European egg sizes. The British eggs of the day sported the Lion crest stamped on the side and were exactly the right size to sit comfortably in the lever collar. The clockwork operated approach locking timer relay for the motor points that sat on the block shelf performed a secondary role as an egg timer.

Food preparation in the box had to be kept simple, so the boiling of eggs in a saucepan of water was a popular choice. So too was anything that simply involved heating the contents of a tin or packet in the saucepan. Soup, baked beans, creamed rice and the like were not only easy to prepare but a tin or two kept in the locker were handy as emergency rations in case relief never came or the shift was extended for some reason.

Microwave ovens and prepacked meals from the supermarket were a convenience of the future but a few slices of corned beef chopped into a saucepan of hot baked beans tasted terrific. I did discover tins of beef curry where the tin was partitioned such that the curry was contained in one end and the rice could be found in the other. The tin was heated in a pan of boiling water, taking care not to let it explode. One end of the tin was then opened to reveal the rice that was duly deposited onto a plate. The other end was then gingerly opened to release the pressurised curry which was tipped on to the rice to create an instant meal. I can't say it tasted that good but it was simple to prepare.

Toast of course was easy, provided you kept an eye on its progress, and I remember a long spell where I would regularly take cornflakes in a Tupperware bowl to eat on nights, enjoying these with a dash of milk for supper around 11pm whilst listening to the radio. I would never cook a fry up as this created too much of a mess from spitting fat but grilled bacon between two slices of bread was just exquisite. Occasionally a long shift at the weekend might mean preparing something more extravagant, perhaps grilling a chop and boiling a few potatoes and carrots. Somehow I never had much luck with the potatoes, invariably they turned to a mush. The resultant problem could be simply solved by draining off the water, adding a little butter and creating mashed potato.

Milk was taken to work in a bottle, just enough for the shift plus a little extra in case of visitors. An old fizzy drink or sauce bottle was ideal, the screw cap ensuring the milk remained inside. During hot weather the bottle would be placed in a bowl of cold water to help keep the contents fresh to the end of the shift.

Late turn I always found a hungry shift for some reason. I was struck with hunger pangs as soon as I arrived in the box, regardless of whether I had eaten lunch before leaving home. It took great will power to hold off devouring all I had brought before tea time and from raiding the reserves in my locker. There were some days when temptation won and all my food was eaten before 5pm. The other shifts never presented me with this problem, indeed on nights I would rarely eat much, except perhaps for the cornflakes and milk around 11pm.

Warmth came from the coal stove in the far corner of the box. I had to learn how best it operated, to achieve the optimum performance depending on weather conditions and wind direction. The coal was stockpiled alongside the down siding, adjacent to the exit trap points. It was delivered twice a year, bringing the spectacle of a locomotive hauling a single wagon. A truck of coal would be ordered for a string of boxes, being shunted off a freight at Taunton East Yard. Then one or both of the Taunton trip engines, a crew and shunter would be tasked to trip the wagon out to the boxes where the contents would be shovelled out into bunkers or, in the case of Whiteball, into a heap alongside the siding. The fire brought a heart to the box. It was only allowed to go out during the summer months, although even then it might be lit at night apart from a few weeks at the height of the warmer weather in July and August.

One Sunday night I rode out to the box to open it as booked before 23.45. The rain was falling like stair-rods, with the result that I was soaked through to my uniform, even before leaving my bike under Black Bridge and trudging up the side of the loop to the dark box. There is something cheerless about entering a signal box that is bereft of a signalman to relieve, and where the fire is out and cold. On this particular night the wretchedness was exaggerated by my sodden state.

Having fumbled for the big black key in my pocket I let myself in, switched on the light and removed my rucksack and coat, all the while dripping onto the polished lino'. My trouser legs, socks and shoes were soaked but the first priority was to riddle the grate, gather the dry sticks and newspaper that had been left out by the Saturday man and set about lighting the fire. Once the sticks had taken I placed a few lumps of coal strategically in the flames before removing my shoes and socks and retrieving my plimsolls from the locker. Padding around the box, I signed on in the Train Register then called Wellington on the omnibus 'phone to see if it was clear to open. "What a night, I'm absolutely drowned" I said to Eric when he answered. "If it keeps up like this we'll need an Ark to get home in the morning" he replied. "You open up and get settled in, there's nothing about at the moment." Having switched-in I set about emptying my rucksack, placing it, along with my shoes, socks and overcoat near the fire to assist the drying process. With a shovel of coal added, the fire was now warming through, the box beginning to feel habitable, as it should.

The Sunday night shift was quieter than a weeknight but traffic by two in the morning was sufficient to justify the box being open. The first trains due to pass after midnight were the 01.00 Mondays only Taunton to Drump Lane mixed freight (6B53) and the 01.15 Mondays only Exeter Riverside to Longport clay (6M55). They usually ran a little early and so it was on this occasion, with the next trains being the "Postal" on the down and the "Waker" on the up, both due to pass simultaneously at 02.08.

In the period between the two freights and the two class 1 trains I put my shoes on top of the stove to accelerate drying them out then relaxed, putting my feet up on the stool which I had positioned just the right distance from the chair. I must have dozed for a few minutes as the sound of "Call Attention" summoning me to the bell sprung me back to full consciousness. At the same moment I became aware of an acrid smell emanating from the direction of the fire. Realising that I had foolishly left my shoes on top of what was now a very hot stove I grabbed them. As I lifted them the rubber soles remained largely attached to the stove, the now semi-molten material stretching between the enamel casing and base of the shoes. Pulling them fully away revealed a ruined pair of shoes and a glutinous mass of rubber bubbling away on top of the stove. Needless to say I learnt a lesson, spent the next hour having to clean the stove whilst ventilating the box and then had to wear my plimsolls home in the morning as well as back again for late turn that day. Fortunately the rain had stopped.

Signalmen were still afforded a degree of respect, reflected in the way that other grades addressed them. From the Victorian days when railway policemen had been the custodians of rudimentary safeworking the terms Officer and Bobby continued in everyday usage on the Western. Whether it was a permanent way man knocking at the door or a driver calling from a telephone the opening greeting always began with one of these salutations. Someone at the door might start his greeting with "Morning Officer" or a driver on the 'phone might begin "Hello Bobby" before asking how long he would be held in the loop. Visitors always knocked before entering, acknowledging the prominent cast iron notice screwed on the door which carried the words "Great Western Railway NOTICE No Unauthorised Person Allowed in this Box".

Although the single needle telegraph had long been superseded by the telephone, the railway still employed many of the telegraphic code words that had been devised to simplify and bring consistency to message exchange. These were perpetuated in the printed notices of train alteration and engineering works that were despatched from the Divisional Office at Bristol and in the transmission of verbal messages over the telephone. Standardised by the Railway Clearing House in 1897 many of the codes employed the names of animals, fruit and vegetables for particular groups of messages whilst rivers and trees were used for general messages. The everyday names of permanent way wagons were derived from the telegraph fish names such as salmon, whale, mermaid and dogfish.

An anachronism perhaps, but a number of code words survived in every day usage and were commonly employed by signalmen. Some of the words referred to train running and these would be used in messages passed from box to box preceded by the code word "Boxer". This particular word carried the meaning "The following message must be telegraphed or telephoned Box to Box to ....". An "Acacia" would refer to a "Special Train" whilst the word "Emcars" described "Special empty carriages" and "Oglo" an "Out-of-gauge load". If a train was cancelled the word "Cape" would be used and, if the "Amber" message was received it meant a previous message could now be ignored.

There were hundreds of words available to specify particular phrases, many were no longer applicable in the diesel age and others had just fallen out of use. Amongst my favourites were "Walnut" and "Rede". These were often run together and carried the meanings "Make all necessary arrangements, as far as you are concerned" and "Arrange and advise all concerned". Another common word used was "Ure", usually in conjunction with special trains or when someone important was travelling on a particular service. It stood for "It is important for following reason that under mentioned trains should be worked punctually. Do all that is necessary so far as you are concerned." Some words, like many in the English language, found their meanings modified over time through common usage. "Blockade" was one of these. It's official meaning was "All lines blocked at ....." but it had become the word used to describe when a line or lines were closed for engineering work. Thus a "Blockade of the Up Main between Whiteball and Wellington" legitimately defined that the up main line between these two places was closed for some engineering activity of one sort or another to take place. There had in fact been

BRITISH TRANSPORT COMMISSION

BRITISH RAILWAYS

STANDARD CODES

FOR

TELEGRAMS

1st July, 1958

The cover of the 1958 BTC code book which was still in force containing words and phrases for telegrams and all types of rolling stock.

specific codes to describe "Up Main Line Blocked" and "Down Main Line Blocked" but for some reason these, along with other codes, had fallen into disuse.

If the Time Office rang with an "Extenso" message the receiving signalman would find his shift extended due to there being no immediate relief available. This usually meant staying on duty for a further four hours until the next signalman was brought on four hours early, both men ending up working 12 hours each. At other times a reliefman going off duty at another box might be asked to fill the gap, in which case the "Extended" man might only have to wait a short time for the reliefman to travel from one box to the other. Alternatively a reliefman might be booked out after minimum rest of nine hours and so the "Extended" man would gain just an hour's overtime.

When relieving it was customary to arrive around ten minutes before changeover time. This allowed for an orderly handover including an update on traffic and a brief chat before the signalman going off duty departed by the due time. This was a courteous ritual enacted the length and breadth of British Railways. Occasionally a relieving signalman might run late due to an unforeseen circumstance. The first time this happened to me was at the end of an early turn at Whiteball. Reliefman Ken Murray was booked to take over from me at 2pm that particular afternoon. The due time came and went but there was no sign of Ken coming up the railway line. Eventually, some half an hour late, he came hurriedly up the track and arrived apologetically in the box to explain that on setting out for work the gear lever in his Cortina had come off in his hand, in Tancred Street, right in the middle of Taunton causing traffic chaos. He had to get another signalman, John Macdonald from Taunton East Junction who was coming off early turn, to give him a lift out to Whiteball. "Well" I said, "if you will drive a Ford what do you expect".

Certain signal boxes were designated as reporting points to the Control Office. Whiteball was the furthest point west within the jurisdiction of Bristol Control and therefore assigned as a reporting box. Every hour or so therefore the signalman was required to report the passing time of all up and down trains, any movements into and out of the loop and any delays or irregularities. The annotation of a tick alongside entries on each page in the train register would mark the last time a report was made. West of Whiteball the railway came under the auspices of Plymouth Control and so Tiverton Junction undertook a similar role on their behalf. A dedicated telephone line, connected to Control, called in at every box. This was effectively an omnibus or party line circuit but each signal box had a unique code to which its selector relays responded. Thus when Control called, only the telephone in the selected signal box rang.

A custom which had grown up was for the signalman at Whiteball to ascertain the destination of light engines heading in the up direction so as to advise his colleagues at Taunton. Such engines could be bound for Taunton itself or travelling beyond to such places as Westbury or Bristol. In order for these to be routed and regulated correctly at Taunton early advice was essential. If information had not therefore been passed ahead about such engines then a call to Control would be triggered. Details about the loco' would then be passed to Taunton West Station box so that it could be dealt with correctly there and, if necessary a 1-5 routing code added to its 2-3 bell signal should it be destined for the Bristol direction at Cogload. Indeed the signalman at Cogload needed to ascertain not just in which direction to send it but, if heading towards Bristol, enough information in order to select an appropriate four digit identity for transmission over the train describer to Bristol Panel. The four digit number corresponded with that allocated in the working timetable for regular trains or with that shown on special notices for the additional and special services. The class of train was shown by the first number with the second digit being a destination or area letter and the last two numbers providing a degree of uniqueness.

One regular light engine ran up every weekday night but strangely was never shown in the timetable. This phantom "Western", originated from Newton Abbot and was destined for Taunton. The signalman at West Station box needed to be sure about this one as it was diagrammed to take the second part of the Paper train forward once this had been split in the station. Until it was needed the locomotive was placed in the old Barnstaple Departure Bay whilst the crew made use of the mess room.

The 00.30 Paddington Papers arrived in the Down Relief platform at 02.42 in the morning. It was immediately split by the shunter, with the existing train engine taking forward the vans for Plymouth and Cornwall, that had been marshalled at the front of the train, at 02.46. First stop would be Plymouth. The last vehicle in the remaining formation was then detached, this contained the newspapers for Taunton and Somerset, whilst the engine that had come up light from Newton Abbot ran forward out of the bay and backed down onto the remaining vans. These left as the second portion of the Papers, hard on the heels of the first portion, conveying vans for Exeter, Barnstaple, Newton Abbot and Paignton. Although not booked away until 02.55 it would leave as soon as it was ready and usually be only five minutes behind the first portion. As it passed Whiteball a rolled up newspaper would be ejected from a window in one of the vans to land in front of the box - the national news arriving with the first person in Devon just after 3am.

CHAPTER FOUR

OFF THE TOP

Promotion took me from Whiteball to Witham in East Somerset, not far from the Wiltshire border. The signal box was situated in pleasant rural surroundings in the valley of the river Frome adjacent to the village of Witham Friary. The village is so named as a Carthusian monastery, the first in England, was founded here in the twelfth century. The monastery has long gone but the village church is adorned with an interesting spire containing a trinity of bells. With the triumvirate name of Blessed Virgin Mary, Saint John Baptist and All Saints perhaps there is one bell per name or maybe the names were chosen to match the trio of bells. The village and surrounding farms had once formed part of the estate belonging to the Duke of Somerset but were sold in lots at auction to pay off death duties in 1952, the local inhabitants and tenant farmers buying their freeholds. In the centre of the village was a farm, the farmhouse doubling as the ivy clad Seymour Arms public house run by John and Jean Douel. This was a real "spit and sawdust" establishment with flagstone floors and wooden trestles, drink being dispensed from the parlour through a serving hatch. It took its name from the family name of the Duke of Somerset. Like the Blue Ball at Sampford Moor, there was a phone box outside. Opposite, at right angles to the railway, was a terrace of ex-railway cottages.

The railway is elevated on an embankment as it passes through the village, crossing the road alongside the cottages and the Seymour Arms. A station had once served the community. It was closed to passengers on 1st October 1966, being subsequently demolished. Only remnants of the up platform and bay survived until track alterations in 1972. As well as the station and sidings, the signal box, dating from 1880, had controlled the junction of the branch to Wells and Yatton and, during the Second World War, had been extended to control new up and down goods loops to the west of the layout.

By the time I went to Witham the layout had significantly altered from its previous days. The Down Loop was gone, although the Down Sidings remained. The Up Loop now formed two of the four Up Sidings and a new bi-directional Up and Down Goods Loop, which had been built by extending the old bay platform line, gave access to and from the branch via a pair of motor operated crossovers some 600 yards to the east. The branch no longer went through to Yatton but was truncated near Shepton Mallet. It still served both a bitumen depot, in sidings behind the closed station at Cranmore, and the huge Foster Yeoman limestone quarry at Merehead in the Mendips via a connecting spur. There were almost as many levers missing in the frame as still remained. Only 36 working levers were in use, there being 31 spaces in the 67 lever frame that dated from when the loops had been provided in 1942. The frame was a GWR 5-bar vertical tappet style, the last of the GW designs. The levers had a 4" pitch but an operating arc that required them to be pulled just a little further than earlier GW frames.

At the high numbered end of the frame was a "hurdy gurdy" provided for the motor points but this was only needed in the event of a mains power failure, as the electricity supply was man enough to normally drive the points. The box lights would dim whenever the points moved, especially if both sets (which were double ended) were called simultaneously. In the Down Yard was a rare, pre 1900 style shunting signal, which was also fitted with a yellow and white enamelled face. This allowed movements within the yard to pass it at danger when shunting, the signal only having to be reversed for moves out onto the main line.

The western extension of the box had obviously been constructed in haste and was not as sound as the original structure. It had to contend with the prevailing weather, the rain and wind always finding their way in around the windows and brickwork. The windows in most boxes would rattle in the wind and often rain water would percolate through, between adjacent windows and around the frames. As in many boxes, strips of folded newspaper were pushed between the frames to minimise these problems.

Not only did the wind cause the windows to rattle. Every evening around 9pm all the boxes from Cornwall to Somerset could chart the rapid approach of Concorde as it raced up the Bristol Channel on its return from New York to Heathrow. The muffled rumbling as it decelerated from Mach speed would produce a resonance that set every box window rattling in succession along the West of England main line.

The box had an illuminated diagram as the layout was extensively track circuited and in the far corner, below the GWR drop case clock was a Tyer's token instrument for the branch, full of tokens engraved WITHAM - MEREHEAD. Compared with Whiteball though, here was luxury. Running water was available,

Witham signal box viewed from the top of the Up Branch Home signal bracket. There are cows in the field behind the box and some of the village houses can be seen beyond. The western extension to the box is evident, alongside which is the termination pole carrying all the various block, telephone and indicator circuits. *(Author)*

together with an inside toilet located in the converted porch cupboard. The water came from a private supply to the village and railway, being fed from a tank on the hills a couple of miles away to the south east and still owned by the Duke of Somerset. There was a large sink mounted on wooden supports, above which was an electric water heater fitted to the wall. Piping hot water at the turn of a knob, modernity indeed! The armchair, positioned alongside the coal stove, completed the home comforts. The train register book sat on top of a train register desk beneath a window at the back of the box. The front edge of the desk lid revealed its age from the worn shape derived over many years of being pressed and rubbed against, especially by waistcoat buttons. Pinned above the desk was a list of trains together with their passing times, drawn up from the working timetable as a "simplifier" for easy reference.

Unlike Whiteball, the box was tall, spacious and had a commanding view of the countryside. It faced north west and so the sun would rise above the railway lines to the east, travel behind the box during the day and set below the branch line that curved steeply away up hill at 1 in 49 through Lower Bitcombe wood towards Wanstrow. During a clear evening the sun's rays would pick out the bright colours of the levers in the box and cast their parallel shadows across the polished brown linoleum on the floor. An ash path alongside the Down Sidings meant I could ride the bike right up to the box steps, bobbing up and down over the wooden ramps that provided continuity across the signal wires and point rodding. Anyone who came by car or van had to park in the yard and walk down the ash path. So, like Whiteball, there were a few minutes grace to tidy the box if needs be and warn either side if the visitor was official like Area Manager Bernard Green, Traffic Assistant Mike Romans or Inspectors Gordon (Pussy) Simons or Jack Creed. If it was Jack (Gentleman Jack) we could relax our guard as, whilst he expected us to do the job properly, he did not insist on rigid adherence to petty procedures that added no value.

The main line traffic passed at speed, especially the class 1 expresses which took full advantage of the 90 mph line speed. A good view of trains was afforded from the box, being as how it was tall and set back beyond the Down Refuge siding. Further up the line the four boxes controlling the junctions to the Frome and Westbury 'cut offs' were positioned close to the nearest main line. Being constructed entirely of wood this meant that Blatchbridge, Clink Road, Fairwood and Heywood Road boxes were prone to the draught created by passing trains. So much so they would physically move when a train passed, particularly when an express thundered by. The rush of air would punch the fabric, shaking the box and even causing the signalman to miss the bell tapper if he attempted to use one at the time.

After a couple of weeks Assistant District Inspector Malcolm Arthurs from Bristol duly spent an hour with me in the box watching me work and testing my knowledge of the local instructions, rules and regulations before handing me the competency slip to sign. Despite attempting to portray a confident air it was quite unnerving to be scrutinised by an Inspector. As at Whiteball I "took on" on nights the next day, the reliefman covering the vacancy being allowed to stand spare.

Beyond Witham to the west, the block section to Castle Cary was quite long at 8.7 miles. An up express would

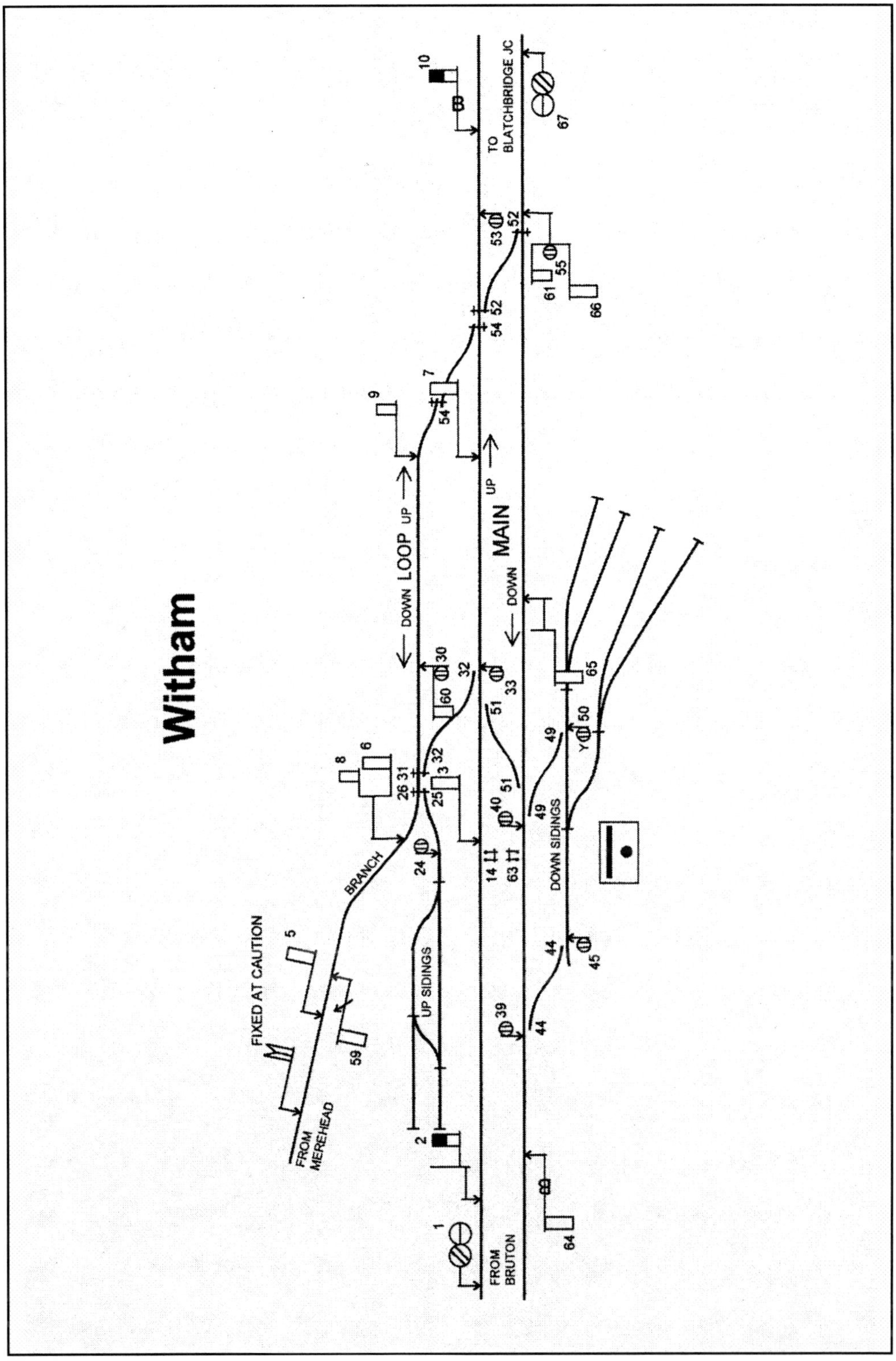
Witham
DOWN LOOP UP
DOWN MAIN UP
BRANCH
UP SIDINGS
DOWN SIDINGS
FIXED AT CAUTION
FROM MEREHEAD
FROM BRUTON
TO BLATCHBRIDGE JC
1
2
3
5
6
7
8
9
10
14
24
25
26
30
31
32
33
39
40
44
45
49
50
51
52
53
54
55
59
60
61
63
64
65
66
67
Y

take 7 to 7½ minutes to traverse this section having to climb Brewham bank on the way, and a Weymouth train, having stopped at Castle Cary and called in-section at Bruton would take 12 to 13 minutes. A couple of the London's in each direction stopped at Castle Cary so these took up to 10 minutes to pass through. Finding a path for a freight train or a light locomotive could sometimes be difficult. There was an intermediate box at Bruton but this was only open on summer Saturdays or for engineering work.

From Westbury through to Witham the complexity of the railway meant that the signal boxes were closely spaced, some boxes "asking on" immediately they had accepted a train, others waiting for the specially authorised "Train Approaching" bell signal 1-2-1. The signalman at Blatchbridge Junction was authorised to send this signal to Witham when he received "Train Entering Section" for down trains from Clink Road or Frome North. If the train was continuing main line it was at this point that the Witham signalman then offered it forward and pulled off. During the periods that Bruton was open then the 1-2-1 was also authorised to and from Witham for all up and down trains.

The regular men at both Castle Cary and Witham learnt Bruton and often worked the box on a summer Saturday on overtime rather than tying up a reliefman. Being closed most of the time, the box was damp with the lever tops rusted, and there was chicken wire across the windows to protect against vandals' stones. But one treasure remained inside. Or two to be precise - the block instruments were both of the GWR Spagnoletti disc type. What a treat to signal main line trains with Spagnoletti blocks. My chance to learn Bruton came one early summer Saturday when Ron Kirby was booked there for the day. Part way through the shift I left Ron on his own to take an hour out for lunch, strolling back to my digs at the other end of the town. In the train register I had recorded all the Londons with the abbreviation "Pad" alongside their starting time, as was my usual practice. On returning to the box I found Ron had added a second letter "d" to all my entries to extend the abbreviation to "Padd", to comply with the way he always wrote them down. Ron was certainly well set in his ways, even continuing to use the old South Western phrase of "Warn" for "Line Clear" having originally been an L&SWR man. He would say "Is he Warned?" and "Warn him on" rather than "Is he Asked?" or "Ask him on".

The former main line from Castle Cary to Weymouth had been singled as far as Dorchester with crossing loops provided at Yeovil Pen Mill and Maiden Newton. The West of England route to Taunton, whilst still double line had long block sections from Castle Cary to Somerton (10.4 miles) and thence to Athelney (9.2 miles). It was thus fortunate that not too many freights were booked to travel beyond Witham. There was a Ripple Lane to Exeter City Basin Shell Mex tank train of bitumen; a Fawley to Plymouth Friary oil; and a Fawley to Tiverton Junction oil, both for Esso; a Salisbury to Meldon Quarry ballast empties; a Westbury to Exeter Central cement; and a Westbury to Truro cement (for Chacewater), both from the Blue Circle works at Westbury; a Sittingbourne to Burngullow china clay empties from Bowaters at Sheerness for English China Clays Ltd (ECLP); an Acton to St Erth milk empties; a Westbury to Yeovil goods; and a Reading West Goods to Exeter Riv-

The diminutive box at Bruton which only opened for engineering work and to split the section on summer Saturdays. There is a lineside telephone cabinet to the right of the box for use of staff, such as train crew, wishing to contact Witham or Castle Cary when the box is shut. Note the fire buckets hanging on brackets on the stairway. *(Author)*

erside general freight. This latter train, which ran late morning, was always heavily loaded carrying a variety of traffic but always conveying a flat wagon loaded with farm machinery, usually three brand new muck spreaders on their way to West Country show rooms. Their pristine, bright red newness I always saw as incongruous with the reality that awaited their ultimate service on a farm. This train was unique as it was now the only timetabled freight which avoided Westbury, coming down the backroad from Heywood to Fairwood.

There were of course the corresponding workings in the opposite (up) direction apart from the Reading West Goods, return traffic being worked back via Bristol and Severn Tunnel Junction but the Meldon Quarry to Salisbury ran in two loaded portions. This meant that 6V80, the 03.55 Salisbury to Meldon, usually conveyed a great long raft of assorted empties such as grampus, salmon and whales, making an interesting sight just after 06.30 in the morning when it would pass through Witham. It was booked to follow 2O51, the locomotive hauled 05.12 Bristol Temple Meads to Weymouth that left Westbury at 06.08. But if Westbury was congested or 2O51 was running late then the Westbury South signalman would get rid of 6V80 first. This meant it often had to be shunted at Witham for 2O51 to pass, backing into the down sidings for its sojourn. A hefty margin was required to let a goods down to Cary as the loop there was before the station with the box situated at the other end by the junction, so it suffered from a similar problem to that described at Tiverton Junction in Chapter 2.

Whilst the loaded Meldons travelled up via Taunton the empties took an even more circuitous route. They would first travel from Salisbury to Westbury, where the locomotive would then run round. The next leg of the journey saw the train run down to Castle Cary where the Weymouth line was taken as far as Yeovil Pen Mill before traversing the connecting spur to Yeovil Junction and joining the "Southern" again for a run down the old London and South Western route to Exeter, then down the bank from Exeter Central to St Davids and into Riverside Yard, before the final leg onto the Barnstaple and Meldon branches.

Like the Meldon empties, 6B22 the 19.07 Westbury to Exeter Central cement also reached its destination via Yeovil, following the 17.45 Bristol to Weymouth passenger. This latter train, 2O61, left Westbury at 18.48 and, whilst calling at Frome, would be overtaken on the avoiding line by the prestigious "untouchable" down "Golden Hind", 1B19 the 17.30 Paddington to Penzance. Leaving Blatchbridge as soon as the "Hind" passed Witham, the Weymouth passenger would often be checked at Witham waiting for the "Hind" to clear the long section to Castle Cary. Meanwhile the cement, formed of a rake of presflo wagons and invariably hauled by a "Western", followed the "Hind" from Fairwood Junction. If it left Westbury on time it would get a clear run to Witham. If it left early it would be held at Clink Road Junction whilst the Weymouth passed clear of Blatchbridge Junction, and it would be checked at Blatchbridge before the Weymouth cleared Witham. Either way, upon arrival at Witham it would have to wait for the Weymouth to reach Castle Cary. It was thus brought from signal to signal at walking pace before the starter was lowered and the driver would cajole the twin Maybach engines back to full revs for the attack of Brewham bank.

The previous day's return empties were brought back as 6B23, the 23.30 from Exeter Riverside via Taunton. With Somerton box switched out at night, Castle Cary worked with Athelney, a long 19.6 miles away. The empties were booked to pass Athelney at around 00.30 and could take anything up to half an hour or more to then pass Castle Cary. The train would be accepted by Witham all this time and I can remember on many occasions becoming concerned around one o'clock in the morning as to whether my mate at Castle Cary had forgotten to put the train "On Line" to me, or indeed had dozed off and missed it passing him altogether, as Castle Cary was a relatively quiet box at night. A telephone call on the box to box circuit was often required just to check on the situation.

One particular night I left it too long and the train arrived at my Up Home signal out at West Barn bridge. Ken Roberts at Castle Cary, having cleared his signals had then fallen sound asleep, never noticing the train going by. Neither had the signalman at Athelney checked with Ken why the train had not reached him in the normal running time. No doubt he was gently dozing too having succumbed to the warmth of the fire and the comfort of the armchair. Having been stopped, the driver came on the telephone at the Up Home signal to enquire if I was awake! I felt just a little indignant but needless to say there was no real problem and the entries in the Train Registers at Athelney, Castle Cary, Witham and Clink Road (Blatchbridge was switched out at night) were all reconciled to portray an uninterrupted journey.

Some time later, when Ken was off for a week, I had Joe Apsey on nights down at Cary working twelve hours. Joe had started with the Great Western and now, in later years, had developed distinctive large eyes which bulged forward from his head giving him frog-like features. His catchphrase when answering the 'phone was "alright cocker". One night, having got the road from me for the Up Sleepers and pulled off, Joe had the 'dos on' in the armchair when he was woken by the driver storming up the stairs to find out why his train had been held at the home signal. Unbeknown to Joe the down rod to the signal had broken after he had pulled off. True to the failsafe principles of the design the arm had returned to danger, which in turn had automatically reverted the colour light distant back to caution.

Another night the Up Sleepers was overlong in the section to Clink Road. In due course the signalman there came on the 'phone to explain that the train had come to a sudden stop beyond the box, the crew reporting that they may have hit something approaching the junction. The signalman and secondman from the sleepers went back to investigate, finding a corpse and various body parts. Someone had evidently jumped from a nearby overbridge to commit suicide - not the first time in that area. The signalman had to be relieved such was the effect on him. He was off for the rest of the week and never the same on night turn after that, being always nervous and twitchy.

One of the first trains to pass on early turn and one of the last on late turn was the empty "bubble car" on its way to and from Maiden Newton. This single car diesel unit was stabled and fuelled at Westbury overnight and manned by Westbury train crew. It spent the day shuttling between Maiden Newton and Bridport, connecting with the Weymouth trains, until the branch closed in 1975.

Sometimes, if there were problems between Bristol and Cogload or engineering work was in progress then we would be treated to traffic to and from the Midlands and the north which would be diverted via Cary, Westbury and the Avon Valley. One such afternoon a couple of trains had been diverted due to an incident in the Bridgwater area but word soon came through that the situation had been rectified. The next up train shortly afterwards, the "Limited", caused consternation however when it showed up hauled by a "Peak" displaying the headcode 1E21. Some frantic double checking with Control confirmed the train really was the "Limited" and not the Penzance - Leeds, otherwise it would have been sent the wrong way at Westbury. It was more than rare for a "Peak" to haul a London, let alone the "Limited". Coming as it did just after diversions had been lifted, carrying a credible headcode for the time of day, had us nearly fooled.

Westbury was a stabling and fuelling point for locomotives, most of which were engaged on the stone train workings to and from the quarries at Whatley and Merehead. Besides a few Brush type '4' (class 47) and "Peak" (class 46) locomotives, the majority of the contingent comprised "Westerns" (class 52) displaced from main line passenger duties on the Bristol and South Wales routes by the English Electric type '4s' (class 50), known as "Hoovers". This latter class were progressively transferred from the London Midland Region following electrification of the West Coast Main Line north of Crewe. These locomotives were outbased from either Bristol Bath Road or Plymouth Laira sheds but by this time, all the "Westerns" were based at Laira creating regular movement of light engines, often two or more coupled, between Westbury and their home base to facilitate maintenance. A box to box telegraph message would be passed along the line over the telephone advising of these movements and their departure time. For example, "Boxer Desloc Libna Laira to Westbury 14.10". "Boxer" meant Box to Box message, "Desloc" described a diesel locomotive and "Libna" meant light locomotive. Hence the message informed that a light diesel locomotive had left Laira at 14.10 bound for Westbury.

When locomotives ran coupled in multiple, each subsequent engine would be belled as "Engine Assisting in Rear" but if one locomotive was hauling one or more dead engines the formation would be signalled as a class 9 freight, accompanied by a boxer message such as "one live, one dead for Laira". The letter F was used in the headcode to denote movements to sheds and stabling points, each having a separate number defined in the Working Timetable. Hence, as examples, 0F77 would be an engine for Laira, 0F74 for Bristol (Bath Road), 0F70 for Old Oak Common and 0F75 for Westbury. Appendix C shows the full list. If an engine was towing a brake van behind it, the combination would be affectionately known as a pony and trap (belled 1-1-3) and a slow engine such as a diesel shunter might be referred to as a donkey.

Three coupled for Laira (0F77). D1005 "Western Venturer", D1072 "Western Glory" and 47 026 head west past Witham on their 130 mile journey to Laira for servicing. (A. Vaughan)

During the seventies most of the trains to and from the quarries at Whatley and Merehead operated as local trips out of Westbury where they often received locomotive changes or crew relief. Merehead was served on a round the clock basis from Monday morning until early afternoon on Saturday with around 18 trips a day each way. A variety of different vehicle sets were employed for a range of destinations and each day saw the trips organised to suit the demands of the customer, Foster Yeoman. A pair of hand-written, roneo-copied sheets were delivered to the box each day detailing the workings for the next 24 hours. These sheets, along with any other notices, were handed down by drivers on the local trips from Westbury when collecting the token for the branch. Trips carried the class 6, 7 or 8 headcode together with the letter B for West of England Division followed by the numbers 71, 73, 74, 76, 77 or 78 depending upon which trip circuit they were working.

Although distributed throughout the 24 hour period, trips often turned up in close succession depending on crew availability, early or late running and last minute amendments. This brought daily variety to the work at Witham, especially as the sidings were often used to stable empty sets between workings. There was room for four sets in the Up Sidings and for a couple of sets in the Down Yard. Stabling in the Down Yard required sets to be split as each of the four roads was too short to take a full consist. At times the sidings could be completely empty and then, on another day, impressively full of stone wagons, bitumen tanks and perhaps a "hot box" wagon detached from a passing goods.

Trains were loaded at Merehead for despatch to a variety of destinations in the South East including Botley, Ipswich, Wootton Bassett, Worcester, Acton, Banbury, Basingstoke, Bletchley, Brentford, Fareham, Leagrave, Northampton, West Drayton, Theale and Aldermaston. The stone was bound for the construction industry, especially road building. There was a great deal of motorway and bypass building going on at the time. Ironic then that the railway was helping to build roads for motor cars

TRIP WORKING - WESTBURY AREA

TRIP No. 4

C1.52(Extract of Laira 131)

	Arr.		Dep.	
		MX		
Westbury Depot			00//30	LD
Westbury	00//35		00.45	6V62
(22.20 Woking)				
Frome North	01.02	FS	01.45	6046
	(To Woking)			
Westbury	02.00		02.40	6B74
Merehead	03.26	FS	03.55	6B74
Westbury	04.58			
		MO		
Westbury Depot			06//22	LD
Westbury	06//27			
		SX		
Westbury			06.42	6B74
Merehead	07.29	FS	07.55	6B74
Westbury	09.00		10.18	6B74
Merehead	11.05	FS	11.35	6B74
Westbury	12.49		14.15	6B74
Merehead	15.02	FS	15.32	6B74
Westbury	16.38		17.45	6B74
Merehead	18.31		19.00	6B74
Westbury	20.08		20//15	LD
Westbury Depot	20//20			
		SO		
Westbury Depot			00//30	LD
Westbury	00//35		00.45	6V62
	(22.20 Woking)			
Frome North	01.02	FS	01.45	6046
Westbury	02.00		02//05	LD
Westbury Depot	02//10			

TRAINCREW:- Westbury 38, 49, 655, 656, 679.

TRIP No. 5

C1.52(Extract of Laira 34)

		MX		
Westbury Depot			04//00	LD
Frome North	04//15		04.35	6B75
Whatley Bridge	05.00		05.35	6B75
Westbury	06.19		07.46	6B75
		MO		
Westbury Depot			07//15	
Westbury	07//2		07.46	6B75
		SX		
Whatley Bridge	08.35		09//00	0B75
Westbury	09//40		10.48	6B75
Whatley Bridge	11.45		12.20	6B75
Frome North	12.50		13//05	0B75
Westbury	13//17		14.40	6B75
Whatley Bridge	15.35		16.10	6B75
Westbury	16.54		17//00	LD
Westbury Depot	17//05		18//20	LD
Frome North	18//35		19.05	6B75
Westbury	19.20			

Then works 19.50 Westbury - W.Drayton.

		SO		
Westbury	06.19		06//25	LD
Westbury Depot	06//30			

TRAINCREW:-

Westbury 55, 67, 665, 669, 691, 697.

TRIP No. 6

C1.33 (Extract of Eastleigh 206)

		SX		
Westbury Depot			19//20	LD
Westbury	19//25		19.43	6B75
Whatley Bridge	20.38		21.03	6B75
Frome North	21.32		22//05	0B75
Westbury Depot	22//20.			

TRAINCREW:- Westbury 56, 695.

A page from the locomotive and crew diagram for trips in the Westbury area.

and lorries. Additionally ballast was also sent out to Woking for use on the Southern Region in 'Whales' and 'Sea Lions'. The Western never used Mendip stone for ballast, preferring that from Machen in South Wales and especially the aesthetic pink stone from Stoneycombe quarry in Devon. Train lengths varied according to destination but typically loaded to between 900 and 1,500 tonnes with most around the 1,000 or 1,100 tonne mark. A similar but slightly smaller Westbury based operation went on in parallel serving the ARC owned quarry at Whatley which was reached via the Radstock branch from Frome. Westbury was therefore a busy railfreight hub.

Whilst the Botley, Worcester and Wootton Bassett workings were formed of smart new air braked privately owned 'Procor' hoppers, the West Drayton and Ipswich services comprised sets of older 21 tonne bottom discharge hoppers. All other trains were made up of 26 tonne four wheeled tippler vehicles. Eventually these were all fitted with vacuum brakes but initially many ran with only fitted heads and a brake van at the rear. These tipplers and hoppers sported a distinctive white stencilled logo on the body side cleverly depicting the word STONE in the shape of a hopper.

The branch was a single line, worked by "No Signalman Key Token" to Merehead Quarry Junction, where it split. Here, a new spur went into the quarry whilst the branch continued on to Cranmore on the former Cheddar Valley route. The empty stone trains would take the spur into the reception sidings whilst loaded trains usually propelled out from the departure roads on another line to a siding at Whites Crossing further along the branch where they would then be facing the right way to join the branch and come forward to Quarry Junction. The quarry layout thus operated as a triangle with the sets and loco's effectively being turned on every trip. The "No Signalman Key Token" system gave control of the branch as far as Quarry Junction to the signalman at Witham. He could remove a token from his machine at any time, provided one had not already been taken out. In contrast, the Chargeman at Quarry Junction had to obtain a release from Witham to extract a token from the machine at his end. Communication was over a dedicated block 'phone, the Chargeman advising the destination of each loaded train when ready to leave and requesting release of a token.

To help one another, the bell on the block 'phone was used in an unofficial fashion to advise when a train actually departed from one end or the other of the section. The code 1-2-1 (Train Approaching) was transmitted by the signalman to Quarry Junction when a train left Witham and likewise the Chargeman would send 1-2-1 to Witham when a train left him. This provided a simple means of keeping one another informed without having to converse. There were two regular Chargemen up at the junction who alternated between early and late turns. One of them, Eric Compton, actually lived in the village at Witham so I would see him from time to time tending his garden or out for a walk. On the night shift, the Chargeman's role was combined with that of the yard shunter and so the junction was only manned whilst there was no train to deal with in the quarry sidings. Thus on nights I always had Leo York on the other end of the telephone and token machine. If one train was already in the quarry then I could send a second up to the junction but it would have to wait there until Leo arrived from

Whites Crossing on the outgoing loaded train. He would then have to send the second train down into the quarry to clear the single line before despatching the loaded and then walk back to the sidings. It was usually more convenient to hold an empty set at Witham and let the loaded run down first. Controlled by a ground frame, Quarry Junction was at the summit of the branch and so when trains left there on their journey down to the main line they were termed as being "off the top".

With the layout and sidings at Westbury being congested at times due to the amount of traffic being handled it was normal for the signalman at Witham to check with his counterpart at Westbury South before letting a loaded stone away, just in case it might cause a problem. Similarly the signalman at Frome North would also check with South before letting a Whatley stone proceed. My regular counterpart at Westbury South was Tom Lambe whose full name was Thomas Oswald Teasdale Lambe. He always gave the impression of fussing and fumbling in the job of working such a busy box. In reality this was a diversion because he was completely on top of his work - most of the time, planning each move well ahead of time like a chess player and working in complete harmony with Ian Wannell in North box as they both went about the business of sorting all the moves through the complicated layout.

Whenever I rang Tom to let him know I had a stone "off the top" he would always go through the ritual of narrating the current and impending situation at Westbury to me in his high pitched Wiltshire accent and in such a way as to surely conclude that there was no possibility he could take another train. His dialogue would go something like this: "Well, I've got the Brentford sitting on the Up Reception, the Fareham empties are on the Up Salisbury, the Bassett's coming over Bradford Junction, the Botley's still on the Down Main waiting for a driver, the banker's coming back from Warminster, the Pilot wants to make a transfer from the down side and the London's off Woodborough - but let 'im come." Tom would never refuse me. Other signalmen often faired less well, especially when trying to persuade Tom to take a train that had already arrived at Witham. His favourite retort to them was "As far as I'm concerned he can stay there 'til the wheels fall off've 'im".

Tom Lambe resplendent in his work attire with waistcoat, tie and pocket watch as he thinks through his next move at Westbury South. The emergency oil lamp hangs from the ceiling. South box, like North had a frame with room for 99 levers.

(Author)

Witham provided plenty of exercise, not just from working the frame but in constantly climbing up and down the stairs to issue and collect the token in its metal hoop to and from branch trains. This meant leaving the box and crossing the Down Refuge Siding, both main lines and the outlet from the Up Sidings on a wooden foot crossing to reach the branch line track farthest away from the box. At night, or when the weather was cold or wet, it was wise, and sometimes essential, to don jacket, coat and hat. There was always the temptation to forego this sensible routine and dash down the stairs and across the tracks without the protection of sufficient clothes but I usually saw sense unless things were really busy. Danger from catching cold or slipping was slim compared to the possibility of being hit by an express at 90 mph that might approach whilst I was out of the box. Care had to be taken and there was many a time that the secondman of a loaded stone had to drop the token in its metal hoop to the ground as he passed as it was either too busy for me to collect it at that moment or there was insufficient time to safely get out and back before an express would rocket past. Both myself and the other regular men at Witham knew that token pick-up and set-down posts would greatly improve operations and safety. The number of moves on to and off of the branch were far in excess of those at many places where this apparatus had been provided. Requests to the Area Manager, laying out the arguments for such equipment, met with sympathy but did not extend to actually spending the £600 quoted by the S&T department to procure and install it.

With up to 20 movements each way a day, the branch was certainly well utilised. Once a train had been advised "off the top" by the 1-2-1 on the 'phone there was no further warning of its approach so, once five minutes or so had elapsed it was necessary to keep an eye out towards the woods. The loaded trains would drop down the 1 in 49, smoke issuing from the brake blocks, as the drivers tried to hold their speed, especially if the signals were against them. If the road was clear out on to the main line they would roll down briskly, stone dust blowing across the fields from the open wagons. The yard at Cranmore usually had a daily visit from a trip conveying loaded bitumen tanks. Cranmore was also the home of the fledgling East Somerset Railway. This provided for the occasional visit of an enthusiasts special to the branch or the movement of David Shepherd's steam locomotives between their base and the main line. He owned two locomotives, both Swindon built. Green Knight was a standard 4MT 4-6-0 numbered 75029 whilst Black Prince (No. 92203) was a mighty 9F 2-10-0. Famous for his wildlife and locomotive paintings, David Shepherd established an art gallery in the defunct signal box at Cranmore. The daily bitumen tanks, run for Shell Mex, travelled down on 6V32, the 02.00 Ripple Lane to Exeter City Basin. Hauled by a silver roofed, Stratford based, Brush type '4' this train dropped Cranmore and Frome traffic at Westbury before taking its reduced load on to Exeter. A Westbury engine, often a type '3' (class 33) working trip No. 2, B72, then tripped this traffic into Frome during the morning leaving loaded tanks and bringing out the Frome empties from the previous day along with the Cranmore loaded. At Witham, the Frome empties would be stabled in the sidings before the trip went down the branch to Cranmore. Having shunted the yard at Cranmore, the empties from there

Under threatening skies a class 33 propels a brake van and a short rake of bitumen tanks through the trailing crossover onto the up main at Witham before heading down the branch to Cranmore. *(A. Vaughan)*

would be brought to Witham and stabled with those from Frome left earlier, the engine then returning light to Westbury.

In the afternoon the return working 6E33 to Ripple Lane from Exeter City Basin would call at Witham to attach these empties. This train was worked by a Taunton driver and guard as far as Acton. They usually arrived comfortably in front of the up "Limited", formed up their increased load, carried out a brake test and recorded the wagon numbers ready to follow it away at 15.01 knowing they would get a good run up the Berks and Hants line before the next express. They were in fact booked to follow the 13.45 Plymouth - Paddington over an hour later but the Taunton men were always keen to get away as they might then get an early path back from Acton with the St Erth milk empties which was their return working.

The wagon numbers and train consist details had to be telephoned through to the local TOPS (Total Operations Processing System) office at Westbury. This was the duty of the guard but I and other signalmen often undertook this task on their behalf if it meant we could get the train away promptly. The box was provided with a Post Office telephone for this purpose, a shared extension being housed in a locked cupboard on one of the lamp posts in the up sidings for the guards.

On one occasion a rather large number of empties had accumulated in the up sidings. Not all of these could be taken forward by 6E33 when it arrived with its load from Kings Ashphalt in Exeter or the train would have been overweight. Advising me of the situation the Taunton guard therefore left a handful of tanks on the stop blocks for the following day. In his haste, he had forgotten to ensure the handbrakes were secure on these wagons so that as the train departed via No. 32 points out onto the main line I noticed the four "left overs" following behind along the siding. They had gathered a fair speed and quickly I determined I had a choice of four courses of action. I could let them follow into the section as a runaway but they were likely to travel some distance as it was downhill. I could try and switch points No. 32 behind the train into the goods loop so that they derailed on the trap points at the far end. This would mean breaking the glass of the emergency release on lever No. 31 in order to unbolt the points and move them between the two sets of vehicles. Not an impossible task but the resultant derailment would see a pile of empty bitumen tanks in the farmer's field at the bottom of the embankment. Alternatively I could stop the train, allow the errant wagons to catch it up and hope the resultant collision did not result in a derailment, or I could try and apply the handbrakes as the vehicles came past the box and stop them myself.

There were no other trains about so I decided to carry out both the latter two options. I threw back the Up Advanced Starting signal (No. 10) rather than the starter, in order to bring the train to a fairly controlled stand before it entered the section - the driver would see it return to danger in the distance. I then ran down the stairs and across to the exit of the up sidings just as the wagons passed at running pace. Being air braked tanks they were fitted with wheel operated handbrakes that proved difficult to turn when running alongside on ballast and whilst trying to avoid all those obstructions of pointwork, rodding, signal wires and the like. In fact it was highly dangerous and my efforts made little impact in arresting their motion as they passed out onto the main line. As I arrived breathless back in the box the guard of the train was already hastily ringing on the telephone from the Advanced Starter, wanting to know why it had been put to danger in front of him. "Well", I said, "remember those tanks you left behind, they're just about to catch you up." And with that the loud bang of meeting buffers came over the telephone, to be echoed by the same sound through the window a split second later.

We were all lucky, as there was no derailment and no damage, the incident replicating little more than a very rough shunt. Following a quick and satisfactory examination by the guard, the wagons were propelled back into the siding and this time the brakes firmly secured. The train got away a little later but no-one, other than the three of us concerned were any the wiser. Between the three of us though that bond of the railway family took on a slightly deeper meaning.

Later that day, just before the end of my shift, the same Taunton men headed home early with the 19.18 Acton - St Erth milk empties at full tilt, the milk tanks hammering out their unique six-wheeler beat on the down main line as they hurried by. The driver switched on his cab light to show himself waving as he passed. I returned a raised arm, smiling both to him and myself.

CHAPTER FIVE

MAKING HAY

The impending demise of the Western Diesel Hydraulic locomotives attracted much photographic attention. The first withdrawals had begun in May 1973 but it was not until February 1977 that the final 'Thousand' was taken out of service. Some renowned railway photographers and authors such as John Chalcraft and John Vaughan visited the Westbury area on numerous occasions, as did many less well known people.

A father and son combination, Tom and Chris Chapman from Bath, pursued their shared interest in photography by capturing many of the "Westerns", and other types of traction, from trackside locations in the area. Befriending many of the signalmen this duo were able to gain vantage points precluded to others. Whilst both learning more about railways and Tom teaching Christopher all about photography, Chris also came under the spell of signalling. So much so that, with particular encouragement from Chriss Burden at Blatchbridge, he joined the railway as an S&T trainee when he left school.

The pair spent summer evenings and Saturday afternoons in or near signal boxes, sometimes at Witham when I was on late turn. For Christopher's fourteenth birthday he was allowed to spend the night shift with me at Witham. This was a treat which enabled him to see and signal trains like the Postal, the Papers, the Sleepers and the return Exeter cement amongst the others which broke the silence of the night hours whilst he would normally be asleep in bed as most folks were.

After pestering him for many years, Chris finally published the best of their "Western" photographs in a volume called *Western Glory* dedicated to his late father.

Chris and Tom were able to see and photograph some of the more interesting activity, as did Adrian Vaughan who was the signalman I normally relieved at Witham. Adrian had moved to Witham from Clink Road Junction, having been accommodated there when the mechanical boxes at Oxford closed under a resignalling scheme. Using black and white film Adrian recorded some excellent scenes of train working at Witham. A selection of these can be found in his book *Signalman's Nightmare*, the third in the trilogy covering his career on the railway. He would often be busy writing when I arrived to relieve him or poised with his camera ready to capture a passing train. Witham was the last box which Adrian worked - signing off in the train register with a suitably final phrase. The romance of the railway had already died for him. He makes mention of me in *Signalman's Nightmare*, on page 116, in connection with the routing codes mentioned in the next chapter. Adrian was replaced by another keen and competent signalman by the name of Nick Jones who came to Witham on promotion from Moreton-in-Marsh.

On transferring to Witham I initially lodged with another signalman, Ian Wannell, and his family a few miles away in the small town of Bruton, famous for its boarding schools - Kings, Sexey's and Sunnyhill. Ian had started as a booking boy at Exeter Middle and West boxes and gone on to be a signalman at Fairwood Junction and then Witham before moving to Westbury North. We were both on the same shift so the arrangement worked well, especially for his wife, Dawn, who had to organise domestic life and meals around work patterns. She made a terrific flapjack and always supplied cornflakes for night shift but I was never keen on the pig's hearts she often cooked for Ian and the family. After a spell at Swindon, Ian moved back to the Exeter area in later life, eventually settling at Exmouth Junction box.

Their small three bedroom cottage, at the end of a terrace in Providence Place, was comfortable and the rent from my lodging assisted with the houseckeeping bills. When the birth of their third child was imminent it was time for me to vacate the spare bedroom by seeking alternative accommodation. I tried a lodging house in Frome for a few weeks but this was less than ideal, so I ended up renting a bedsit flat over a toy shop in Shepton Mallet. A mattress in front of the hearth back at Providence Place sufficed occasionally after an evening in Bruton. Some months later the Wannell's moved to a rented four bedroom house in Warminster and I was invited to become their lodger once again.

Moving over the border to this small Wiltshire town reminded me of my old acquaintance at Aylesford, Eddie Twitchen and how he had proudly told me of his early years in and around this part of moonraker country. Amongst his unprovoked and often repeated repertoire had been the question "Can you name the five Deverills?" and the statement "Did you know that 26 families can sit on the Westbury White Horse and have a picnic?" Well, on moving to Warminster I visited Longbridge, Brixton, Hill, Kingston and Monkton Deverills strung out along the river Wylye, but on closer examination of the White Horse - or Old Grey Mare as it was locally known - discounted the picnic theory on the basis that the slope of the hill was far too steep. Picnickers there were though on the grassy areas above the Horse from where, off the top of the escarpment, spectacular views could be had, not just of Wiltshire and East Somerset, but of the railway junctions around Westbury. Travelling to and fro to work between Wiltshire and Somerset took me via the picturesque village of Horningsham and through the edge of the Longleat Estate.

Whether from Bruton, Shepton Mallet or Warminster, the journey through the lanes was pleasant in the summer and undertaken in daylight at all changeover times but the morning trips could be hazardous from wildlife. What is it about birds that makes them obstinately sit in the road in the early morning and why is it that rabbits always run the wrong way? As the seasons changed so did the journey. In the summer farmers would mechanically hack the hedgerows, widening the lanes by feet on either side but leaving debris strewn across the road. In the wet winter months the muck dragged out of the fields by tractors or from the farm yards by cattle would make riding treacherous, especially in the dark. On dark mornings it was not unknown for me to find myself beginning to fall asleep during the journey, being jolted back to consciousness by a brush with the hedgerow! Autumn brought mist and fog, neither of which were conducive to navigating around Somerset lanes. There was one stretch of lane in the autumn where, in the evening, hundreds of migrating frogs would swarm making passage almost impossible.

Riding to work one afternoon the narrow lanes were particularly treacherous with wet mud dragged off the fields. As I turned left from one lane into another a large tractor emerged from the direction I wished to go. Taking avoiding action I missed the tractor but hadn't bargained for the trailer it had in tow behind. The slippery conditions ensured that I made contact with the trailer. With no apparent damage to the bike and to the relief of the farmer I was alright and so continued on to work.

On climbing the box stairs however I found my right leg had become extremely stiff. Closer examination revealed a tear in my trousers under which there was a nasty gash to my upper thigh. Adrian was concerned as to whether I would be alright to which I assured him that as Nick was learning the box with me I could relax in the armchair and leave the job to him. Nick arrived so Adrian hastily departed before I could change my mind. It was not long before further examination convinced me that the gash would need a few stitches. Nick agreed to ferry me into the cottage hospital in Frome in his car but first we had to wait for a suitable period to switch-out. This came about twenty past three once the 13.30 Paddington cleared Castle Cary. The next down passenger would be the 14.30 Paddington whilst the next up due was the 13.55 from Paignton. These would not be affected by extending the section provided stone traffic was temporarily halted. One trip had already gone down the branch and would be a while at the Quarry so after making all the necessary 'phone calls Nick switched-out. The nurses at Frome fixed me up a stitch in (no) time such that we were back in business at Witham in just over an hour.

The Honda had enabled me to leave home and get around Somerset but it was not really the most ideal form of transport, especially in the winter. So, while living in Bruton I decided it was time to learn to drive a car. Ian had allowed me to put the 'L' plates on his mini a few times when we went to Yeovil which gave me some initial practice. To learn properly I enrolled with Mr Elliot, an instructor who lived at Evercreech Junction. Weekly lessons took me on the open road to Yeovil where town work and manoeuvres were practised. Yeovil was where the test centre was located and eventually my instructor deemed me ready to take the test. I took it on a Friday, which was market day in Yeovil, so the traffic was at its busiest around the town. The examiner was highly critical of other drivers, cutting short the session and asking me to return to the test centre. Fortunately, and to my relief, he advised me that I had passed when we got back. Two weeks later I bought my first car, a Wolseley, from a garage in Shepton Mallet making a bit of a dent in my savings. What a difference it made to my journey to and from work and for travelling at other times. No more freezing hands. No more the need for wet weather clothing and no more the encumbrance of a helmet to carry everywhere.

However, there were new drawbacks from car ownership. The thrill of a frosty morning I expound elsewhere but this was tempered by the newly discovered chore of having to de-ice the windows of the car at five in the morning. It was helpful to place newspaper or an old blanket across the windscreen the night before, held in position by the wiper blades in mid stroke but the side and rear windows still had to be hand scraped. Pushed for time, cold and not very awake served to make the situation a real pain whenever it occurred. Then there were times when a forecast frost was followed by rain arriving earlier than expected. This would result in having to peel sodden newspaper from the windscreen and dispose of it as it assumed the consistency of papier mâché.

On many occasions, especially during the peak of the summer timetable, Witham was open during the daytime on Sundays to split what would otherwise be the long section between Blatchbridge Junction and Castle Cary. This day shift was worked by the late turn Saturday signalman who would return after rest and who would also double back again to open the box at 5am on Monday morning. If there was no Saturday night turn for engineering work then this signalman would work three successive shifts, closing and reopening the box each time.

Whilst living in the bedsit in Shepton Mallet there was little incentive to travel to and fro on such weekends. On more than one occasion I just set up home at Witham, sleeping there Saturday and Sunday nights between the three shifts. After all, it was warm, there was plenty of coal, there was hot running water and the armchair could be very comfortable. The only disturbances to slumber would be the sound of the few trains that passed in the night, usually little more than the sleepers and sit up passengers in each direction and the newspaper trains on the down (there were two on Saturday nights), a need to chivvy up the fire once or twice and the onset of cramp or "pins and needles" that called for a change in sleeping position. It was a strange phenomenon to be in a signal box where trains passed without intervention, without bells heralding their approach or levers being replaced behind their passage. It was as if ghost trains were passing in the night, like a scene from Arnold Ridley's famous play.

After opening again on Sunday morning out would come the radio from the locker so that a leisurely breakfast, looking out on the surrounding countryside, could be accompanied by a chat show. A typical Sunday shift might see the box open from 07.00 to 13.00, or perhaps longer, largely to help move the timetabled and extra trains heading to the West Country and to Weymouth. Following breakfast a stint of cleaning would see the box brought to a polish. Once switched out again a walk along the quiet branch towards Wanstrow, perhaps as far as Witham's fixed distant signal, made for a pleasant afternoon. On the way back the elevated view down towards the village, junction and signal box beyond provided a different perspective of the locale.

One of the signalmen who had moved on from Witham before I arrived there had obviously made it a home from home as he had kept a television in his locker for entertainment. Whilst this had been against the rules as far as the railway was concerned he had taken the unusual step of ensuring that his viewing was legal by purchasing a television licence, registering the signal box address! This caused myself and the other signalmen no end of problems when his next annual renewal came around. Notices and demands were received in the post, Trevor the local postman having to cycle all the way down the yard to the box to deliver them. Then, one evening a telltale "detector" van arrived in the yard to monitor the signal box. The blue Commer van parked at the end of the down sidings, its rooftop aerial trained on the box in an attempt to detect a television in use. It left after an hour or so and eventually the authorities were satisfied that the signalman in question had moved on and that no one else was using a set in the box. The episode of course had to be kept secret from our local management at Westbury for fear of them starting their own investigation and taking action against our departed colleague.

Here I am, with sleeves rolled up, relaxing between trains in the window at Witham. There were excellent views to be had of the railway, the village and surrounding countryside. Note the lever cloth tucked inside my left pocket.

The village, railway and signal box were surrounded by fields. These were given over to grazing cattle for the most part, dairy farming being the mainstay. The field behind the box, which reached across to Kerry Croft, usually played host to a lowing herd, giving rise to the unnerving nocturnal sounds of bovine coughing, grass munching and digestive action. During the winter, despite having a noticeable slope, it also doubled as the local football pitch. In certain parts of the fields, usually in the shadowy and damp corners, wild mushrooms would thrive in the autumn. The field opposite the box, below the embankment where the branch began to curve away and through which the young river Frome meandered, was a particularly good spot for mushrooms. Early morning, at first light, as the mist began to rise from the damp grass, was the best time to leave the box, clamber down the bank, climb through the wire fence and fill a bag with plump juicy fresh mushrooms. The Westbury train crews certainly knew about the mushrooms at Witham. There were occasions when the secondman on an empty stone heading for the quarry, either the 04.15 or 05.50 trip from Westbury, would drop off the locomotive as his driver collected the token. He would then gather a harvest big enough for the two of them, the signalman and for their mates back at the depot before coming to the box for a cup of tea to await the return of his driver from Merehead with a loaded train.

In spring the grass in many fields was left to grow and by the end of May this was ready to be cut for haymaking. The meadow below the embankment opposite the box was always used for hay, the farmer often getting a second cut in late June or early July if the weather permitted. Once cut the grass would be left to dry in strips, being tedded every few days to aid drying before finally baling would start. Cutting and turning using tractor and implements would often take place on balmy long sunny evenings, the farmer's daughter driving the tractor up and down along the meadow in parallel runs. The smell of the mown grass would fill the air and rise up to the box window.

As signalmen we "made hay" regularly too. There were staff shortages in the district so rest days were usually worked, the weekly roster being issued with the letters RDC against the day, meaning Rest Day Cancelled. The shortage was exacerbated by reliefmen such as Ron Reynolds being away temporarily for handsignalling work on the Badminton line between Wootton Bassett and Westerleigh for five months. The work was in association with upgrading of the route to 125 mph running in readiness for the new High Speed Train (HST) service. Sunday turns were paid as overtime and twelve hour shifts were not uncommon. Working seventy plus hours a week meant that grossing twice the basic pay became a regular occurrence. It was even possible to break the £100 barrier once the overtime rates were added on. The first time this happened for me was after working a 72 hour week when I accumulated £109.17 but of course the actual take home amount in the pay packet was always back to two figures once the Chancellor of the Exchequer had extracted his cut. Holidays were rostered to control the number of men on leave at any one time. These were arranged as two consecutive weeks summer holiday and separate winter weeks, one early in the year and one later. We may have received four weeks holiday a year but invariably each man worked overtime at some stage to cover when another was away. So effectively we all worked our holiday hours as overtime either before or after our own leave. Holiday pay was enhanced with ALP (Annual Leave Pay) which was calculated as an average of overtime from previous weeks. Bank holidays had to be worked too. These registered for overtime payment and a lieu day. These LBH or Leave in lieu of a Bank Holiday days accrued over a period of time and if not used could build into a sizeable number.

I much preferred twelve hour nights as opposed to days. The night shift somehow never seemed to last as long, perhaps because the extra four hours was worked at the start of the shift, not tacked on to the end. To swap shifts at the weekend meant doubling back from twelve hours on Friday night to late turn Saturday, made worse by the 1pm start, and then doubling back again to the day shift Sunday. For the man on days, the early finish Saturday was followed by having to return at 10pm the same day and then again at 6pm on the Sunday to assume the twelve hour nights. These were tiring weekends but the chance to make hay while the sun shone. Whether starting a night shift at 10pm or being relieved at that time, changing over at around ten to ten on a June or July evening had a special pleasure with it still being daylight.

The job of course was solitary and shift work was not conducive to having a social life either. On late turn the evening was spent at work, on nights the evening was cut short by having to set off for work after 9pm and then on early turn, a late night meant minimal sleep before having to rise around 5am. Social aspects aside I preferred the late turn as it allowed a lay-in and provided the ability to carry out any other chores during the morning such as shopping or going to the bank or library. Twelve hour shifts left little time for anything other than work, sleep and travelling to and fro. Twelve hour days prevented the ability to do any shopping, other than at a late night convenience store.

Such was the addictive habit of working every single day that when a rare day off materialised this gave a sense of injustice and caused bewilderment as to what to do with the free time. Providing it did not infringe minimum rest periods, signalmen were allowed to mutually exchange shifts should one of the men need to be off for personal reasons when rostered to be on duty. Usually this would occur when a man on late turn required the evening free and so he would seek to swap with the early turn man that day. Such mutual assistance normally balanced up over a period but one of my colleagues at Witham, Graham Warnecke, took more interest in activities outside of work than the job would bear. There were a biased number of occasions, especially Saturdays, when the relationship was stretched beyond acceptable limits.

As we were short staffed and working most rest days, the Rest Day Reliefmen (RDR) like Jack Richards and Mick Elliott who were based at Castle Cary, spent most of their time off-roster undertaking general duties in the same way as the General Purpose Reliefmen (GPR). Jack always amused me as he seemed to be tone deaf. Whatever box he was in he would have trouble distinguishing between the tone of the block bells. At Witham we only had the two but still Jack would tap both bells with his finger to judge which had rung - and then still choose to answer the wrong one! I have seen other men with a similar problem attach a clothes peg to a bell to change its tone or to dangle a string from the hammer to see it dance when rung. Not Jack, he relied upon tapping each one to compare the pitch. It could be mildly amusing if he was on at Cary with a train offered to him on the Witham - Cary block, to suddenly see the indicator flick to "Train on Line" accompanied by two beats on the bell, even though the train had yet to pass. I would have to call him on the 'phone and suggest that perhaps Somerton had just sent him Train Entering Section for an up train.

As with the Taunton area, the Cary, Frome and Westbury reliefmen comprised a wide variety of characters. As well as Jack and Mick, there was Fred Wilkins, nicknamed "Tiny" because of his near seven foot height. He would greet everyone with the words "how was we?" There was Ron Kirby an ex London and South Western man, Ken Russell, Ron Reynolds, Bob Baker, Bob Cruse and Tom Baber, a master sponge cake maker with his magnificent sandy moustache and matching sideburns. Tom was one of three signalmen who hailed from the tiny village of Batcombe, between Bruton and Frome.

The reliefmen, a few in particular, seemed to be able to influence the weekly rosters to their advantage. There were some documented local agreements that favoured relief staff but even unwritten arrangements appeared which went unchallenged. Some complicated manoeuvres went on between the reliefmen to ensure they got plenty of overtime. Mick Elliott spent much of his spare time helping out in a fish and chip shop in The Butts in Frome. The lady proprietor could often tell us the next week's rosters before we knew ourselves! During a rare period when the Rest Day Reliefmen were able to resume their roster I was on late turn one particular week when the box rest day fell on the Saturday. This was followed by the rest day of the next week being on the Monday. Tom Baber was not one of the RDR men for Witham but he was covering the job as the RDR man was on leave and so was rostered to Witham for the Saturday late turn and Monday early turn vice myself.

Now the box was booked to be open on the intervening Sunday, the turn normally falling to the Saturday late turn resident man which, in this case was me. Tom decided that as he was covering for me on both days then he would claim the Sunday in between, convincing the roster clerk to place his name against the turn. Ordinarily I would have been quite happy to forego the Sunday, rather than interrupt an extended weekend off that would allow me to go away somewhere. However, I had not been consulted on the matter, so I put the roster clerk right whilst suggesting he pay more attention to the agreed national rostering procedures than to the local reliefmen. Tom rang me on the Friday from Clink Road to try and brow beat me but I was having none of it. The simple truth was that he had no entitlement to the turn unless I, or indeed any of the other resident men at Witham, declined to work it. Tom knew this, despite his yarn spinning, so when I suggested we both turn up but that I would be the only one to get paid he conceded the situation. If he had asked me first I reckon I would have been happy to let him have the Sunday and then I could have taken advantage of three days off in a row to go away somewhere for the long weekend.

An occasion that I would never be allowed to forget happened one night at Witham. Following a long weekend off I was due to resume for a week of nightshift at 10pm one Monday. Having had a busy day this particular Monday I thought it prudent to gain a couple of hours sleep before heading off to work and thus offset the necessity to remain awake for 24 hours. The idea was doubly important as squadron tamping was booked to start that night between Witham and Castle Cary so it would be a busy shift with lots of people about. Shortly after tea I retired to bed setting my trusty alarm clock for 9pm. At this time I was still renting the bedsit flat in the middle of Shepton Mallet. There were streetlights lit outside and a fair level of noise rising up from the street below as people went to and fro. Not being particularly tired I suffered the frustration of laying awake for well over an hour, finally deciding that trying to sleep would be fruitless on this occasion. I switched off the alarm clock but laid in the bed for a little longer. My next recollection was looking at the clock and seeing, to my horror, that the time was a few minutes to ten. Amazingly I had fallen asleep moments after believing slumber was to evade me all evening. Witham was a 20 minute drive away, I would be well late.

I leapt from the bed, threw on my uniform, grabbed my rucksack, food and milk and dashed downstairs to the street. My car was parked in the public car park to the rear of the shops. I dashed through the alleyway and made straight for the public 'phone box in the car park, thinking how fortunate it was that Witham was one of the few boxes that had a GPO telephone - I could ring and advise the late turn signalman not to worry, I was on my way. I dialled the local code for Upton Noble and then 441 - the box number. Mick Elliott answered in his Somerset brogue and I pushed twopence into the slot. It would be Mick wouldn't it, one of the Castle Cary reliefmen! I had learnt the box with Mick and so knew he loved to tell a good tale. He was in fact an ex Somerset & Dorset Railway employee, having begun his career at Cole station not long before nationalisation. Naively appraising Mick of my reason for being late he answered with "that'l be alright me boy". He always addressed fellow railwaymen as "me boy". I then raced out of Shepton Mallet on the A361 to Nunney Catch and through the lanes to Trudoxhill and Witham Friary. It was nearing 10.30 as I turned into the yard to find yellow vans, permanent way men and a siding full of yellow Plasser machines, their engines running and spotlights blazing. It was then I remembered that squadron tamping was on this week.

Having walked quickly up through the yard I climbed the box steps to be greeted by Mick and the local ganger, Mac, who was waiting to take possession of the line after the last passenger train. They both enjoyed pulling my leg, Mick finding his additional half hour at work well worth the inconvenience. He extracted great mileage, right up until his retirement over twenty years later, from the story of how I was the only man he knew who could oversleep for nights.

Squadron tamping was a phenomenon introduced in the 1970s to regularly maintain the main line network by mechanised means. As the name suggests, a squadron of tamping and lining machines would blitz a stretch of track, completing a few miles each night, progressively working their way up or down the line. Whilst this was the theory, in practice the process was less successful as the machines would often break down, usually through some hydraulic failure, the machines comprising an array of actuators, valves and hoses that were prone to breakage. From a squadron of perhaps seven, one machine might not even go out whilst one or two would probably fail during the night. By the end of the week the squadron was often completely grounded.

Witham's down sidings frequently played host to these yellow machines. It was an ideal place at which to base them when the six monthly tamping cycle came round on this stretch of the West of England main line. Road access into the yard allowed the night time crews easy access to the machines. Similarly during the day the maintenance fitters could attend to the casualties from the previous night and refuel the machines by hand pump from drums of diesel. Their stores and materials added to the assorted permanent way materials such as sleepers, fishplates, keys and packing stone that normally littered space around the yard.

The squadron operated from Monday to Friday as the machines were dispersed to relaying and other maintenance activities at the weekend. This meant the machines would congregate at a base like Witham during Monday morning, dispersing again on Friday morning after four nights work. They were slow travellers, having to be let away with a good margin but often having to be sidelined during their journey in order to be overtaken by revenue earning traffic. Sometimes, to enable faster movement, at least to Westbury or Castle Cary, a possession of the line would be taken as far as their destination by the engineer early on Friday. By this means the whole squadron would travel together in convoy through each block section taking care to avoid collision with one another. Even allowing for the time to take and give up the possession this was a much quicker way of moving such a large number of machines compared to signalling each one individually in the conventional manner.

15

SECTION B—continued

At or between	Line affected	Remarks
2. READING TO COGLOAD VIA WESTBURY AND FROME—continued		
MONDAY, 6 JANUARY		
74—Savernake and Woodborough	Down BLOCKED	02 30 to 07 00. Tamping and lining between Pewsey and Woodborough. 76½ and 78½ mp. DIVERSIONS VIA SWINDON. Savernake Signal Box open.
TUESDAY, 7 JANUARY		
75—Woodborough and Haywood Road	Down BLOCKED	02 35 to 07 30. Tamping and lining between Woodborough and Lavington. 83¾ and 86 mp. DIVERSIONS VIA SWINDON. Lavington and Heywood Road Signal Boxes open.
WEDNESDAY, 8 JANUARY		
76—Woodborough and Bedwyn	Up BLOCKED	00 05 to 04 45. Tamping and lining between Pewsey and Bedwyn. 70¼ and 66½ mp. DIVERSIONS VIA SWINDON. Bedwyn Signal Box open.
THURSDAY, 9 JANUARY		
77—Newbury Middle and Thatcham	Up BLOCKED	01 00 to 05 15. Tamping and lining. 51½ and 50¼ mp. DIVERSIONS VIA SWINDON
FRIDAY, 10 JANUARY		
78—Thatcham and Ufton Crossing	Up BLOCKED	01 00 to 05 15. Tamping and lining between Colthrop and Aldermaston. 48¾ and 45½ mp. DIVERSIONS VIA SWINDON.

A typical page from Section B of a K2 Weekly Notice showing tamping and lining taking place progressively along the Berks & Hants line between Heywood Road and Ufton Crossing over successive nights.

As well as squadron tamping, other engineering operations involving the blockage of one or both lines between trains might take place on week nights but more extensive work was usually programmed for Saturday nights. Sometimes, single line working would be involved, bringing additional men to the box in the guise of Responsible Officer, Pilotman and Groundman. Every chair and stool would have an occupant. Between trains tea would be brewed and local gossip exchanged.

A possession also meant having a member of the permanent way gang stationed at the box to put out the detonator protection and red flags or lamps before the possession could be granted and to take them up again at the end of the work, before the possession was lifted. If works train or machine movements were to be made into or out of the possession then this "handsignalman" would undertake the removal and replacement of the protection for such moves. In between these activities they would make themselves comfortable in a corner of the box and "get their head down" to enjoy some sleep.

If track laying were involved then the army of assembled men, with help from an earth moving machine or two and a series of spoil and material trains, would set to work. Having cut and lifted out the old track panels to pass the point of no return, they would then remove the ballast, level the formation, drop new ballast, lay the new track and connect it up. For a while the resultant scene was one of a distorted, uneven mess, as the line meandered uncontrollably up, down and from side to side across a sea of new ballast. Once the "yellow machines" got to work lifting, lining and tamping the whole would once again begin to resemble a main line. At the appointed hour, the line would always be back open ready for traffic, albeit with a speed restriction imposed.

Writing out the possession record in the train register at the start and finish was a tedious task but the words always looked good in long hand across the page. In time, special rubber stamps were introduced that printed the standard wording, requiring only the specific line and location details to be interjected by hand in the right places. These were a great boon but the end result never looked as elegant.

Both the Up Sidings and the Down Yard could be illuminated by electric lighting controlled from the signal box. This was useful at times when shunting or stabling took place after dark. The series of lights were normally left switched off when there was no shunting activity except for the one mounted on a wooden pole adjacent to the signal box. This was angled to provide floodlighting of the box steps and the foot board crossing that went across the tracks to the branch line. This was a powerful light that cast its illumination onto passing trains, being also useful for number catching. During the warmer months this light was a magnet for a myriad of moths and other flying insects. At dusk and into the early night a bat would circle around the lamp to feed on the throng of insects, providing a distraction for the signalman to watch its swirling, swooping and diving.

Many insects would find their way into the box too and be drawn to the one light that would be illuminated over the train register book. This was most inconvenient, as they would crawl across the book or fall onto it when exhausted, getting in the way of making entries and becoming potential smudges on the page. On particularly warm nights it became preferable to keep a different light on, elsewhere in the box, to avoid this problem, only switching the one over the book on when making an entry or even using the Bardic hand lamp for this purpose. On sweeping up the floor in the morning, before being relieved, the dust would largely comprise of a host of small dead insects and a larger moth or two. I would wonder at the amazing numbers of insects created every day and the tragedy of their short lives.

There were some long hot summers in the mid 70s that led to balmy nights after glorious days. I enjoyed them all, whatever the shift, although sleeping during the day when on nights was difficult because of the heat. The tinder dry vegetation resulted in lineside fires that caused delay to trains. The inevitable water restrictions that were a feature of the time were unpopular with the public, leading to hose pipe bans and even rationing. The image of the railway suffered as locomotives and coaching stock were prevented from being washed. At Witham the private supply was something of a luxury, exempt as it was from restrictions.

During the day the heat would shimmer off the rails and ballast, blurring the image of approaching trains. Signal wires would be wound in to their maximum to compensate for their expansion in the heat. By late afternoon the rail temperature could reach very high numbers prompting permanent way men to patrol the continuously welded rail with thermometers, looking for buckled rails, ready to slap on an emergency speed restriction if the temperature passed certain limits. At night, as the rails cooled down, the contraction would result in longitudinal stresses that eventually caused the rail to move all of a sudden in its chairs. The movement would precipitate a noise like the crack of a rifle shot that would shatter the otherwise quiet and usually frighten the life out of me.

The telegraph poles stood like equally spaced sentries down the side of the line and the wind would sing in the wires. There was a termination pole alongside the box with 74 wires meeting on its cross-arms. Even a mild breeze would set up an eerie whistling that could conjure the belief of a force ten gale if you closed your eyes and just listened.

It was at Witham that I was cured of any fear of lightning. A signal box operating floor, being elevated and surrounded by glass, not only affords excellent views of the railway and surrounding locality, it also exposes the incumbent signalman to the full excitement of a storm. To watch the spectacle of forked lightning bringing alive the countryside in white flashes and to see the random jagged bolts discharge to earth whilst isolated alone in an elevated glass building was out of this world. I experienced some particularly violent storms that brought torrential rain, loud claps of thunder and spectacular lightning. Late evening and night time storms were of course the most impressive, especially as these could be enjoyed with the lights out for much of the time. As the storm approached it would induce reaction into the exposed wires on the pole route, often sending blue sparks dancing along their length. The bells and instruments would click and ting simultaneously and sometimes the bells would ring with the false certainty that they were receiving a legitimate signal from the adjacent box.

The open pole route through the long section to Castle Cary meant the circuits were susceptible to damage from lightning, strong wind and fallen branches. More than once Regulation 25 had to be brought into play when the bells or instruments failed to operate. Usually at least one of the telephone circuits remained available so that absolute block working could be maintained in preference to introducing time interval. Indeed Castle Cary, like Witham, enjoyed the luxury of a post office telephone and so this diverse medium could always be used as a last resort.

Throughout the railway, semaphore signals were illuminated by long burning oil lamps, the oil being replenished every week. Most places were served by a lampman who looked after a string of boxes. Fred was the lampman who came to Witham. He carried the lamps and oil in the boot of his own car. He would turn up at 5am so he could be finished by mid morning in order to get back to Frome to open the antique shop he ran with his wife on Catherine Hill. His car and clothes reeked of oil and he was a smoker. We all had visions of Fred vanishing in a puff of smoke like a wizard or his car suddenly exploding in a ball of flame like a dramatic scene from a Hollywood movie. If a lamp blew out at any time it was the signalman's job to walk out and relight it - not a pleasant task on a wet and windy night. This usually meant bringing the lamp down to ground level and then, huddling round it to protect it from the wind, strike the match through the open door of the case towards the wick. Success might take two or three attempts and then, before reaching the top of the ladder, a gust would blow the flame out and the process have to be started all over again.

The temporary speed boards placed by the permanent way department to mark the approach to, and commencement and termination of, temporary speed restrictions were also lit by oil lamps or gas. These boards were placed following renewals whilst the track settled in or when a defect was found until such time as it was repaired. They too were prone to being blown out in the wind, resulting in trains having to be stopped and cautioned at the signal box until a member of the gang, called from his home, had been out and relit them. Sometimes they might even be blown completely over in a gale when not secured sufficiently. If an errant board was close enough to the box then the signalman might trudge out to it, perhaps in the wind and rain, in order to rectify the situation and so minimise delay to trains.

The stove at Witham was tall and narrow, enclosed in a black enamel skin. It could hold enough coal to stay alight for ten or more hours so could be banked up before the box was switched-out on a Saturday night allowing it to burn through but still be alive on Sunday when the box reopened. All it would need was a thorough riddle before the air drew through to brighten the remaining coals. Meanwhile the overnight chill would have been kept away so that it did not take long to bring the temperature of the box back to a comfortable level. It did have a tendency to clinker up on the grate at the bottom with a poor batch of coal which meant it could be difficult to keep the embers alive sometimes, especially if it had not been cleaned out for a while. Use of the poker could usually get the air drawing through but there were times when the fire needed extra help if it had been left to die for too long. A few dry sticks inserted into the coal and a sprinkling of lamp oil usually did the trick. The oil would fume and smoke from the residual warmth, then all of a sudden ignite, the gas exploding up the stove pipe in a roar to leave the fire invigorated, ready for a good riddle and some fresh coal.

Sometimes it was difficult to judge whether the initial application of lamp oil would be sufficient. On one occasion I closed the stove door and waited a few minutes but the muffled conflagration from within the black enamel casing did not materialise. I opened the door. Evaporating fumes were rising but the part burnt coals looked grey and lifeless. Hoping there were some red embers below I sprinkled on a little more oil. That did the trick. With a terrific whooshing sound the whole mass burst into flame. A ball of exploding gas leapt from the open door, singeing off all the hairs on my right arm before I could slam the door shut. What a horrible smell burnt hair leaves behind! Just a few seconds later a signal telephone rang. It was the driver of an empty stone waiting in the loop for his turn over the single line to Merehead calling in. Having seen tongues of flame issue forth from all four outlets of the H cowl sitting on top of the stove pipe protruding from the signal box roof, as he idly surveyed the otherwise tranquil scene, he was concerned for my welfare.

CHAPTER SIX

COMMUNICATING

Every signal box was provided with a megaphone which could be described more appropriately as a speaking trumpet. This was a useful device for calling instructions to train crew or to anyone on the ground in the vicinity of the box. Made from a fluted rolled sheet of steel about three feet long and fitted with a handle half way along the length, these devices were simple but very effective in directing the voice. For those on the receiving end there was no reciprocal arrangement. They would have to respond using cupped hands or, more usually, hand signals. Using the megaphone to communicate with a driver was an alternative to going down on the ballast but often the latter course of action was best to make sure the message was properly understood. Stopping a train outside the box meant bringing it in from board to board, lowering each signal purposely slowly as the driver approached and then holding a red flag or lamp from the window until the driver acknowledged with a toot. Before then proceeding, the driver would wait to see a green handsignal.

I am reminded of an amusing story concerning Percy Darch at Silk Mill Crossing box whose shift rota had coincided with mine at Whiteball. Silk Mill had only home signals in both directions, these acting also therefore as the section signals. On the Down Main the home signal was some distance on the approach side of the box, almost 300 yards away. One day, due to a problem with the automatic crossing at Victory, in the section towards Wellington, Percy was having to stop and caution down trains. Having closed his own crossing for an approaching train and then gently lowered the Down Home signal Percy went to the window with his megaphone but watched in dismay as the train accelerated away past the box, its driver oblivious to Percy's shouts.

A mile or so short of Bruton, on a tight bend subject to a 70 mph restriction, was an accommodation crossing linking a farmer's fields. At one time it had been busy with the haulage of timber from woods below the railway lower down across the river Brue necessitating that it be manned. Known as Sheephouse Crossing it was now used regularly by the farmer and his wife, Mr and Mrs House, when herding cattle to and from milking twice a day. The name (taken from Sheephouse Farm) seemed misplaced therefore but the cast iron nameplate fixed to the adjacent hut bore the name out. Indeed the nameplate was longer than the diminutive building to which it was attached, extending in both directions beyond its wooden form. Inside the hut was a telephone which the House's would use to gain permission to take the herd across the line. This 'phone was connected to the box to box circuit and so the signalmen at either Castle Cary, Bruton or Witham would respond to their request and to their subsequent advice that all was once again safe after a crossing. Authorisation to cross would only be given if there was no train approaching and delay would not be incurred.

Signalmen watched each train as it passed, looking for signs of alarm or anything untoward. The Regulations dealt with emergency situations but to communicate with the driver or guard meant stopping the train, usually at the next signal box. The train crew could however communicate with the signalman without having to stop. They did this by writing a note on a scrap of paper, often a blank page torn from a weekly notice, hurling this towards the signal box as they passed. I have had many messages thrown to me from passing trains. From drivers these would often relate to problems with their locomotive. At Witham for example a note thrown out by the footplatemen of an up express requesting a fresh locomotive at Westbury would ensure actions were put in motion to have the replacement engine off shed and waiting at the north end of the station just as the train ran in, thereby reducing delay to the minimum.

For the signalman at Witham such a note would trigger a number of 'phone calls to ensure subsequent actions further up the line. If the train was a "backroader", not therefore booked to run via Westbury, the first call would be to Fairwood Junction to get the train turned into town. Dave Richards was the regular man there on my shift. "Right oh matey" would be his reply. The Fairwood signalman would know to then call Westbury South to appraise his mate there of the reason for the diversion and to also advise Heywood Road Junction at the other end of the Westbury Avoiding Line. The second call would be to Westbury North to explain the situation. The North man would then directly contact the shed foreman to organise the replacement engine. Planned movements in and around the station and yard would be modified to accommodate the arrival of the express and its loco' change. The third call would be to Control, at Bristol, to advise the actions that had been put in place in order that the event could be logged, assessed and any subsequent actions initiated.

Obviously a driver intending to throw a note out needed to ensure he attracted the attention of the signalman. This would be achieved by sounding a series of short blasts on the locomotive horn. For a guard intent on ejecting a note, it was a little more difficult but usually accomplished by waving an arm from a window, sometimes accompanied by shrill blasts on his whistle.

There were many reasons why a guard might wish to transmit a message. Typically, it might be that a passenger had been taken ill and required medical treatment, thus an ambulance was requested to be waiting at the next stopping point. Sometimes the police were required to meet the train to deal with a miscreant on-board. Perhaps a connection needed to be held or someone had been over carried beyond their destination. In some instances the train might be forced to make a special stop for these attendances, with signals being held at danger, as the driver would be oblivious to the need, there being no form of on-train voice communication between the guard and locomen. For the signalman at Witham this may again have meant getting an up train diverted into Westbury or ensuring that the staff at Taunton were informed in good time of what was required for a down train.

A paper note being thrown from a train travelling at 90 mph could end up anywhere. The turbulence would pick it up and toss it in any direction. Train crew knew this and took precautions to ensure their message landed as close as possible to its target. Screwed up in a tight ball, the sheet of paper could be projected clear of the train's slip-stream giving it a chance of landing somewhere in the vicinity of the box. The signalman had to track the movement to see where it fell to earth amongst the ballast or alongside the line.

Some guards and drivers kept a piece of ballast in their bags for just these occasions. No doubt this was a substitute for the lump of coal they had learnt to use in steam days. The paper wrapped around the ballast, perhaps secured by an elastic band, made an excellent weighty missile that always reached its target, hitting the ground close to the signal box or ricocheting off the wall. At other times the missive has been rolled and then tied with the driver's cloth or written on the back of a rolled up Weekly Notice book. On one occasion at Witham I can recall when a secondman launched a paper aeroplane from the cab window of an express passenger train as it passed at full speed. He was obviously good at his origami. The fashioned paper shot out from the window, soared high into the air, like a gull facing into a stiff on-shore breeze, then, escaping the draught effects of the train glided gently past the box, down across the fence to settle in the field behind where the grazing cattle took no notice of its arrival. The bull in the field took a keen interest in me though when I climbed through the fence and negotiated the cow pats to retrieve the paper aeroplane. That message was the most difficult I ever had to contend with.

If an up train was nearing Fairwood or a down train approached Heywood Road before its footplate crew could alert the signalmen to their desire to run into Westbury then the driver would slow the train and blow the horn continuously to attract attention whilst the secondman leaned out from the cab pointing an arm to the left or right depending which way they wished to go. The same pantomime would be enacted on the rare occasion that a signalman at Heywood or Fairwood inadvertently pulled off along the backroad for a train booked to call at Westbury. Quick action could recover the situation with very little delay and without the need for anyone, other than those involved to be any the wiser.

Westbury train crew rarely got the chance to work express passenger trains, these usually being the domain of London, Taunton and Plymouth depots. There was one Westbury link however that contained a turn which saw Westbury men travel up passenger "on the cushions" to collect the 15.30 Paddington, taking it to Exeter. As this train was non-stop from Reading to Taunton it ran via the Westbury Down Avoiding line giving the men the opportunity to travel over the backroad between Heywood Road and Fairwood Junctions missing their Home Station altogether. They always seemed to enjoy the run, waving enthusiastically as they passed Witham. No doubt they relished these rare occasions with a class 1 train, especially as it was the only time they ever got every backboard off for them throughout the whole Westbury area. Their return working saw them take over the Perishables at Exeter and bring it up as far as Westbury where it picked up traffic and they were relieved.

Apart from Bruton, all of the signal boxes open at this time in the Westbury area had control of one or more junctions and hence responsibility for the correct routing and regulation of trains. Some routing bell codes had existed between Westbury South, North and Bradford Junctions but with the blessing of the local management, the signalmen devised a more extensive arrangement that assisted operations throughout the area. This saw the codes 1 pause 2, 1 pause 3 and 3 pause 4 added to the "Is Line Clear" code between certain boxes to identify specific routings. So, for example, a local passenger train for Weymouth would be belled from Westbury South to Fairwood and Clink Road Junctions as a 3-1-1-2 signifying that it was to run via Frome. The Clink Road signalman would retain the 1-2 on the end when asking to Frome North to signify that the train was to take the Yeovil line at Castle Cary, the 3-1-1-2 therefore being continued on by Frome North, Blatchbridge Junction and Witham. If a train was to take the Yeovil line at Castle Cary but was not booked to run via Frome then it would leave Westbury with the 3-4 suffix. The 19.07 Westbury Cement was just such a train, being belled as a 5-3-4 as far as Clink Road. The signalman here would send the train via the Frome Avoiding Line but ask it forward to Blatchbridge as a 5-1-2, i.e. a fully fitted company block train to be routed over the Yeovil line at Castle Cary.

In the up direction Castle Cary would add 1-2 for trains booked to run via Frome and at Witham we would add 1-3 for anything that should take the Westbury Avoiding Line, the "Avoider" or "Back Road" as we called it. Thus a straight 4 bells would be an express passenger running via the Frome Avoiding Line but taking the Main Line into Westbury whilst a 4-1-3 was an express passenger running via both the Frome and Westbury Avoiding Lines. The code 1-3 was also applied between Westbury and Witham in the down direction to signify a train for the Merehead/Cranmore branch. So a light engine for the quarry, for example, would be sent out as a 2-3-1-3. The 1-2 code was continued through Westbury to Bradford Junctions for "branch" trains heading towards Bathampton and used in the opposite direction to signify trains heading towards Salisbury at Westbury South. Thus the Cardiff – Portsmouth trains (Pompeys as they were known) were all belled as 3-1-1-2.

Keeping the traffic moving in the most efficient manner, especially ensuring that the passenger trains had a clear run, meant that every signalman needed to know what was happening throughout the area. There was no benefit, for example, in letting a Merehead stone train away towards Westbury from Witham with the barest of margin in front of a fast (usually ten minutes) if Clink Road had already accepted a Whatley stone from Frome North. Both could not make it to Westbury without causing delay to the passenger. But if the Merehead had to go, perhaps because an empty stone needed to be run into the loop out of the way of a down passenger, then a quick call to Max at Frome North would determine if the Merehead could be run that way whilst the fast passed it on the Frome Avoiding Line. By belling the train out as a 5-1-2 Chriss or Tony at Blatchbridge would know to turn it into Frome. One had to be careful to let Clink know what was happening, especially if Ken Russell was on there because he was just as likely to accept the stone from

Frome North, rather than refuse it, and let it straight back out, defeating the whole object of the exercise. Whilst 10 minutes was the absolute minimum margin to let a stone away when there was an up London to follow it into Westbury, a couple of minutes could be shaved off this if the London was a backroader, as once the stone had been turned in at Fairwood the fast had a clear road ahead. It was important to know how traffic was approaching too. It was no good, for example, starting a shunt move at Witham from the down sidings across to the up side if a passenger train was only five minutes away.

The selector telephone was the medium by which we all communicated. Indeed at busy times all of us along the line might have our receivers left off the hook, thus enabling us to listen to activity in one another's boxes and so determine the minute by minute picture of what was going on. We knew the tones of the block bells in each box, could hear trains passing and ask questions of whoever was listening or conversing. Attached to the back wall of the box, the selector and omnibus 'phones would be busy clicking and ringing in the background as signalmen called one another for information or to pass on messages. Only when the appropriate code for Witham rang out would it be necessary to respond.

Before ringing-out it was courteous to first ask if there was "anyone on?" to check whether there was a call already in progress and to warn anyone listening that they should move the receiver away from their ear so that the subsequent ringing-out would not deafen them via the earpiece. At quieter times, often in the late evening, or early hours of the morning these 'phones were used for group conversation to pass the time on any number of topical or general interest subjects and to put the railway and the world to rights. They were a means of contact between solitary signalmen and the medium by which the men were able to recognise themselves as a team. During conversation the strict protocol of exchanging bell codes might lapse a little with one man for instance telling his mate at the adjacent box to "take on the up" as he left the receiver to deal with a passing train or another might say "give us the road for the Weymouth" as he received two beats from the box in rear. When coming back to the 'phone the conversation would be resumed with a "yeah" to pick up from where it had left off. When having to interrupt a conversation to deal with a train the signalman concerned might whistle a tune so that his mate at the other end of the 'phone could hear that the line was still open and that dialogue would resume shortly. At 11.00 every morning the bell on the omnibus 'phone would rattle out a series of rings to signify the time as being precisely 11am so that all the signalmen could check and, if necessary, adjust their signal box clock. This time signal and whether the clock had been correct, fast or slow had to be recorded in the Train Register book. This was another railway ritual enacted across the length and breadth of the British Railways network as clerks in dozens of local Time Offices across the nation synchronised railway time as they pressed the ring buttons on hundreds of 'bus 'phone circuits. The signal box clock was an essential element of the working equipment which demanded its own ritual of winding once a week, usually on a Saturday morning.

Such was the level of traffic at times through Witham and the Frome/ Westbury area that a degree of ingenuity was required to keep it all moving, especially if delays to passenger trains were to be avoided. The normal method by which to send empty stone trains down the branch at Witham was to route them through the facing crossovers onto the Up and Down Goods Loop. If there was a loaded stone train to come off the branch first, then this would be run into the loop and the empty train routed around it by running it down the Up Main and onto the branch from there. It was often possible, if the timing was right and with co-operation from the drivers, to keep both trains gently rolling, effectively crossing them as if at a long loop on a single line.

Occasions arose when an empty stone might only just have time to make it across into the loop before an up express was due to pass. The section from Castle Cary took seven minutes to traverse for a class 1 passenger but with the Up Distant some 3,182 yards out from the box this signal would need to be at green after five and a half minutes or there was a risk the driver would see it at caution. If the down stone empties was "on line" from Blatchbridge before the up train was put "on" from Cary then there was every chance it would make it across into the loop in sufficient time to normalise the points, clear the up line signals and set the distant to green just before the five and a half minute mark was passed.

At other times the empties would have to be held at the Down Home to wait for the up to pass. However, if there was a down fast hard on the heels of the empties it would be imperative to keep the empties moving. I would do this by lowering both the Down Home and Inner Home signals (Nos. 66 and 65) for the approaching empties. The Westbury drivers knew what this meant, especially when they saw the up line signals were already "off". They would run their train straight down past the box within the protection of the two signals and beyond the clearing point, allowing me to see the tail lamp, clear back to Blatchbridge and take on the following express. As the locomotive passed the box I would hold my arms in a cross shape to confirm the manoeuvre to the driver and guard.

The signalman at Blatchbridge could then lower his signals and, if the fast was only just passing Clink, give it a green distant. This was known as "dropping the distant down the chimney" which described the action of lowering a semaphore distant just as a steam locomotive was about to pass it, hence narrowly avoiding delay to the train. Many such phrases lived on into the diesel era and in this instance even referred to a colour light distant. At the same moment the up express would pass Witham and I would put it "on line" to Blatchbridge. The trailing crossover outside the box would then be reversed and the empties signalled to propel across to the Up Main. Two beats on the bell from Blatchbridge would signify the down fast was less than three minutes away and only one and a half minutes from the Witham Down Distant. Prompt work by the crew of the empties would see their train propelled back over to the Up Main in double quick time.

With the crossover normalised and the down line signals all at clear (having dropped the Witham distant out at Bunns Lane down the loco's chimney too!), the route would then be set up for the empties to go onto the branch. I would go across with the token to hand up to the driver as he drew his train forward and, on getting back to the top of the stairs and re-entering the box the down fast would roar by at

90 mph with the driver playing a thank you tune on his locomotive horn wondering, having only just passed the up train half way between Witham and Blatchbridge, how the stone could have got across to where it was. Exhilaration, not just from the thrill of a passing express streaking by at full speed, hammering out its beat, but enhanced by the slick working of dedicated railwaymen.

Blatchbridge would then "knock-out" for the up, and I would "knock-out" for the down at the same time. The first few times this happened the Blatchbridge signalman would come on the 'phone and ask "How'd you get those empties across?" I always replied nonchalantly that "I just used the flyover". Neither Tony Page nor Chriss Burden at Blatchbridge could fathom the move. Some years later when Chriss progressed to becoming a very competent relief signalman he was able to learn the flyover move at Witham for himself.

The railway was a great place for banter between the grades and for leg pulling. One morning the Cranmore trip engine was hooked up to a dozen tanks when the crew came up the box to get a can of hot water to brew tea. The guard was a newcomer, not yet fully conversant with the local workings, so his driver, looking for a bit of fun in front of an audience, asked what load they were allowed to take down the branch with the type 2 engine they had. The guard had to admit that he didn't know and that he was not carrying his "Working Manual" so couldn't check. "Well you'm best ring the Yard Master at Westbury to find out" retorted the driver as he winked across the box in my direction. The Yard Master was of course none too pleased at being asked the question by the young guard but replied that a load of 400 tons was allowed behind a type '2' and therefore, at 46 tons each when laden, only eight tanks could legitimately be taken forward. The guard conveyed this wisdom to his driver who, by now, had filled the tea can with boiling water. "That's interesting" replied the driver, glancing a smile in my direction, "cos I was planning to take all twelve just like we did yesterday - eh Bobby?"

Drivers were usually co-operative in making unusual or quick moves when necessary but occasionally one or two adopted the view that they were the only train on the railway or that they could choose when and how they moved. At such times these drivers had to be brought back to reality by the signalman. One regular ruse, where a driver was getting near the limit of his shift, or there was a delay to a freight train, was for him to abandon the train and take his engine light to shed post haste and book off. Unlike steam days when a loco' might have run short of water there was no excuse for this behaviour. I recall just such an occasion at Witham when a delayed stone trip received an extended wait in the loop before there was an opportunity to let the train away to Westbury. The driver, already frustrated, protested at the wait, declaring that as he'd been on for nearly seven hours he would leave his train of 'Procor' wagons in the loop and cut off his engine to go light immediately to Westbury shed. Being some way into yet another twelve hour shift I was unmoved by his desire to leave my loop occupied by a dead train, just so that he could escape home in less than seven hours. He persisted, cutting off his engine, demanding to go forward. I explained that he was quite at liberty to move but that the only place he would be going was through the trap points and down the embankment into the field until such time as he recoupled to his train and I was in a position to let him leave with it. By the time this pantomime had been played out I was able to let the train proceed. The angst had been unnecessary, only serving to raise tempers and remove enjoyment from the job.

On another afternoon the return trip from Cranmore dropped its empty tank cars in the up sidings before the loco' drew up to the disc signal to wait the road back to Westbury. Meanwhile, a light engine from Merehead had followed the Cranmore up the branch, once the section was clear. This dropped down the gradient to arrive at the bracket home signal, coming to a stand just before the Cranmore loco' halted alongside it in the sidings. Neither of them could go anywhere for a while as the 11.00 Plymouth to Paddington running a few minutes behind schedule had just entered the section from Castle Cary. Behind this would be the 12.15 Weymouth to Bristol (Temple Meads) stopper that would be waiting to follow. Although this second train would take twelve minutes to come through from Cary it would only be possible to let one movement out between the express and the stopper.

With this in mind I went across to the driver of the light engine on the branch to collect the token and ask him to draw forward and then set back to couple to his counterpart in the siding. By travelling in multiple together they would both make it back to Westbury before the Weymouth. My request proved unpopular, the driver determining that he had come to a stand momentarily before the Cranmore engine, that he should not be required to couple to anyone, and that I should give him priority to go first. Having thanked him for his views I returned to the box with the token.

A few minutes later the Plymouth rushed past the two engines on its way to the capital, momentarily creating a triple line up of juxtaposed traction. The Weymouth was duly offered and put straight "on line" behind by Ken down at Castle Cary. I lowered the Branch to Loop Home signal to let the Merehead light engine trundle up the loop which it duly did, the driver surmising that I had heeded his views. I then reversed and locked the Branch to Up Main points, then reversed the Up Siding to Branch points, before clearing the disc signal for the Cranmore engine. The driver gave the short customary toot before moving forward out onto the main line, he and his guard waved knowingly as they passed the box. I lowered the Starting signal to allow them to pass their Merehead counterpart and continue to the Advanced Starting by which time the up London had sailed past Blatchbridge and I was able to get the road for them.

The Merehead loco' and its crew had to languish where they were in the loop for another ten minutes thanks to their obstinacy before I let them away behind the Weymouth which they then had to follow to Westbury, being checked at Blatchbridge and Clink Road behind it. By the time they arrived on shed the men from the Cranmore had been booked off and gone by twenty minutes.

With the bi-directional goods loop only providing facing access to and from the branch it was not very practicable for use in refuging a through freight travelling along the main line. In the event that one had to be shunted for a passenger train to pass then it would be pushed back into either the Up or Down Sidings as appropriate. Such a manoeuvre took time and was not liked by train crews because of the reversing. In the case of down freights it was possible to signal these directly through the mains facing crossover and bring them to a stand on the Up Main, provided they would not be in the way of an up train for the duration of their stay. Once the down express had passed, the freight regained the Down Main via the trailing crossover which, for this move was traversed in the facing direction thus no reversing was required at all. The 11.00 Reading West Junction and the Yeovil goods were often treated in this fashion, avoiding the need to propel back into the sidings.

The rescue of a failed train was one of those situations rarely photographed and although there were less failures than I had been exposed to at Whiteball they did still occur from time to time, sometimes for inexcusable reasons such as the locomotive running out of fuel. Communicating with a failed train, so that regulation 14 could be put into action, usually meant waiting for the guard or secondman to ring in from a lineside 'phone - there were a few of these strung out mid-section connected to the box to box circuit. In walking to thc 'phone they would put down the prescribed detonator protection in accordance with Section M of the rule book. This required detonators at ¼, ½ and three at ¾ mile to the rear of the failed train but only three at 300 yards to the front. The signalman could only wait for news, unless there was a train travelling in the opposite direction on the adjacent line which could be stopped and the footplate crew asked to travel cautiously through the section to make contact with the overdue train. Caution was paramount as the non-appearance could be the result of something far more serious such as derailment or landslide. Once the means of assistance had been agreed with the train crew concerned there was always a willing set of Westbury men around, happy to abandon their stone train in the sidings in favour of the more glamorous option of going to the rescue of a failed express out in the section as if they were the Tracey family in Thunderbird 2.

Not long into a late turn I took a call from the 'phone at milepost 123 which was near the top of Brewham bank not far from the site of the long defunct Strap Lane Halt. A rather dejected Old Oak secondman from the 13.55 Paignton declared "We're a failure mate - no power - we'll need assistance". "Right, where exactly are you failed" I asked. "Just this side of the 123¼ milepost" came the reply. "Tell your driver he's not to move and I'll arrange to get an engine back onto the front of you, then come back and call me again." I knew I could rustle up an engine pretty quickly as the loaded Brentford trip was edging its way down the bank from Wanstrow. I had expected to let it trickle out behind the Paignton but now its class 47, still in faded two-tone green livery, had a more urgent task to undertake. When the secondman returned to the 'phone I made sure he had put down the protecting detonators and had a red flag with him. "Wait at the dets to stop the engine and escort it to the train" I finished. "How long do you think it'll be?" "Not long, he'll be leaving here shortly."

Ken at Castle Cary had listened in on the 'phone circuit to what was going on and gave his agreement to the manoeuvre. I replaced the main line signals to danger and sent the cancelling bell signal to Tony at Blatchbridge, which meant another call to explain why. On relinquishing the token to me, the three men on the Brentford were more than happy to play rescue service, refuging their train in double quick time. I had to look away as they propelled 1,400 tonnes over the points into the Up Sidings as if they were traversing a high speed junction. The guard jumped down, split the pipes and unhooked the moment the vehicles came to a stand. The loco' then drew out onto the main line. Whilst I changed the road, the three men changed ends so that they were in the west facing cab. They saw my handsignal to drop back to the box and paused outside to receive instructions. "Where is she then Bobby" called the driver. I went across to them to make sure they heard my instructions properly. "123¼ right oh, see you in a few minutes" replied the driver and with a toot they shot away down the up road towards the stricken Paignton as if they were in a race against the clock.

An early morning scene at Witham as a couple of empty stone trains each wait for their turn to go down the branch to Merehead. The one in the loop is headed by D1040 "Western Queen", the one on the up main by 47 060. The latter has been drawn across to allow 6V32 the 02.00 Ripple Lane - Exeter City Basin tanks to pass on the down main behind 47 019. (A. Vaughan)

Back in the box I watched the short berth track circuit at the Up Home signal occupy and clear momentarily and was left with my thoughts that had visions of the mad crew missing the secondman, exploding the detonators and happening upon the train at great speed. There had been instances of assisting engines colliding with the failed trains they had gone to rescue turning a minor incident into a major catastrophe. I hoped this would not be another. Putting aside my nightmare thoughts I rang Westbury North to advise Ian that the Paignton would need a fresh engine in due course and then got the road to Blatchbridge again and pulled off. Next I called Control to keep them in the picture. We often got things in motion locally like this before ringing Control as invariably their early involvement led to delay. This was inevitable, being tucked away as they were in a remote office in Bristol without the benefit of being able to see the immediate picture. But it was in our interests to maintain a good relationship with Control as they could always overlook or cover up an error that a signalman might make which caused train delay. "The 13.55 Paignton's fallen down at Brewham". "Right, leave it with me, I'll see what assistance I can organise and get back to you" said Alan at Bristol. "Hang on a minute Alan, I've already sent an engine in on the front". With that I heard a clunk from a relay downstairs and looked up to see the berth track at the Home signal occupied again. "And she's just about to come by". I went to the window to watch the cavalcade go past. The train passed at full speed, the 47 positively hammering, its three animated occupants beaming from ear to ear, pointing six thumbs-up towards me. In contrast, the dejected pair in the dead 50 behind were sat with their feet up resting on the console. From leaving me to passing the box again, barely ten minutes had passed. They really were in a race.

Forty five minutes later, having dumped the class 50 at Westbury, the 47 and its men arrived back light engine to collect their Brentford. I couldn't resist strolling across to them to call them a mad lot. "We're not mad, we just wanted to show them cockney boys a bit of railway work".

Failures didn't always occur remote from the box. If an ailing train made it to within station limits before expiring the recovery operation was usually simpler. However, I recall a morning when the Ripple Lane tank train had not called at Westbury but run straight to Witham to detach vehicles before going forward to Exeter. On drawing out of the down sidings to go on its way the locomotive expired across No. 44, the exit points, unable to move. The simplest way to clear the main line was to admit an engine into the down sidings behind the train via No. 49 points near the box, attach it to the rear of the train and drag the formation back clear inside. I had a loaded stone from which to borrow its unusual traction - a pair of Brush type '3s' - but with 44 points sitting reverse under the failed train the interlocking held the levers for both the main line trailing crossover and for No. 49 points in the normal position.

Having been detached from their train in the goods loop I was able to get the locomotives across outside the box on the Down Main by running them out over the facing crossover, blocking back outside my Home signal. With the axe and poker from the fire I was able to disconnect No. 49 points from their lever at the crank on the lead-away from the box, bar them across and clip them to allow the engines into the sidings. Before doing this I had telephoned John Taylor, the signal lineman at Frome, who promptly made his way down to Witham with his mate Eddie Hucker to properly reconnect No. 49 and ensure all was in order before resuming normal working. They came out in their yellow Vauxhall Viva van, a familiar railway vehicle. What satisfaction railway teamwork engendered! Whilst all this had been going on I had dealt with an up express and run an empty stone through onto the branch - the railway had to keep moving. Later in the morning the failed loco' was towed away to Bath Road and a replacement Westbury engine worked the tanks down to Exeter.

The interlocking between levers was of course an essential part of the mechanisms in place to ensure safe operations. Knowing the constraints of the mechanical interlocking, the electrical track locking and the interlinking with the block instruments was a key part of being a good signalman. This was especially the case in the larger, complex boxes but there were often tricks to be learnt almost anywhere. An example at Witham was the Down Branch Starter (No. 59) which rearlocked points No. 32 in either position. This was a standard piece of locking provided to prevent the points being moved under a train running towards the cleared signal. However, in the same section of track was point No. 25 leading into the up sidings. This was fitted with a facing point lock operated by lever No. 26. This lever was electrically locked by track circuit whilst any movement was traversing the points. Hence a rearlock between the Branch Starter and these points was not necessary. If points 25 were set reverse then there was also no need to enforce the mechanical rearlock between the Branch Starter and points 32.

When passing a stone empties down the Up Main through No. 32 reverse onto the branch in order to cross with a loaded stone standing in the loop, it was often necessary to get these points restored to normal as soon as possible so as to clear the signals for a train approaching on the Up Main. Having to wait for the empties to substantially pass signal 59 added unwanted seconds to the manoeuvre and could result in the up train catching the distant at caution. By unbolting the siding points as soon as the track circuit was vacated by the train and reversing these the rearlock on 32 could be broken down and the lever normalised. All perfectly safe and legitimate, saving vital seconds and perhaps making the difference to an up express getting the distant "off". Arriving to relieve me at ten to two one afternoon, Tom Baber witnessed this move as he took his coat off. "Well I never knew e could do thik" said Tom, "are e sure tis legal?".

Widely installed, following an accident at Welwyn in 1935, involving two trains in the section at the same time, was "Welwyn Control". This ensured that, having pegged "Line Clear" to the box in rear, another could not be given until the train for which the first had been given had been proved to have arrived. This proving was achieved by the occupation and clearance of a track circuit on the approach to the home signal. While the track was occupied the relevant block indicator was forced to the "Train on Line" position and, if the commutator for that instrument had not been turned to "Train on Line" already then the

The Bruton block instrument at Witham with its bell to the left, below which is the Welwyn control winder in its circular housing. To the right of the block instrument are the two switching out boxes. Also on the front of the shelf are two lock plungers and associated sealed emergency releases for FPLs.
(C. Chapman)

signalman would have to do so, in a catch up fashion, before being able to return the indication to "Normal" once the train had passed clear.

To allow for situations when a train did not proceed into or through the section from the box in rear or suchlike, an emergency release device was provided, mounted on the block shelf near each block instrument. These comprised a mechanical winder which had to be turned until the letter "N" appeared in a small window. The winder was geared such that a certain number of turns was mandated which would take two minutes to complete. One version came with a proper winding handle which allowed continuous turning, although the gearing restricted the speed. The other type, which we had at Witham, came with a lozenge shaped turning handle. This had to be gripped by the hand and thus only allowed half turns to be made before having to remove the hand and start again. This needed less turns but the enforced half turn action still meant that the operation would take about two minutes. To help beat the system where this version of the device was fitted a homemade handle, fashioned from a piece of copper track circuit bond wire was kept hidden in a handy place. This could be hooked over the lozenge and turned vigorously to effect a release in about ten seconds flat. Witham had one of these illegal aids tucked away in the train register desk to help make life easier.

In many boxes, including Witham there was an even quicker and simpler way to beat the system. Power for the signalling circuits in Western Region boxes was generally provided by a battery (trickle charged where mains existed) that was centre tapped to earth. By this means both positive and negative feeds were available whilst all the return circuits used a common earth wire. It was possible therefore to drive polar circuits by selecting the appropriate feed. The positive and negative looping that fed all the various circuits and indicators was protected by resetable circuit breakers known as Nalders. These Nalders were located on the block shelf so that in the event of one tripping, for whatever reason such as a power surge or through lightning, the signalman could reset it. These Nalders proved useful in helping to bypass some of the modern electrical safeguards such as the "Welwyn Control". By manually tripping and then resetting the Nalder that fed the circuit to the track repeater relay for the home signal approach track circuit it could be momentarily set to occupied and cleared again. This fooled the system into registering the arrival of a train thus enabling the block to be normalised without recourse to winding the emergency release.

Right:
The view of Whiteball Siding from the adjacent accommodation bridge in 1974. Nestled into the side of the cutting, the box was of minimal height to give the signalman a good view under the bridge and back along the cutting the other way towards the tunnel. The adjacent corrugated lamp hut was a feature at most boxes, housing spare signal lamps, wicks and lamp oil. Note the concrete troughing route being installed on the up side of the line, the lids are laying haphazardly near the sleeper ends. A new telecomm's cable will soon render the pole route redundant.

(Author)

Right:
The cramped conditions inside Whiteball signal box. The block instruments, bells, telephones and other instruments are evident on the block shelf. Towards the left hand end is the block switch. Hanging from nails above the end window are the red, circular, Workman Disconnected reminders for placing over levers when equipment is being worked on by the Lineman.

(Author)

Above:
The signalman's view of an up train from the window of Whiteball box. D1048 "Western Lady" heads an up Plymouth to Paddington evening train under the accomodation bridge and on towards the tunnel. The roof of the corrugated iron lamp hut is visible, as are the down siding and loop entry points. *(T. Chapman)*

Below:
The 09.55 Exeter Riverside to Walton Old Junction mixed freight (7M67) hauled by a Brush type '4' passes Wellington box situated on the defunct up platform. *(Author)*

Above:
D1009 "Western Invader" draws the 19.07 Westbury to Exeter Central cement train past Witham box on 25th May 1976 having had to wait the road behind a light engine. The Fireman has his fingers in his ears and the driver is pointing to his mate whilst exchanging a joke with me as I lean out of the box window. It was a beautiful spring evening and I was working my rest day - again. *(T. Chapman)*

Right:
Having returned from Cranmore and dropped tanks in the up sidings for the Exeter to Ripple Lane to collect later, a Brush type '4' draws up towards the siding exit signal ready to return light to Westbury. Meanwhile a "Peak" drops down off the Merehead branch with a rake of loaded stone tipplers, their brakes squealing. Neither are going anywhere for a moment as an up express hauled by an English Electric type 50 powers up the main line en route to Paddington. *(Author)*

Above:
Jim Murray, the Frome Signal Gang Foreman steadies the ladder as he sends his assistant Dave Whittington to replace the cowl on the top of the stove pipe at Witham. The previous cowl had come crashing down one night the week previous during high winds, frightening the life out of me as I huddled next to the stove in the small hours.
(Author)

Above:
The spaces in the frame are evident in this interior shot of Witham. It must have been a warm day as the corner windows are open and I am working with sleeves rolled up as I operate lever 54, the mains facing crossover. The telephone handsets on the block shelf connect directly with signal post telephones at the more remote signals. Between the two block instruments are a pair of switching-out boxes and at the far end of the frame, half obscured, is the emergency hand generator. Hanging above this is the megaphone. The lever tops are well burnished and the levers themselves recently repainted by myself. *(C.J.L. Osment)*

Right:
The token machine at Witham with telephone to Quarry Junction above and token carriers hanging from the wall behind. *(C. Chapman)*

Left:
The driver of 47 087 "Cyclops" has some notices to hand down as he collects the Merehead branch token from me on his way to the quarry with an empty train one late summer's evening. The bell tower of Witham Friary church can be seen beyond the locomotive whilst the cows have returned to the fields from the milking parlour.
(C. Chapman)

Right:
Detonators, ready for action, strapped to the block shelf bracket at Blatchbridge Junction by their lead straps. The blue det's are dated 1973 and the orange det's 1975. Sitting on the block shelf are two generations of lever collar.
(C. Chapman)

Left:
Smoke drifts from the "roll-up" in Tom Baber's hand as he sits in the spare armchair at Frome North. On this occasion Tom is resting between trains whilst acting as Pilotman. He is wearing his signalman's grey summer jacket over which is placed an orange high viz vest - a new innovation in the 1970s. A collar sits over lever 33.
(C. Chapman)

Right:
Witham's Down Goods Loop to Branch Starting signal at "clear" with its associated elevated disc alongside that read into the Up Sidings. On the left hand side can be seen the Down Main Inner Home and in the distance is the signal box. A rake of hoppers is stabled in the Down Sidings.
(Author)

Below:
With customary shiny buffers, a Brush type '4' hauls empty royal carriages through Exminster as the 09.10 Liskeard to Wolverton on 24th May 1978. I have a learner in the box, Dave Barnett - seen studying the train from the window. Once a learner had shown sufficient ability to work a box, leaving them alone for a while but not straying too far away, did wonders for their confidence. The wide gap between the Up Loop (which by this time had become a siding) and the Up Main, where one of the island platforms had once stood, is evident in this picture. *(Author)*

Above and below:
Dawlish Warren box sat behind the wooden down platform and backed onto the Warren Golf Club. A high net fence extends along the platform to catch errant golf balls. The platforms were provided with their own lines, the main lines running through the middle of the layout. The wooden surface of the platform could be treacherous in damp and wet weather. The rear view shows just how substantial a structure the box was, having to be built up from the ground below the level of the railway. (Author)

Above:
Sunday single line working. Bemused passengers wonder what is happening as a Brush type '4' backs a down train through the crossover at Teignmouth ready for the Pilotman to take it through to Newton Abbot East over the up line. The Groundman is unclipping the far end of the crossover points and will move to the other end to clip them normal shortly. Above the third vehicle can be seen the tail lamp mirror on its post capped with a finial.
(Author)

Right:
At the end of the down platform Teignmouth signal box sat in the shadow of Shute Hill bridge, although here it catches some late afternoon sun. Dating from 1896 it was constructed from hard blue-grey Cakemore brick. Unusually it retained its brick chimney - many boxes had stove pipe replacements. The wooden end finials remain in place at ridge level. Note the coved and recessed lower corner at the rear of the box and the recessed waste pipe that allowed walking space when there had been a dock siding tight behind the box. *(Author)*

Above:
A view of Newton Abbot West box from the road with its array of Down Home signals. A Holbeck based "Peak" is departing from the Down Main (Platform 3) with the 06.42 Leeds to Paignton and is routed towards the Down Relief line. The old wooden coaches in the background are owned by, and stabled alongside, David and Charles the publishers. *(Author)*

Left:
At the left hand end of the frame in Newton Abbot West resided a small 3-lever detonator placer frame. These levers numbered 1, 2 and 3, operated placers for the Down Main, Down Relief and Down Through lines and stood alongside the real levers 1, 2 and 3 in the main frame. Being just inside the door, the coal buckets were kept behind this frame, above which can be seen faded green and red flags standing in the flag bracket beneath the window. *(Author)*

Right:
The last 18 levers in the frame at Newton Abbot West all had their handles cut short to remind the signalman that they controlled electric signals. These operated all of the up direction running and shunt-ahead signals, the distants and homes were colour light whilst the starters were motor worked semaphores. Those with white stripes half way down the levers were released by Line Clear from East box whilst those that have their lower halves painted black worked relief line signals. The floor mops and bucket reside behind the levers. *(Author)*

Above:
The lever frame inside Newton Abbot West box makes an impressive sight. Light reflects off the polished linoleum floor - cleaning was undertaken on Saturday mornings being a joint effort between the signalman and booking boy. There were two illuminated diagrams, two coal stoves and five block instruments. Sandwiched between the Up Relief and Up Main Lines just off the platform end the box was long but narrow. *(Author)*

Above:
The brick built Aller Junction standing proud over the junction that it controlled. This box included an inside staircase and, because it faced west, had a sunny perspective on fine days. A mile or so out from Newton Abbot, reliefmen were allowed 30 minutes to walk each way. *(Author)*

Below:
Two pairs of banner solenoid discs controlled by Newton Abbot East reading back through the scissors crossover between the Down Relief and Down Through lines. *(Author)*

Right:
Aller Junction was crammed full of instruments, even on the window ledge, to supplement the illuminated diagram and colourful lever frame. With 2-lever detonator frames positioned at each end of the main frame, the hurdy-gurdy at the far end of the box and an inside staircase there was little room left once the modern amenities of running water and a hot water geyser were added. Note the Bardic lamp at this end of the block shelf and three blue detonators affixed to the shelf bracket ready for instant emergency use. Behind these is a glass fronted cabinet containing the Nalder switches. Between the two nearest block instruments is the clockwork timer associated with the loop exit motor points. *(Author)*

Above:
Communications facilities at Aller Junction. There are nine telephones ranging from omnibus through selector to auto types. The framed cards provide information on what codes to ring on the omnibus and selector circuits. Notices are pinned behind bulldog clips and a Railway Convalescence Home calendar hangs by the window. Sitting on top of the three lockers is the Train Register Book. Above this, on another clip, is the hand written timetable extract or simplifier. *(Author)*

Below:
The illuminated diagram and part of the block shelf at Paignton South. The double block instrument handled traffic on the Up and Down line. The down direction needle and commutator show a train has entered the section from North box, verified by the red lights illuminated on the diagram. The single (or half) block was used for the Down line. To the right of this is a lever collar hanging on the lower hook of a double hanger and the block switch which allows the box to close. *(Author)*

Right:
The height of the three storey Torre box is evident in this picture, particularly as the lower floor extends through the platform to track level. This was the only remaining intermediate box on the branch between Aller and Paignton at the time. (Author)

Left:
Backing onto Station Lane, Paignton South looked after the south end of the station, the north end of Goodrington carriage sidings, Sands Road level crossing and the connection to the Torbay Steam Railway. It retained wheel operated gates and a separate two-lever frame for the wickets, the levers of which were painted blue. (Author)

Right:
After dark at Paignton North. Peter Davis, dressed in his casual summer gear, leans against the gate wheel and gate lock lever. The paper sellotaped in the windows is to restrict the view into the box by pedestrians crossing on the old footbridge. (C. Chapman)

Left:
The modern flat roofed "Plywood Wonder" structure at Dainton Tunnel which replaced the earlier Saxby and Farmer design of box. Note the glass door and end panels. The signal is the Down Home. Sidings had once existed on the level ground behind the box accessed via facing points at the tunnel mouth.

(Author)

Right:
The compact frame and block shelf set at the back of the box inside Dainton. The only levers in use are those for the running signals, the crossover and associated discs plus the two detonator placers. The diagram is of the non-illuminated type, the three track circuits being provided with indicators on the shelf.

(Author)

CHAPTER SEVEN

TWENTY MINUTES A MILE

As a regular signalman, the life of the reliefman had seemed a little less than satisfactory to my way of thinking. I much preferred being able to set up home in one particular box and furnish it with my possessions, filling a locker with the comforts required to sustain continual long and unsocial hours. The maverick existence of the roving men that came when you were on holiday, sick or when you should be so lucky as to have a rest day off, appeared a little lacking in compensation.

However, after gaining experience at Whiteball and Witham the chance of a move back west to a relief signalman's post could not be passed up, not just for the promotion, but to fulfil a desire to experience that type of work and compare its benefits should it have any. Most regular men remained regular whilst most reliefmen remained on the relief. An observation which I believe shows that there are, in the main, two types of signalmen. My transition from one to the other came easily and enjoyably. The post I went to at Newton Abbot had become vacant following the promotion of Ken Waldron to Plymouth Panel but Ken could not leave until I arrived.

A vacancy in a high grade position invariably set off a chain reaction of subsequent vacancies down the order of seniority as eligible applicants followed one another up the promotional ladder until a low grade box was filled by a shunter or booking boy getting their feet on the first rung. The release of each signalman by his local area manager was reliant upon the replacement signalman being available. Of course, not all signalmen aspired to move, many being quite happy to remain resident at a box where the work and location was to their liking. Before being released to move to Newton Abbot my replacement at Witham had to be found. There were no internal applicants so a person was sought from "off the street", in the shape of Charlie Beatson. He already knew the basics of the job, having been friendly with Dennis Davey during his time at Somerton, so it was not long before he "took on", allowing me to be on my way. Charlie made a good signalman at Witham, then a few years later went on to win Jack Richards' Rest Day Relief post at Castle Cary when Jack retired. Eventually he too landed at Newton Abbot, as a resident in West box.

Having travelled up and down the West of England main line and visited most of the boxes along it I found that the railway was more traditional the farther from London one went. There was greater pride and sense of duty the more westerly the location but also less flexibility in attitude. Previously on moving east from the Taunton area to the Westbury area I experienced a lesser sense of tradition but a more easy going approach. Now, leapfrogging beyond Taunton and Exeter to Newton Abbot I found myself in a railway environment closer to 1948 than the 1970s. My relatively tender age compared to the other signalmen heightened this image for me but my age also came as a surprise to the many incumbents that had seen service with the Great Western Railway.

My job as a General Purpose Relief signalman was one of a number on the Newton Abbot district, which normally covered the area from Exeter exclusive to Plymouth exclusive and down to Paignton on the former Kingswear branch. We could be found elsewhere outside this area when demand arose, usually during engineering works. A quote from Norman Marlow's *Footplate and Signal Cabin* aptly sums up my time on the relief: "Never in my life have I seen so much of dawn and darkness nor been acquainted with the face of nature at such strange hours". Names of my relief colleagues (both GP and RD) that I remember from around the district include Frank Casely, Bryan Warren, Bill Moore, Cliff Balment, Peter Davis, Dennis Hawkins, Nigel Turner, Mervyn Arscott and Jack Eveleigh. Jack had a claim to fame as he was the only signalman we knew who had managed to snap a lever in half whilst pulling it over in the frame, an achievement he accomplished during his time as a resident man at Kingswear.

The number of boxes and the traffic that they handled in the Newton Abbot area were much reduced from the days of steam, yet it was still an enjoyable and various part of the railway world. Fourteen boxes on the district survived, ranging from the ten remaining working levers at Dawlish, which was normally only open on summer Saturdays or other times as required, up to the 206 lever double manned Newton Abbot East.

On arrival I eagerly set about learning the simpler boxes so that I could take on the role quickly. I learnt one box a day. In the first week I went to Teignmouth on the Monday, Exminster on Tuesday, Dawlish Warren on Wednesday, Aller Junction on Thursday and Dainton Tunnel on Friday. The following week I signed for these with the District Inspector on the Monday then learnt Stoneycombe Siding, Paignton North, Paignton South and Torre before signing for these and going to Bristol to see Chief Inspector Forrester on Friday. I then spent a few short afternoons learning Totnes but left Newton Abbot until later. Inspector Tom Earlam conducted my final exam in a carriage compartment on his way back to Exeter. By the time the train drew into St. Davids he had signed my competence slip leaving me to catch the next train home.

It was necessary to know a lot of information to be able to do the job well. To help with this I consolidated the relevant contents of the Mandatory and Conditional timetables with that of the Newton Abbot Station Working book into a single notebook, together with my own additional comments, particularly about movements at Newton Abbot and Paignton, plus the realistic timings for freights. This meant I had a simple, helpful guide to the running of trains throughout the district that I could carry with me.

Besides relieving in signal boxes the reliefman's job involved many other tasks. In fact, following my initial two weeks of learning, I spent the next two as a "groundman" or hand signalman on the level crossing at Paignton North, where the signal works engineers were busy replacing the capstan wheel operated gates with hydraulic lifting barriers. I was rostered with Peter Davis, a Dawlish Rest Day Relief signalman who also happened to live in Teignmouth which is where I had taken up digs. We travelled to and fro together in his Hillman Humber for the two weeks. Between us, under the signalman's instructions, we would close the crossing off for each train by halting road traffic and then stringing a row of red and white pennants on a rope across each side of the line. One of us would then proceed to the relevant signal and exhibit a proceed hand signal to the driver of the train.

I was to spend many subsequent hours out on the ground clipping points and flagging trains at one location or another, even acting as a temporary block post to protect the Royal Train one night. Extension of the new M5 motorway to beyond Exeter produced handsignalman work north of Exminster in connection with the construction of the bridge that spanned the Exe and the railway. The plant and workers crossing the line and working alongside it and over it required strict control to protect the safety of trains.

Amongst the most enjoyable tasks was that of donning the red arm band to be the Pilotman during single line working, especially around the infamous sea wall stretch between Teignmouth and Dawlish Warren. Sometimes this would be due to damage caused to the wall when the sea was at its roughest. At other times a pleasant Sunday could be spent in the cabs of diesel locomotives like the "Westerns", "Peaks", "Brush Type 4s" or latterly the "50s" travelling up and down as a human staff beneath the red cliffs and above the beaches and through the five tunnels, during routine maintenance or track renewal.

There was one weekend when much of the pointwork at Newton Abbot East box was disconnected so that the signal gangs could renew cranks on the lead-away outside the box. An army of signalmen were drafted in to act as groundmen to hand bar and clip the points for each movement. I was placed in charge of the group on the Saturday night working to the signalman's instructions, ensuring that each route had been correctly set and that the points were clipped and padlocked.

Major work like this occurred rarely but was always well planned so as to impact as little as possible on the train service. On another occasion the 3-pin bow bridge which carried the Torquay Road over the railway just west of Newton Abbot station was demolished using explosives on a Saturday night in March in order that it could be replaced with a new structure. In true railway tradition trains ran on the Sunday and a normal service operated on the Monday.

When a vacancy required to be covered the roster clerk invariably strove to share the job around, placing reliefmen in three week stints to work a round of lates, earlies and nights each, before moving them on to somewhere else. If the vacancy remained for any length then a return stint or two would duly follow. Covering a vacancy often meant playing host to the learner signalman. Depending on the box and its grade the learner might be a promoted signalman, or perhaps a railman (porter) seeking to enter the signalling grades. Very rarely was it someone from outside the railway, particularly in this part of the world, such was the strict promotional system, based on step seniority, that was in force.

A grading formula existed by which signal boxes were classified. This took account of, amongst other things, the amount of equipment, the level of traffic, the hours of opening and the number of men on duty per shift. The lowest graded boxes were designated class A, the highest class F, with B, C, D and E in between. Relief signalmen, depending on the highest class of box they relieved in, were allocated to grades 1, 2 and 3. For purposes of establishing seniority these nine classes were slotted into five promotional steps. Accrued service in each step established the position in respect of each person for the purposes of evaluating relative seniority.

The Western Region was divided into a number of promotional areas for Conciliation Grade staff which covered the likes of shunters, station staff and signalmen. The West of England promotional area covered all the way from Heywood Road Junction at Westbury through to Penzance and branches. Staff employed within this area had first call on applying for vacancies that occurred in it. Only if there was no suitable applicant would the job be thrown open to the rest of the Region, it being deemed "exhausted" within its promotional area. This of course brought a degree of protection to the men within each area but virtually prevented promotion between areas. It also led to the absurd position that a signalman employed at say Bradford Junctions near Trowbridge could seek promotion to Plymouth but not to nearby Swindon or Bristol, unless the vacancy had become exhausted, for these places, although nearby, were in the Bristol promotional area.

At one time a vacancy arose at Teignmouth for which there were no applicants. In due course it was filled by a lively Londoner, Fred Rooke. Already a signalman, he transferred from the London Midland Region, coming from Silkstream Junction near Hendon on the Midland main line out of St Pancras. Fred had decided to move his family to Teignmouth in preference to waiting to be made redundant at Silkstream by the impending construction of a new power box at West Hampstead. He learnt the box with me, acclimatising very quickly to the environment in Teignmouth finding it far preferable to that of north London. Indeed he was able to supplement his signalman's wages by helping out at breakfast or dinner time in one of the local hotels, depending on his shift. Eventually, when Exeter power box was built, Fred was one of those who found a job there until his retirement.

Each of the boxes had an appeal and atmosphere of its own. Just like the English pub, no two looked or felt the same, inside or out. They were unique in a lot of different ways. They might have all had levers, instruments, furniture, a clock, a stove and all the other things that comprised a signal box but the way these were all arranged was different at every place. Then there were detail differences like the variation in fire tools and how home made brackets might be fitted to the wall on which to lodge them. There might be a toasting fork made from bond wire or useful little shelves upon which to place things or linoleum fitted to locker tops or the train register desk to give these a smooth surface. Each box had its own set of signalmen too, characters every one. No one box could be a favourite, I enjoyed each for its own merits. After a week in somewhere busy like Newton Abbot West with its 153 levers and five block instruments, it became a pleasant change to spend a shift out in the rolling Devon countryside at Dainton merely passing trains or a twelve hour Sunday at Dawlish

Warren collecting golf balls off the track which had strayed from the nearby course! The line and station at the Warren were at a higher level than the links and a 15' high wire fence along the length of the down platform gave added protection against stray balls. There was always a good Sunday's collection to be gathered though in between trains. Remembering to keep the Train Register up to date at a new box, after spending a while at Newton Abbot West was always a problem, because here booking boys were provided, allowing the signalman to concentrate on just working the frame, bells and blocks.

The overtime and unsocial hours enhancements paid to all signalmen were complicated. Between Monday and Friday the first three hours of overtime paid on any one day was at the rate of time and a quarter with any subsequent hours beyond three, at time and a half. Any hours worked on a Saturday between 6am and 12pm or on a weekday between 9pm and 2am were paid at the rate of time and a quarter, enhanced to time and a half if overtime and on weekdays between 2am and 6am at time and a third but when overtime at time and seven twelfths. Only one rate was paid for Sunday work with all hours attracting time and three quarters. In addition to this an Irregular and Unsocial hours Payment (IUP), calculated as a percentage of basic rates depending on the degree of irregularity and timing of turns was added to the gross figure as an allowance.

These rates sometimes led to bizarre situations, such as when working beyond 6am in the morning. A 10pm to 10am twelve hour turn would yield time and a quarter for the four hours from ten until two, then time and a third between two and six but the four hours beyond 6am, at the end of what was otherwise a night shift, saw the hourly rate revert back to time and a quarter, the standard daytime overtime rate. Even more odd would be if an eight hour shift, that was not overtime, finished after 6am. For example, an 11pm to 7am turn would see time and a quarter paid for the first three hours until two, time and a third for the next four until 6am but then only flat (single) time for the last hour until seven. Therefore an eight hour night shift starting later than 10pm would pay less than a normal 10pm to 6am night shift despite being probably as, or indeed more, unsocial.

Reliefman's work was comparatively well paid. It had to be to compensate for the irregularity of the shifts and the fact that more time was spent on back and night shifts than early turn. In fact many Saturdays were spent on late turn somewhere because of its dislike by most railwaymen who found it far preferable to go to the football or make a long weekend off. Being on the relief meant that I could be rostered for a variety of duties from week to week and even these might change as the week progressed due to unforeseen events. The hours that signalmen were allowed to work and the rest periods between turns were governed by both national and local agreements. Even within these rules it was possible to work a significant number of hours and to "double back" to book on for a second shift in one day. The most lucrative time for this would be on a Sunday which, as mentioned, attracted time and three quarters pay. So a "double back", generating perhaps two eight hour shifts would be rewarded with 28 hours pay. Double time was not paid to Signalmen on Sundays as the work was not classed as manual! I feel the National Union of Railwaymen failed to provide due representation for signalmen in their negotiations on this and a number of other matters. The only time it was possible to receive double time was after midnight on a Saturday night if the turn had begun before midnight and it was your rest day on that Saturday that you started working!

When travelling from "Home Station", to the next box or site of work the reliefman booked on in time to catch a convenient train or otherwise to walk, or perhaps journey by a combination of both to a remote box. An allowance of twenty minutes a mile was given to any walking. The man could use his car, pushbike, bus, or indeed walk but by using the fair system of a basic time per mile payment, no room for argument was left with regard to actual cost or the time involved in getting to work. Indeed a man could hardly claim inability to get to work through a private transport problem for he was paid to walk! If working at the same location on consecutive days then a lodging allowance was paid in lieu of travelling, although at most times reliefmen would always return home. Where, in fact could onc have lodged at many of these locations, especially for the paltry sum involved of £1.82?

The emolument for the reliefman could become well enhanced through travelling time. In fact, when travelling across one's district there were often insufficient hours in a day to book travelling to and from, say, a twelve hour shift. I remember when subsequently moving to a panel job at Oxford that the higher rate of pay barely covered for the loss of travelling time I had enjoyed on the relief!

This system might appear anachronistic but it would be hard to find one as fair, even with its anomalies. For instance my home station was Newton Abbot and therefore I received no travelling time to take up duty there. So, by living at Teignmouth five miles away, I had to reach Newton Abbot in my own time using train, car or bike. There was a box at Teignmouth of course, just a few minutes walk down the hill. To work here I could book on an hour and forty five minutes earlier than the start of my shift and book off likewise later afterwards or claim lodging for consecutive days.

The agreed walking times for the area are laid out in the list opposite. For some journeys, combinations of these times would need to be added. So, for example, a journey right across the district from Totnes to Exminster amassed eight hours.

These were times of high inflation (up to 20%) but rather than provide pay rises to match, the cash starved railway relied upon government introduced fixed allowances to top up the weekly wage. There were various schemes including Threshold Payments with acronyms such as NES, SEE and SES. When these ceased large rises in the rates of pay were negotiated by the unions, including a massive 18% rise in 1978 and a further 17% in two stages during 1979.

Very occasionally I would get a "spare" day when there was no shift to cover. At these times I would often accompany the Newton signal technicians (Gordon Holman and his mate) allowing them to perform a few routine renewal jobs that needed the assistance of a traffic department flagman such as changing a signal wire or semaphore arm. Whenever Gordon went to a signal box to do his routine maintenance or to perform a renewal or repair he would always sign the train register *G.F. Holman Signal Dept*. Another occasional job would be a nice day shift with the DI visiting a

LIST OF OFFICIAL WALKING TIMES

From	To	H. M.
Paignton	Goodrington	.10
"	Torquay	.45
"	Torre	1.00
"	Dainton	2.00
"	Newton Abbot	2.40
"	Totnes	2.00
Newton Abbot	Totnes	2.55
"	Dainton	1.20
"	Stoneycombe	.50
"	Aller Junction	.30
"	Teignmouth	1.45
"	Dawlish	2.40
Dawlish	Dawlish Warren	.30
Dawlish Warren	Starcross	.40
Starcross	Exminster	1.15
"	Exeter St. Thomas	2.35
"	Exeter St. Davids	2.50
Exminster	Exeter St. Davids	1.35

couple of boxes to relieve the resident men for an hour or so whilst they were taken aside for their bi-annual rules exam. Rest days off were rare and to be cherished and if I did not leave home for the day by 8am, a visit from the porter at Teignmouth station or a taxi driver from the station rank would bring a message of a late turn shift that had arisen somewhere on the district. But at least working rest days paid time and a half, even for the travelling!

On one particular "waiting orders" day a message was brought to the door from the station Chargeman asking me to go to Dawlish. A rock fall had closed the up line during the morning so single line working had been introduced over the down. By opening Dawlish the single line could be split to allow two trains to follow one another in the same direction and hence improve the traffic flow. I packed a bag for a long shift prior to making my way over to Dawlish. Before opening I had to wait for the Pilotman to come to the box whilst the train he was escorting paused in the station. He issued a Single Line Working form allowing me to join in proceedings and I duly switched in to split the block. The weather at Dawlish was foul with a strong south westerly wind blowing spray right across the station from the sea below. So much so that it was landing across the box windows, percolating through the sill by the action of the wind, so as to then trickle down the inside wall before collecting in puddles on the linoleum.

I had in fact been on nights at Aller Junction, finishing at 6am that morning so the message asked me to book on as quickly as possible having already had the minimum eight hours rest. Having never actually worked Dawlish box before, this first shift was rather unusual, acting as a break section on the single line, working

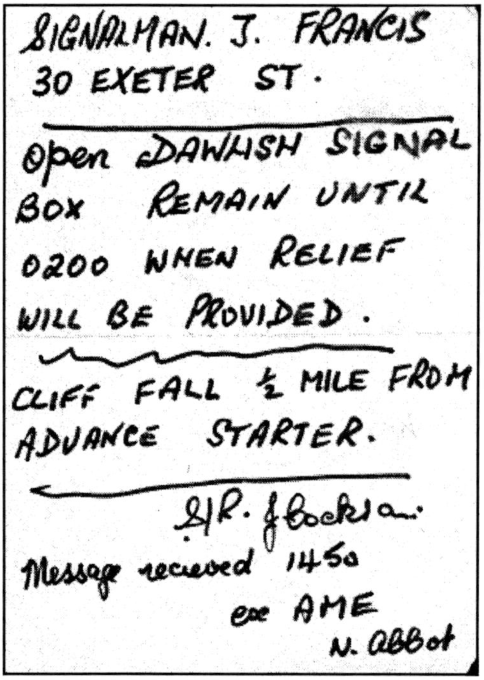
SIGNALMAN. J. FRANCIS
30 EXETER ST.

Open DAWLISH SIGNAL
BOX REMAIN UNTIL
0200 WHEN RELIEF
WILL BE PROVIDED.

CLIFF FALL ½ MILE FROM
ADVANCE STARTER.

[illegible]
Message received 1450
exe AME
N. Abbot

Here is an actual message, typical of many received, brought to my lodgings one winter's afternoon by a taxi from Teignmouth station. This one refers to a rock fall that had blocked one line and Dawlish box was required open to split the remaining single line into two sections and hence allow two trains to follow one another in each direction to ease delays. I packed my bag and made my way to Dawlish as quickly as possible. Another reliefman, Dennis Hawkins, came out at 2am in the morning to relieve me.

the up line signals for trains travelling in the wrong direction over the down line. It was 2am the following morning before welcome relief arrived in the shape of Dennis Hawkins. I was glad to get home to bed, especially as my next shift was 15.20 to 23.35 at Paignton North later that same day!

High tides coupled with onshore winds often caused track circuit failures at Dawlish. So long as the box was switched out these were not a problem. At Teignmouth a similar problem existed with the track circuits either side of the Down Home signal, out on the exposed sea wall. Failure of the track circuit beyond this signal prevented clearance of the Down Home. The foul weather precluded the provision of a hand signalman out on the exposed wall and so a special instruction allowed drivers to be issued with a written order by the signalman at Dawlish or Dawlish Warren, authorising the passing of the signal at danger. Under these circumstances the clearing point, before which a train could be accepted, was extended through to the Down Starting signal.

Thursdays were an important day for not only did the week's pay arrive but usually a telephone call or note from the roster clerk at Newton Abbot was received too. There was little chance to plan far ahead, for on a Thursday the work from Sunday onwards would be allocated. Timesheets also had to be compiled by Thursdays ready for collection, a definite task and more when a reliefman. All the relevant boxes on the sheet had to be filled with the correct hours worked at the various rates of pay for different times of the day, different days and sometimes different jobs. Travelling time by train or walking, lodging and shift allowance had to be recorded too. All then had to be calculated and accumulated to reflect the truth or at least come close to it. The pay clerks would double check the accuracy of all the entries, rarely giving much away.

Having to live out of a bag was one of the disadvantages of life on the relief. Rule books, cutlery, crockery, the large and heavy signal box key and anything else had to be carried every day, as well as food and milk. The big old key fitted

Area Manager's Office,
NEWTON ABBOT.

5.MAY 77. 19

Memo. to Relief Signalman/~~Porter~~ J.FRANCIS 30,EXETER ST TEIGNMOUTH

Duties for Week Commencing 8.May 77.

Sunday

Monday 2245-0700 H/S DAWLISH WARREN X/O

Tuesday 2300-0715 H/S DAWLISH WARREN R.D.C.

Wednesday 2315-0715 H/S NEWTON A. EAST X/O

Thursday 2215-0730 H/S TOTNES

Friday 1700-2200 NEWTON A. WEST VICE HAMMACOTT

Saturday 0910-1715 DAWLISH BOX.

PLEASE ACKNOWLEDGE RECEIPT.

for Area Manager.

Here's a typical note from the Roster Clerk. There's no Sunday turn for me but my rest day on Tuesday is cancelled to enable four nights of handsignalling in connection with single line working where tamping is taking place. In actual fact Bill Moore, who preferred handsignalman's duties to those of pilotman asked to swap with me so I had four nights riding on engines instead on this occasion. Despite finishing at 07.30 on Friday morning and being allowed to travel back on the next available train at 08.43 to home station at Newton Abbot I was rostered to do a short late turn at West box from 17.00 on the same day, the early turn man being extended to wait for me. Then, on Saturday, I enjoyed a day shift at Dawlish.

the lock on any Great Western box and was stamped GWR on the ring. I had to invest in a plastic mug, having broken so many china ones carrying them to and fro. Transporting the portable radio added to the weight too, made worse by the three varieties of electrical systems that existed throughout the district requiring conveyance of a range of plug adaptors. The boxes that had been recently wired employed the modern standard square 3-pin socket whereas those with earlier vintage wiring had either large round pin or small round pin sockets.

The digs in which I stayed in Teignmouth could not have been better. The owners, Kate and Arthur Treen, had migrated down to Teignmouth from West London where Arthur had been an electrician. He now worked as a clerk-cum-driver for the Ministry of Agriculture, Fisheries and Foods (MAFF) at their Starcross facility. They had hoped to open up the three storey house they bought as a bed and breakfast business but their application for a licence had been turned down by Teignbridge Council. Turning to plan B, they decided to take in lodgers. Arthur was well placed to find these lodgers, as university students received regular placements to MAFF at Starcross. They had to be found accommodation for the duration of their stay and who better to help them than Arthur, who collected them in a Ministry car from Exeter St Davids station on their day of arrival.

The turnover of students was steady and reasonably constant but a more long term lodger was also sought. Kate and Arthur placed a small-ad in the local paper just once. This happened to be in the week when I took a rest day off from Witham to visit Newton Abbot with the express purpose of finding somewhere to live. Having drawn a blank from the adverts in newsagents' windows and not found anything suitable in Newton Abbot itself, I came across the Treen's small-ad in the local paper but thought twice about calling the telephone number as I had always regarded Teignmouth as being a drab, undesirable place. This was an impression gained purely from passing through on the train, I had never actually been outside of the station. The granite station buildings dating from 1884 and deep stone lined cutting that ran from the sea wall to Old Quay with its many overbridges were dark and grey, hiding any view of the seaside town beyond.

It was getting late in the afternoon and I was due to take up my new posting on the Monday week so I decided to ring the number. Arthur took the call and we agreed I should drop by to see if I liked the room and for him to decide if I would make a suitable tenant. So I caught the next stopper up to Teignmouth and followed Arthur's directions up the hill from the station to the three-storey house on Exeter Street. We had a chat, during which I explained how I would be working shifts and that these would impact on the domestic arrangements. This was not seen as a problem and, after looking around the house, we shook hands on a price for board and lodging with the expectation that I would move in on Sunday week.

And so it was that I was able to discover a popular seaside town and vibrant little fishing port beyond the grey stone station and the railway line that cut through the red hill between the spectacular sea wall and the equally beautiful river Teign. Despite first appearances the station was attractively designed, sporting ornate ironwork, long awnings and other architectural features. Indeed, like the town it served, its character far outweighed that of its nearby neighbour Dawlish. Teignmouth literally had two sides to it. There was the sea front promenade known as the Den with its deckchairs, gardens, bowling green and pier along with hotels, the usual seasonal shops, the Riviera cinema and the Carlton theatre and then, behind the spit of sand that pointed out into the Teign estuary towards the Ness at Shaldon was the old part of town. Here were the back beach, the quay with its commerce of boat builders, fishermen and coastal merchant ships. There were narrow streets, small painted houses, hostelries like the Ship, the New Quay, the Endeavour and the King William, lock-ups and little shops. On Northumberland Place was the house where the poet Keats had looked after his ailing brother in 1818 and is said to have written his works of Endymion and Isabella. This was the all year round Teignmouth, rather than the resort Teignmouth. As if to confirm this split nature, the western side of the town had its own church, St James's, overlooking the harbour rather than sharing St

Michael's which looked out to sea on the eastern side.

Beyond St Michael's the northern end of the sea front met the railway line where it hugged beneath the red sandstone cliffs on its manmade ledge. The promenade carries on around the sea wall towards Dawlish right alongside the railway line, providing the route for bracing walks and unique views of passing trains. Part way along is the grassy bank at Sprey Point where the name TEIGNMOUTH is cast in large concrete letters to greet the passing trains. A similar distance on is the rocky outcrop of The Parson and Clerk where the railway dives through the cliffs, one of five occasions between Teignmouth and Dawlish. I remember learning the tunnel names when first familiarising myself with the area. In order, travelling West, they are Kennaway, Coryton, Phillot, Clerk and Parsons. There was a permanent way gang based here along the wall just to upkeep the track and sea defences. They were never short of work, constantly fighting nature, and must have seen their job as the next most indispensable to the Forth Bridge painters.

Wherever I was on the district the sea was never far away. It brought a cleanliness and taste to the air and a brightness to the blue of the sky when the weather was fine. But it also brought persistent seagulls and, in the summer months, hordes of "grockle" holidaymakers, many with their motor cars clogging up the West Country roads.

Kate's cooking was excellent, she catered for my special meal times when I could not fit in with normal breakfast and dinner and always provided a packed lunch for me to take to work. Together, Kate and Arthur were a double act. He knew just how far he could go with his risqué jokes, innuendo or commentary and she knew how to start him off and just when to intervene to stop him. They enjoyed entertaining the MAFF students, especially around the dinner table and would play on the students' adolescent beliefs that they were worldly wise. Of course the students knew little of the true realities of life and so provided good amusement to the pair. When at the dinner table I would be drawn into the banter. Despite being only a year or so older than the students I found that my short working life experiences, straight from school, highlighted the naivety of youth, especially of those who had yet to stand on their own two feet. A swear box was kept in the dining room to control the enthusiasm of the conversation. Somehow though it was always Arthur that had to contribute to it from his over zealous opinion on the state of politics, morals or the nation in general, rather than any of the rest of us. Pranks were commonplace, not all of them attributable to the students!

The atmosphere at 30 Exeter Street was home from home and Kate referred to everyone as her family. This family feeling was complemented by the coming and going of Kate's mother and younger sister, together with her three young nieces, they having moved down to Teignmouth also. From time to time their son, "Young Arthur", his wife and daughter would come to stay from Buckinghamshire, as would old friends from almost everywhere in the summer holiday period. Council or no Council, the house was always full. In due course I had a spell in most of the single rooms as Arthur set about decorating each in turn. I preferred sleeping at the back of the house as there was a school across the road at the front which meant there could be noisy children outside during the day when I was trying to sleep.

Kate and Arthur were both mad about cats. This they expressed by loving and pampering a Persian named Pearl. This cat possessed an expressive face through which it was never shy to portray its disgust at being disturbed at 5am when I switched the light on in the kitchen to make a cup of tea before leaving for an early turn somewhere. She would blink her eyes at me slowly, scowling from her basket whilst I would say to her that she looked like I felt and she should consider herself fortunate that she was not about to have to leave the house like I was.

There was an active social life in Teignmouth too, the proceeds from the swear box financing convivial evenings at the Spanish Bar down near the sea front from time to time. So all in all it was a lucky coincidence that the one and only advert was placed in the week I went to look. Many of the student "lodgers" kept in touch with Kate from that era in Exeter Street proving that they enjoyed the experience. Sadly Arthur died not long before he and Kate would have celebrated their Golden Wedding Anniversary. I found that profoundly sad for Kate but know she treasures their years together through all the good and bad times. It is sad also to know of so many signalmen who, having worked until the age of 65, enjoyed undeservedly short retirements for such long and loyal service.

Unbeknown to many, behind the up side platform at Teignmouth, was a triangular area of yard that had once contained a goods shed, sidings and through goods line. The land had first housed an Atmospheric Railway Engine

The remnants of the former S&T depot behind Teignmouth station in the old up side yard. Bits and pieces of abandoned signalling equipment lay strewn about in the vicinity of a hut constructed from signal box parts. *(Author)*

House, long since demolished, unlike those at Exeter, Starcross and Totnes. Since that era it had seen busy days as a permanent way depot and then as a signal depot, covering all the way from Burlescombe to Brent and branches. This lasted until 1962 but there were still signs of this usage in the 70s with an extant wooden building constructed from tell-tale box parts and various items of signalling hardware discarded around the yard.

The stretch of railway between Exeter and Newton Abbot, which opened in 1846, established Dawlish and Teignmouth as tourist destinations, connecting these seaside towns and others to the west, with the rest of the country. It has featured in several writings, many of them about summer Saturdays when the line was strained beyond capacity. In fact the whole of the route between Taunton, Paignton and Plymouth struggled to meet demand on these days but the Exeter - Newton Abbot section bore the brunt. Even in the 70s, Saturdays in the summer were exceptionally busy with dozens of holiday expresses to and from all parts of the country. Every last rake of Mk 1 vacuum braked, steam heated coaching stock was hauled out of sidings and pressed into service behind freight locomotives for the weekly round trip to Paignton, Newquay or Penzance.

Traffic would start to build up during the early hours of Saturday morning as Friday evening departures from originating stations in the north such as Nottingham, Newcastle, Manchester, Sheffield, Liverpool, Hull and Bradford slotted in with those from London. These overnights, often loaded to twelve coaches, had leisurely timings but many began arriving well before breakfast and long before guest houses and hotels would be ready to receive the weary holidaymakers that stumbled onto the platforms at Dawlish, Teignmouth, Torquay and Paignton with their bulging suitcases and high anticipation of a fortnight's break. Indeed, the vanguard of these trains were already passing around the sea wall not long after 3am heading for Cornwall. For those destined for the Devon resorts, arrivals began, incredibly, from 4am onwards through until 8am, although the one overnight service from Edinburgh did not start to deposit its survivors until after 10am. The noisy seagulls would welcome the arriving holidaymakers as they headed for town and the nearest café, leaving them in no doubt that they had arrived at the seaside.

The seagulls were always noisy. In summer they were far worse as, at first light, they would scavenge the waste bins that awaited the council workers who had yet to arrive to empty them. In high summer the gulls would begin around 4am as the sky began to lighten, dragging the previous night's fish and chip leftovers from the bins, strewing the paper across pavements and car parks. I can recall many a beautiful sunrise being punctuated by the squeal of gulls as they dragged and fought over their pickings in Teignmouth station car park behind the signal box. Today, whenever I hear the wheeling and screeching of seagulls I am immediately transported back to Teignmouth, Dawlish or Paignton, to blue skies, blue seas, blue trains and the most enjoyable job in the world.

The overnight trains, once cleaned and watered, formed the first morning workings back to London or the North, returning holidaymakers of the previous fortnight back to their homes. As Saturday progressed so more and more trains arrived in the west. The down line was busy throughout the morning and afternoon whilst the up line traffic peaked by late morning but sustained well into the afternoon. Trains were run as best as possible but once a late service arrived in the west the result was to throw much of the timetable out of the window. The knock on effect to the return workings would then begin to bite and play havoc with the up line. On many occasions trains would be worked from signal to signal as they followed one another block to block. Indeed, on a summer Saturday at boxes like Exminster, Dawlish Warren, Dawlish and Teignmouth the block needles spent most of their time at "Train on Line", briefly passing to "Line Clear" but never sitting at "Normal".

Many of these Saturday trains called at Dawlish and Teignmouth and some at Dawlish Warren too adding to the period of time they occupied the line. To help to keep them all moving Dawlish box would be manned by a reliefman for the day, splitting the section between Teignmouth and the Warren. There were thus many Saturdays when I would find myself working Dawlish box looking out to sea across Lyme Bay, boats on the water and perhaps a tanker on the horizon, with the sounds of the waves and children playing rising from the beach, whilst dealing with the endless procession of trains snaking their way around the sea wall. I reckon we could have done with the long abolished box at Parsons Tunnel open too.

Perched on the up platform the narrow brick base of Dawlish box arched forward to carry the wider wooden top half. This meant the lever frame was

A beautiful summer's day at Dawlish with the sun streaming in the open windows. See how the wooden top half juts forward from the base, supported by arched brickwork. *(C. Chapman)*

unusually accommodated at the rear so that the signalman had to work with his back to traffic. This was reputedly the first Great Western box to be built with its lever frame at the back. Above the frame was the block shelf carrying the instruments, bells and plungers suspended by the usual X brackets extended down from the roof timbers. Unusually a second shelf rested above this in the crossovers of these brackets upon which were mounted the signal and lamp repeaters. In the up direction the timetable included diverse combinations of calling points. Sometimes Dawlish was the last stop before running fast to Sheffield. Other trains were fast from Torquay. On the Paignton branch the box at Torquay had similarly been retained for summer Saturday purposes. Again I would sometimes find myself here for a Saturday day shift, splitting the block between Paignton North and Torre. The box was situated on the down platform of the expansive station, with its well kept flower borders befitting the resort's slightly upper class nature. It was a brighter, grander and more open version of Teignmouth.

To help with regulating and to sort out any problems with stock, locomotives or train crew, it was usual for local traffic managers to spend Saturday morning and early afternoon in key boxes. This usually meant having company in Newton Abbot West, often from Bill Herne, the assistant at Newton Abbot. To us signalmen he was known as Mr Pastry for his similarity to a well known circus clown. Providing all went to plan these temporary visitors only assisted in drinking tea. Summer Saturdays brought a completely different working to Newton Abbot compared with weekdays. As well as much preparation and servicing of stock and locomotives, fewer trains actually called at the station as many ran through non-stop to and from the holiday resorts. By way of example, in the gap between the 10.52 and 12.38 departures on the up no less than ten intervening expresses all ran through non-stop, four from Penzance, one from Newquay, one from Falmouth and four from Paignton.

Just like the Taunton area, there were special bell codes at Exeter and Newton Abbot. For up express passenger trains not calling at Exeter St Davids these were sent forward from Newton Abbot as a 3-3-3. Similarly on the down, express passenger trains not calling at Newton Abbot and running via Dainton were belled from Exeter West onwards right through to Aller Junction as 3-3-3. For those running via Kingskerswell these were signalled 3-3-1. Such trains were known as "runners" by virtue of them not calling. At Newton Abbot itself, the two station boxes and Aller Junction had to contend not only with these codes but similar codes for up trains and a variety of distinguishing codes for other moves in and around the station. The full set was as follows:

Up Express Passenger not booked to call at Newton Abbot via Dainton
3-3-3;
Up Express Passenger not booked to call at Newton Abbot via Kingskerswell
3-3-1;
Down Express Passenger not booked to call at Newton Abbot via Dainton
3-3-3;
Down Express Passenger not booked to call at Newton Abbot via Kingskerswell
3-3-1;
Up Express Passenger booked to call at Newton Abbot via Kingskerswell
2-2-4;
Down Express Passenger booked to call

at Newton Abbot via Kingskerswell
2-2-4;
Light Engine via Kingskerswell
2-3-1;
Light Engine for Aller Junction (e.g. a bank engine)
2-3-2;
Kingswear Line Empty Coaching stock train
3-2-1;
Kingswear Line Parcels Train
5-1;
Blocking back inside your starting signal between East and West
3-6-2.

In addition the local branch services used the standard branch codes such as 1-3 for a stopping passenger and 1-2 for a goods. Curiously, because the 3-3-1 and 2-2-4 codes were started in the up direction at Paignton, the standard 4 bells only ever saw use on the branch for down trains.

Summer weekdays brought additional local trains for holidaymakers, advertised relief trains, and specials, such as the Saga (senior citizen holiday) trains which ran on the shoulders of the season, during May and September. Another feature of the summer timetable was the running of motorail trains comprising passenger stock with car carrying flat wagons (carflats) marshalled behind. There was a daily daytime service, except on Tuesdays, between Kensington Olympia and St Austell. A portion of carflats was detached at Newton Abbot from the down service and re-attached later in the day to the up working. On Tuesday and Thursday mornings, an overnight service from Stirling to Newton Abbot arrived. This train, which included sleeping cars as well as the carflats, also ran on Friday nights as did a Crewe to St Austell, alongwith a Saturday morning train from Worcester to Penzance. The latter pair called at Newton Abbot to detach whilst the back workings later in the day called to have these portions added. The shunting involved with these trains added to the interest of the two Newton Abbot boxes, the carflats, with their colourful cargoes, being positioned alongside the old Moretonhampstead bay which had a new lease of life as the loading/unloading dock, handy as it was to the station car park.

At Bank Holiday times significant changes were published to the working timetable with extra passenger and relief trains operated to cope with the increase in travellers on the days leading up to and following the holiday weekends. Then, across these weekends in the spring and summer, would run excursions for day trippers. Through the Newton Abbot area would come Charter, Advertised Excursion (Adex) and Mystery Excursion (Mystex) trains travelling to Plymouth, Newquay, Totnes, Torquay or Paignton. These would come from all manner of places up country such as Treherbert, Bromsgrove, Southend, Ramsgate, Worcester and the like, towns which did not normally see long distance engine hauled trains. Once in the west country these trains often resulted in additional light engine or empty stock movements to and from Newton Abbot for fuelling and cleaning.

In fact stock and loco' movements made for much of the regular activity at Newton Abbot, there being a fuelling point, carriage washer and carriage sidings. During the evening and early part of the night empty stock would be propelled through the washplant, shunted and berthed and then, from the early hours of the morning, drawn out again ready for the day. Amongst the sets maintained at

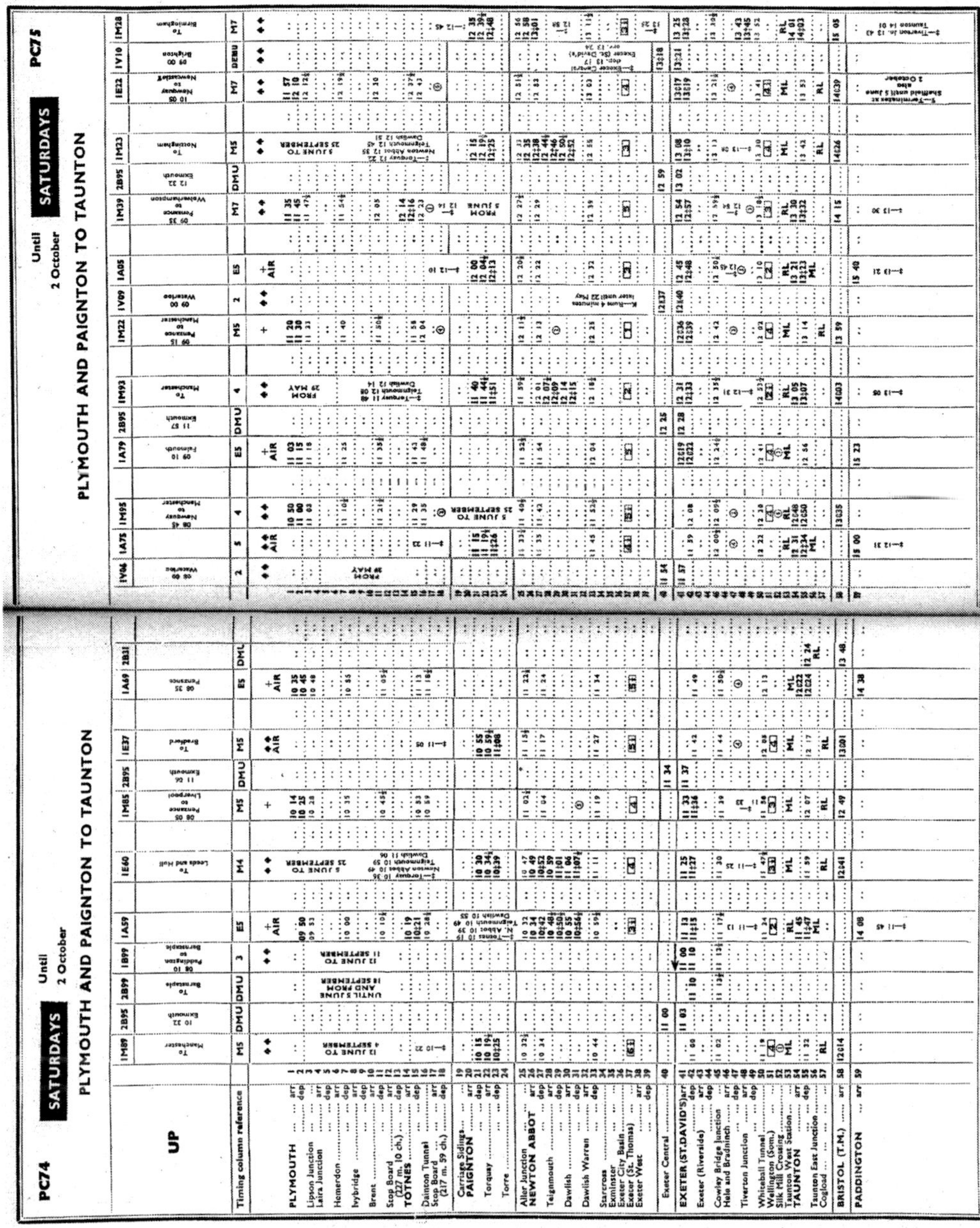

Two pages from Section PC of the Western Region Working Timetable for 1976 showing up trains through Newton Abbot between 10.30 and 13.00. Note the ten "Runners" following 1E60 at 10.52 before the next train calls at 12.35, which was 1M23.

Newton Abbot were those dedicated to the Exeter - Waterloo services that ran via Salisbury and the old Southern route. These worked to and from Exeter either as local stopping trains or as empty stock. One of these, the 05.05 Newton Abbot ran empty as a double headed 16 coach formation to form the 06.15 and 10.10 departures from Exeter St Davids to Waterloo. The locomotives for these were fuelled and stabled on the shed and at this time were Birmingham Railway Carriage & Wagon Company type '3s' (class 33) bringing variety to traction in the area. Similarly the class 1 trains which started or ended their journeys at Paignton ran either as locals or empty stock from and to Newton Abbot. There was always something incongruous to my mind about ten coach formations being belled as branch stoppers, conveying just a handful of people.

PRIVATE AND NOT FOR PUBLICATION

NOTICE No. SPL.3.

D.M.,
BRISTOL.

27th April, 1978.

NOTICE OF MANDATORY TRAIN ARRANGEMENTS.

MONDAY, 1ST MAY.

06.55 (Mystex) Treherbert and return, 1Z08

	Arr.	Dep.	Arr.	Dep.
	As shown in Manuscript Notice No.59 to:		Thence as shown in Manuscript Notice No.59	
Bridgwater	09/33		20/29	
Taunton	09/48		20/17	
Whiteball Tunnel	10/03		20/07	
Exeter St.D.,	10C25	10C28	19C46	19C47
Dawlish Warren	10/40		19/36	
Dawlish	10.42	10.44	19.31	19.33
Teignmouth	10.48	10.50	19.24	19.26
Newton Abbot	10/58		19/17	
Totnes	11/11		19/04	
Plymouth	11.45	12/10	18/07	18.35
Mount Gould Jn.,	12/16	12/26	17/54	18/00
Laira C.S.,	12/30			17/50

Load: 11 VB/SH.

ARRANGE AND ADVISE ALL CONCERNED.

J.R. BARKER.

Example of a special traffic notice giving details of a Mystex from Treherbert.

CHAPTER EIGHT

THE WESTERN WAY

Newton Abbot was a spacious station, having been modernised in 1927 by the Great Western Railway. As well as the Moretonhampstead branch bay there were two wide island platforms one giving two up and the other two down faces 1,375 feet long, sufficient to hold two trains each, plus through lines in each direction around the outside. Scissors crossovers existed between the through lines and adjacent platform lines halfway down the station, and a trailing crossover connected between the two inner roads. By this means the station could be worked as if it had eight through platforms, indeed it was numbered as such.

These arrangements had been provided to facilitate the splitting of down trains and the joining of up trains as Newton Abbot was the junction station beyond which the line to Paignton and Kingswear left the main line to Plymouth and Cornwall. During steam days many expresses ran with portions to and from both routes. The mid-platform crossovers provided the flexibility to position the trains and locomotives to enable the splitting and joining. By the 1970s dual portion working had ceased but the lavish layout at Newton Abbot continued to be essential to handling the many movements that took place around the clock.

There were two signal boxes to control the station, yard and sidings, one at each end of the layout. Both wooden and built when the station had been expanded, the larger of the two, housing 206 levers, was the massive East box which measured almost 80 feet in length. Having once required two signalmen and a booking boy on each shift, traffic levels now only required double manning during the daytime and a single signalman at night. Nevertheless, its sheer size and dominating position was impressive. The amount of walking and lever pulling made the box unequalled in the west country. Whilst the facilities had been reduced, especially in connection with the Moretonhampstead branch, there were still some particularly complicated moves such as when making transfers between New Yard and Hackney Yard. In addition to the original six permanent spaces there were now a further 17 spaces and 62 spares in the frame leaving 121 levers in use. Having said this, because lever 1 was used to operate an additional (acceptance) Home for East when Hackney box was abolished in 1971, then the new colour light distant was controlled by a switch placed on the block shelf numbered 300. When two men were on duty one would normally look after the low numbered end of the frame, generally dealing with down direction traffic whilst the other took the high end and the up direction moves, together with operating the block instruments and making the entries in the train register book. On such a big frame two men, working together, could set up moves very quickly, fitting the shunting, loco' changes, run-rounds and detaching between the through moves. To assist the signalmen, repeater bell plungers were fitted further along the block shelf from the block instruments in order to reduce the amount of walking. This was particularly helpful for the man at the low end or the one man on nights.

The vast, barn-like interior of Newton Abbot East. By this time only 121 of the 206 levers were in use but the box still required two men to work it during the daytime such was the amount of lever pulling and walking required. (Author)

The box sat on the outside of the curve between Hackney Yard and the junction with the Moretonhampstead branch alongside the bridge which carried the lines over the river Teign. Glazed virtually all around, it's height provided a commanding panorama of the railway and surrounds giving, in particular, an enviable view of Newton Abbot racecourse which adjoined the line. The resident men were Ted Kirk, Sid Yendall, Derek Old, Trevor Hazeldine and Russell Wilmot. Russell had secured his post at East box on promotion from Totnes but prior to this had come from Truro West and was seen as rather unique having arrived from outside of the local area. Derek's father had been a signalman and District Inspector in the Westbury area. When Tom Earlam retired as DI at Exeter and Clem Chapman, his assistant, moved up to the DI role, Derek carried on tradition by securing Clem's job.

Being such a tall box, the task of replenishing the coal buckets for the two fires called for a labour saving system. This took the form of a rope hung from the railing of the end window, above where the coal pile lay below. One signalman would go down to the pile and fill the buckets, attaching these, one at a time, to a hook on the end of the rope so that the second signalman could haul them up to the operating floor. This was easier than carrying the full buckets up the steep flight of 22 steps at the back of the box. These steps ended at a porchway cantilevered from the superstructure of the box which contained the privy.

Both ends of the station sported a plethora of single, double and triple discs, some of which were "running shunts" which had to be pulled before the main signal reading over them could be operated. In fact there were more "dummies" than main arms. At East box there were 54 discs. As all three up lines through the station converged into one at the East end, the layout was organised to permit simultaneous acceptance and departure of trains. This was achieved by an additional home signal on the Up Through and by two short dead end sidings in the middle of the layout. These sidings were designed to hold pilot loco's detached from incoming trains or fresh locomotives ready to take up trains forward but, when empty, could be used to establish a reduced clearing point for the acceptance of up trains that were booked to call. One of these, known as the Middle Siding, extended onwards from the Up Relief line whilst the other, which went by the name of the Engine Siding, ran forward from the Up Main. This was however curiously located on the opposite side of the Up Through, reached by a diamond crossing. Thus its use prevented any movement on or along the Up Through. So, by accepting a train on the Up Relief into the Middle Siding, another train could still depart from the Up Main or Up Through. Similarly, by accepting a move on the Up Main into the Engine Siding a parallel departure could take place from the Up Relief. Accepting into these sidings also meant that moves across the junction to and from New Yard or the branch could be made at the same time.

With the station effectively split into two halves by the centre pointwork the working between the boxes was quite interesting. The scissors connecting the Down Relief and Down Through lines were motor operated from East box, protected by East's starting signals and provided with ground mounted electric backing discs. The mirror image on the Up Main and Up Through lines was mechanically operated from West box and protected by West's signals. The trailing crossover between the Up Relief and Down Main was mechanically worked from West but of course protected by East's Down Main Starting and West's Up Relief Starting. This crossover was electrically released by East box but both sets of double discs in each direction were worked by West.

The mid-platform signals were unusual in that the arms and spectacles were of a unique design. Also they pivoted directly on the spindle of the Westinghouse motor to which they were attached. The motors were thus mounted on the side of the wooden dolls behind each arm. These signals always looked unique and appealing as the dolls were painted white and the arms, being wooden, were brightly painted in their respective red, white, yellow and black. A single doll carrying stop, distant and calling-on arms is now preserved at the National Railway Museum in York. The electric ground discs were also of Westinghouse origin, being akin to a banner signal with a red arm housed inside a circular casing behind a glass front.

The position of the starting signals in the middle of the station resulted in one half of the down platforms being within station limits of East box and the other half being in the block section. Likewise, one half of the up platforms was within station limits of West box and the other half was in the block section. The up and down sections were thus staggered which meant either box could admit a train into their half of the station in the right direction without requiring a "Line Clear" from the other. Thus a terminating or reversing move did not always require co-operation between the signalmen.

Dropping vehicles or movements into the station in the wrong direction did however require co-operation as this involved occupying the section. So a wrong direction move, belled as a 2-3-3, or a blocking back outside home signal (3-3) had to be acknowledged and the relevant block instrument then placed at "Train On Line". The mid-platform crossovers and signals complicated the situation if the blocking back manoeuvre was to push back partly beyond these in order to position the train near the platform stairs. In this case a special code of 3-6-2, "May I Block Back Inside Your Starting Signal?", was used.

The combination of lever movements in co-ordination with the bells and block instruments ensured that the traffic was kept safely moving whilst all the shunting, attaching and detaching went on around and in between, such that the best was achieved from the layout. The exchange of bells between the two station boxes and the operation of the block indicators was undertaken in such a way as to ease the working and convey information that was helpful. So, for instance, if a locomotive was running round a train, or a unit detaching from the front of a pair, the 2-1-3 "Locomotive Arrived" signal would be transmitted on the appropriate bell immediately following the signal, either "Line Clear" or "Wrong Direction Movement", for the return move. In this way the receiving signalman knew to associate the locomotive or unit with the one being detached. Similarly if it was not possible to accept a train or movement for a while, rather than just not respond to the bell signal it was customary to flick the block indicator to the "Train on Line" position momentarily a couple of times thereby giving positive indication of the refusal.

Large station boxes, like these, with their short sections, were never prone to the sorts of problems which beset most other boxes. Trains did not fail in isolated places, animals did not stray onto the line, drivers did not report bumps in the track and, if a problem did occur, it would always be nearby and someone would be handy to be called upon to deal with it. There were a myriad of different railwaymen in and about the place, of all grades and departments. One location where many of them came together was at the railway club. The railway staff association ran a network of clubs right across the country at major and many smaller centres. Drinks were cheap and regular social activities were organised. These clubs could usually be found close-by depots and the larger stations. Taunton had a branch, as did Westbury, Exeter, Plymouth and of course Newton Abbot.

West box was sandwiched between the Up Main and Up Relief lines at the Plymouth end of the station just off the platform ramp. This meant the box was narrow but nonetheless still impressive, with a frame of 153 levers, five block instruments, two illuminated diagrams and a pair of coal stoves. Here there was a single signalman per shift assisted by a booking boy, or telephonist as they were known locally, rostered on early and late turns. Gerald Palmer, another outsider, from Taunton, Charlie Hammacott and Arthur Davies were the resident signalmen. Arthur lived in Teignmouth just above the railway cutting in Salisbury Terrace a few streets away from me. He had never really got used to the large frame and would try to pull levers before others had been correctly set. "Testing the locking" we called it. Gerald obtained promotion to Exeter West being replaced by another Taunton immigrant, Ken Marney. The two "boys" at West, Stan and Charlie, were both "green carded" signalmen from the box. Railwaymen who became "green carded" were deemed by the railway doctor to be unfit for certain roles and hence were accommodated on light duties. The term was a euphemism derived from the green label applied to wagons that were found to have a defect indicating they should be returned to the workshop for repair. Stan Rowe had recently developed a back problem and so could no longer pull levers whilst Charlie Lloyd had failed an eye sight test at a routine medical some years earlier, being then declared colour blind. Both men continued as booking boys until their retirement. Charlie in particular knew the box inside out and would always climb off the stool to help out on the frame and bells when things got busy. Stan replaced a "real" boy, Vince Lang who, on reaching the age of 18, was able to move to his first signalman's job, at Dainton.

West box was special for me, having looked down on it from the bridge as a boy promising myself to work it one day. In fact I found working West box was more preferable to East as the signalman could concentrate on the frame, blocks and bells, having them all to himself whilst the "boy" took care of the booking in the train register and the telephones. It was also the duties of the "boy" to collect the pay from the booking office on a Thursday, run errands and bring in the coal, clean out the ashes and put the broom round at the end of the shift.

Two class 08 shunting locomotives were employed as Pilots to manage most of the shunting activities in and around Newton Abbot. One of these worked largely as the passenger pilot, busying itself with coaching stock movements in the station, carriage sidings and through the wash plant. It also performed a little freight shunting when vehicles destined for New Yard were detached from down goods trains and moved vans to and from the NCL Depot. The second (freight)

Long and narrow, Newton Abbot West was sandwiched between the Up Main and Up Relief lines at the Plymouth end of the station. The signals, with their route indicators, read from these two lines back to the Down Main and Relief lines. *(Author)*

pilot spent most of its time shunting Hackney and New Yards and the NCL Depot, tripping clay wagons to Teignbridge and Heathfield on the branch, forming up the evening goods to Exeter, which left at 19.40 from the Down Through line, and then helping out with coaching stock moves later in the evening. On the days when the Motorail trains ran then this Pilot found additional work dealing with these, responsible for detaching and attaching the Newton Abbot portions, ferrying them to and from the Moretonhampstead bay.

There was a fair amount of attaching and detaching of vans and coaches in the station which required the services of one or other of the pilot engines. Detaching usually took place from down trains whilst attaching was made to services on the up. Thus East box handled the former and West the latter. A regular move every evening was for the freight pilot to pull out the day's loaded parcel vans from the NCL Depot and take these West end ready to tail the three evening perishable and parcel trains - the Penzance to Crewe, Plymouth to Bristol and Penzance to Paddington. With two or three vans for each, the pilot drew the whole lot down the Up Through and into the Up Siding. From here the vans, already assembled in the right order, were attached to the rear of each train as it stood in the station. Between East and West boxes the Pilots were authorised to move around under the "Shunting into Forward Section" regulations, even if expected to run right through to the other box. The 3-3-2 bell signal was thus well used along with the miniature shunt arms on the mid-platform signals. These were not released by "Line Clear" and so free to pull at any time. Some of the more mischievous signalmen would just clear the signal and bash out 3-3-2 on the bell without waiting for acceptance. In fact one or two would relax the "Call Attention" signal altogether with the argument that things were far too busy to be concerned with niceties. With the activity constant and the men in the two boxes on their toes working as a team there was something to be said for dispensing with the "Call Attention". Indeed, their attention didn't need to be called, and having rattled out the code one could move on to the next action without having to wait by the bell for a response.

It was rare to undertake any complicated shunting activity out on the running lines but one Sunday when I was on duty there was a ballast and spoil train that needed to be reformed before it went on its way from West box. With the train stood behind the box on the Up Through the shunter suggested the quickest way to rearrange the formation would be to use the pilot and carry out the shunt under control of the box. So we set about the exercise using all three up lines in full view of passers by and inquisitive spectators out on Station Road, including to my surprise, a few "double shunts" employed to knock wagons into different roads to save a bit more time. This called upon improvisation on my part and a degree of educated guesswork to ensure that the shunt concluded safely and to the satisfaction of the shunter.

Unlike East box, West did not have the luxury of facing sidings into which clearing points could be established for the acceptance of down trains. The existence of four lines on towards Aller did however mean that clearing points could be established on the parallel Down Relief and Down Main lines thus allowing simultaneous acceptance, or the acceptance of one train and departure of

ADDITIONAL TRAINS.

6.Z.33 19.45 Cardiff to Hoo via Badminton.

6.Z.26 08.09 Dover to St.Blazey - Will run in the following times and convey 22 Empty Polybulks and call Tavistock Jn. D.S., to detach 11 Polybulks for Marsh Mills:-

	Arr.	Dep.		Arr.	Dep.
Challow	14/10		Exeter	17C52	17C54
Swindon Tfr.,	14EC25	15EC13	Newton Abbot	18AE22	18AE57
Wootton Bassett	15/22		Hemerdon	19*01	19*18
Parkway	15/52		Tavistock Jn.,	19D26	19D46 *
Bristol T.M.,	16C01	16C04	Plymouth	19EC55	20AE15
Worle Jn.,	16/26		Par	21C32	21C35
Taunton East G.L.	16EC56	17EC15	St.Blazey	21.45	

55 SLU's SPECIALLY AUTHORISED.

* DETACH TO UP SIDINGS.

6.Z.22 19.40 Gloucester to Ince UKF., via Craven Arms (SN.84574).

6.Z.92 17.30 Oakdale to Beighton Jn., via Barnt Green.

8.Z.32 07.00 Radyr to Corby via Barnt Green.

8.Z.46 19.00 Radyr to Treeton via Barnt Green.

4.Z.87 18.55 Tilbury to Pengam via Badminton
10 F/L Set with 8' 6" containers.

An extract from a traffic notice showing an extra freight, 6Z26, from Dover to St. Blazey. This was booked to receive an additional locomotive at Newton Abbot signified by the letters AE in the timing column. Note how 22 Polybulk wagons equates to 55 SLUs.

another on a combination of two of the three down lines from East. For non-stopping trains (runners) a full clearing point of 440 yards was required, meaning this fell beyond all of the west end pointwork. In the case of trains booked to call or terminate a shorter clearing point was allowed such that the line only had to be set and clear as far as the Torquay Road bridge. This meant the line beyond the bridge could still be fouled by other movements. It was thus possible to continue to make some crossing and shunting movements, or bring engines off shed until such time as the train was ready to depart. In the up direction regulation 5 (the Warning Arrangement) was authorised in respect of non-passenger trains so that locomotives, empty stock or van trains could approach from Aller despite other moves taking place.

Some of the work at West box involved locomotive changes or the addition of second (pilot) engines to assist the trains over the South Devon banks. The 06.39 Leeds to Paignton was an example of one such train that was booked a loco' change whilst in the station at Newton Abbot. The fresh engine was usually brought off shed shortly before the train arrived and allowed to stand out on the Down Main line beyond the Torquay Road bridge. The Leeds would then come to a stand in the Down Relief platform, its engine being uncoupled by the shunter and taken forward on the Down Relief. From here it would reverse into the shed sidings whilst the new engine was already moving back onto the train in a parallel move. The Holbeck engine which went to shed was serviced and fuelled before being used locally on trips until the next day when it would become the fresh engine for that day's train from Leeds.

The assisting engines for freight trains heading west would come up light from Laira or, more often, St Blazey. They usually arrived well before their train was due and so would be put over on the shed until required. Freights requiring a pilot engine would normally be sent down the through line from East box where they would receive their second locomotive, largely out of the way of other movements. The 17.09 (Sun) Ince and Elton to Truro with its "Palvans" full of palletised bagged fertiliser, its 17.28 (TO) counterpart to Plymouth Friary and the 22.58 (MWO) Fawley to Plymouth Friary oil train were regular recipients of a pilot. The Avonmouth to Friary ammonium nitrate tanks was another of the regular trains that took on additional traction power. East of course dealt with the removal of pilot engines from up trains such as those on the Burngullow - Sittingbourne clay and the Milk. Our old friend 6V53 the clay empties from Stoke stopped during the afternoon to pick up a travelling shunter to assist with the dropping off and picking up of wagons at Ivybridge. The shunter came up from Plymouth Friary on the 12.55 from there to Riverside which slowed to let him drop off at West box.

Night time saw its fair share of shunting moves such as when the second portion of the Papers would arrive at the East end of the Down Relief platform at 04.05, twenty minutes after the first half had run through fast on its way to Plymouth and Cornwall. The locomotive which had travelled up to Taunton to collect this second portion would be cut off and taken to shed via the scissors crossover and Down Through. Meanwhile another loco' with a single brake compartment carriage had come from the sidings and been positioned at the West end of the Down Relief. These pushed back onto the remaining paper van to form the 04.25 to Paignton which also carried mail transferred out of the up and down Postals. Belled as a 5-1 Parcels train for the branch this was the last regular user of this particular bell code.

The specials that went to Torquay and Paignton in the summer and the summer Saturday trains to Paignton were cleaned and watered in the sidings at Goodrington. The locomotives off these specials and many from the Saturday trains ran light to Newton Abbot for fuel before returning to Goodrington to take up their back working. This made additional work for the signalmen, especially at Newton Abbot West where the loco's had to be got on and off shed. A fair number of lever movements were involved, particularly to get a locomotive from the Up Main across onto the shed. No less than 33 pushes and pulls were required. The reversing movement from either the Up Main or Up Relief lines to the down side of the layout was controlled by a pair of signals on a bracket just in front of the box steps. Although merely a few yards away they were the heaviest signals to operate, needing a hefty swing to get the arm to show a decent "off" angle. This was the result of long wire runs that went out to the farthest points to the west of the box before returning to the signals through mechanical detectors on all those points which had to be proved closed and locked in the correct position. The consequent friction together with loss of travel from the raising of an associated mechanical route indicator before the relevant arm would drop conspired to cause the difficulty. Their reluctance to lower was matched by their aversion to return fully to danger and hence propensity to hold up a set of mechanical detection somewhere in the run that would prevent the restoration of a set of points. Having put half the point and lock levers back they would all have to be pulled again to retry the signal in an attempt to clear the blockage.

One of the throwbacks from earlier times, a lack of sequential locking, remained in most of the boxes in the area, indeed the phenomenon still existed from Hele and Bradninch box westwards. Without it there was no enforcement of replacing the lever of one running signal before the lever of the signal reading up to it could be pulled again and so it was possible to signal a second train into an already occupied section. This was not a problem provided signalmen took care, in accordance with the rules, to operate the levers in correct sequence. What it did allow was for the signalman to "pull off" backwards towards the distant by lowering the advanced starting before the starting and the starting before the home, for example.

I was surprised to find even the two Newton Abbot boxes were not equipped with sequential locking, especially West box where the Up Home signals had been renewed as 4-aspect colour lights in 1969. Extra vigilance was required here in order to avoid a catastrophe. If a train was standing on one of the up lines with the starting signal still showing "off" behind it then it was perfectly possible to operate any of the Up Home signals which read towards it, providing the relevant track circuits were showing clear, thereby displaying a double yellow aspect to the driver of an approaching train as if the line was completely clear right through the station to the gantry carrying East's Home signals. Even the track circuits were proved clear in the aspect level of the signals rather than via lever locks, thus the levers were free to be pulled at any time and hence the signal primed to clear. Where care was needed was when a second train was to be admitted from a different line from the first as, having changed the position of the points behind the first train there was nothing to prevent the home signal lever for the second being reversed.

With the Up Homes and Distants being colour light (the Distants were combined with Aller Junction's Starters as 3-aspect signals) and the Up Starter mid-platform signals being worked by motor, all of the up line running signal levers had cut short handles. This gave a unique appearance to the far end of the lever frame as all the levers from number 134 to 152 were treated in this way.

As I have mentioned earlier, I am not the best of early risers. Indeed by late morning, most of the way through an early turn, I would often feel more tired than at any other time, manifested by the feeling of an empty stomach and no energy in the limbs. To compensate for lack of sleep I would sometimes go to bed for a few hours in the afternoon after completing an early turn. This allowed some freedom to stay up later in the evening, especially if I wanted to go out socially. There were times when the shift patterns and sleeping times could be disorientating. I recall an occasion, one winter's week on early turn, when I went straight to bed on getting home just after 2pm in order to catch a few hours rest. I set the alarm for 5.30pm so that I would be fully awake, washed and ready for dinner at six. Being exceptionally tired I found no problem in falling asleep. The alarm clock roused me at five thirty from a dream and, fumbling for the light switch, the time and darkness fooled me into believing that it was the next morning. Thinking I was running late I hurried to the bathroom, had a quick wash and dressed in my uniform before going downstairs with my bag to collect the sandwiches that my landlady would have prepared. Kate was in the kitchen making final preparations for dinner. My initial surprise was soon superseded by the realisation of how I had tricked myself. The story was shared with Arthur and the students around the dinner table that night creating much humour.

The Royal Train was a regular visitor to the West Country, bringing members of the Royal Family on their official engagements to Somerset, Devon and Cornwall, especially the Prince of Wales as owner of the Duchy of Cornwall estate. Departure from Paddington, always platform 1, was usually late evening with the train heading for one of a number of regular stabling points depending upon final destination. These stabling points were reached late at night or early in the morning allowing the regal occupants to enjoy a period of undisturbed sleep before completing the remainder of their journey. These places were chosen for their quietness and remoteness, secrecy and protection being prime considerations.

The north curve of the triangle at Bradford Junctions was one of the stabling points for destinations in Wiltshire, Somerset and Bristol. This was a quiet spot just north of Trowbridge, being a single line spur connecting the Avon Valley branch with the former main line, but within station limits of Bradford Junctions signal box. Further west branch lines such as that between Totnes and Ashburton or between Newton Abbot and Heathfield, part of the old Moretonhampstead branch, were used for destinations in Devon and the Bodmin or Newquay branches for those in Cornwall.

The Royal Train ran under special double block arrangements whereby the section ahead had to be clear before it could be accepted from the box in rear. Given the headcode 1X01, with an "Is Line Clear" bell code of 4-4-4, it ran under the code words "Grove" or "Deepdene" depending which Royals were on board. All shunting had to cease ten minutes before the train was due to pass. With its distinctive plum coloured carriages, always hauled by a recently outshopped locomotive sporting silver painted buffers, the train looked the part drawing curiosity from those that saw it pass.

Methodical planning went into the operation of the Royal Train, a comprehensive special notice being distributed on each occasion that it ran detailing not only the main movement but also those of the locomotive and the empty stock before and after each trip. The coaching stock was kept at Wolverton carriage works, sometimes being returned there empty as 1X00 all the way from the West Country once the Royal party had been delivered to their engagement. Being strictly confidential the special notice was always hand delivered by an Inspector on the day. In addition to the timings of the train it contained details of many other things including platform stopping positions, to ensure the appropriate carriage door lined up with the red carpet and station exit, special protection arrangements if overnight stabling was involved and supply of newspapers. The latter always caused amusement as, not only were multiple copies of the daily and particular local papers to be supplied to the train but also the time honoured tradition of a single copy of Sporting Life.

One night, when the train conveying HRH The Duke of Edinburgh was booked to stable on the Heathfield branch, I was rostered to work my rest day to set up a temporary block post at Teignbridge Crossing, a couple of miles along the branch from Newton Abbot. The shift was from 01.00 to 10.00 plus travelling time. The hand gates at the crossing were normally operated by the shunter who accompanied the trip workings that collected clay from Heathfield or the weekly block oil train from Waterston in South Wales, the resident crossing keeper role having been made redundant when the passenger service was withdrawn. Normally the branch was worked as a siding in accordance with table C.2 of the Sectional Appendix under the control of the Newton Abbot East signalman. The crossing keeper's cottage was still there. This would be my home for the night.

BRITISH RAILWAYS - WESTERN REGION

STRICTLY PRIVATE - FOR USE OF STAFF CONCERNED

NOTICE - 74TP 0803

Chief Operating Manager,
Paddington

Extn. 076 - 2765/2226

JOURNEYS OF H.R.H. THE DUKE OF EDINBURGH :
(1) PADDINGTON TO TORRE : WED/THURS 8/9 MARCH, 78
(2) PAIGNTON TO PLYMOUTH : THURS 9 MARCH, 78
(3) PLYMOUTH TO STOKE ON TRENT : THURS/FRI 9/10 MARCH 78

The arrangements in connection with the above journey are as follows :-

MEMBERS OF ROYAL PARTY

H.R.H. The Duke of Edinburgh
Captain D. Christy - Miller, Equerry
Police Officer Chief Inspector C. Hagan
Valet, Mr. B. Lovell

FORMATION OF TRAIN (Leaving Paddington)
(Air Braked/Air Conditioned - 100 m.p.h. Stock)

Power Brake	2905	
Saloon	2900	
Saloon	2904	(H.R.H. The Duke of Edinburgh - principal door trailing)
Escort Vehicle	2906	

Load 4 - 161 tonnes

GENERAL NOTE

The maximum permitted speed of the coaches is 100 m.p.h., subject to temporary and permanent speed restrictions on the line of route.

In the event of failure of the electrical supply from the locomotive for train heating etc., the generator in Power Car 2905 may be used whilst the train is in motion. In this event, smoke will be emitted from the four exhaust outlets fitted in the roof of the vehicle, which might give an illusion of the coach being on fire. The situation should be regarded as normal and the train should in no circumstances be delayed to carry out an examination for this cause.

CLIPPING OF POINTS

All points which become facing for the movement of the Special Train or its locomotive, must be clipped, unless secured by facing point locks and bars or track circuits in lieu.

The front page from a Royal Train notice. This is the one associated with the visit of His Royal Highness The Duke of Edinburgh to Torre referred to in the text. The notice ran to 16 pages covering the details for this and subsequent movements of the tour to Paignton, Plymouth and Stoke on Trent.

Initially I went to Newton Abbot East to collect the key to the cottage and the keys to the crossing, the gates of which were secured by chains and padlocks. I also collected an oil hand lamp, as there was no electricity out there and I would need to conserve the battery in my bardic lamp. I also took some dry newspaper but knew there would be sticks and coal as the permanent way gang used the cottage on occasion for shelter.

Once the fire was burning well in the hearth I lit the tail lamps that were used for the red lights at the crossing and then telephoned the Newton Abbot East signalman to advise of my presence. Chief Inspector Forrester was on duty there to ensure points were clipped and that all went well with the operation, adding some gravity to the proceedings. The STOP boards protecting the crossing then had to be covered with sacks. At least it was a dry night and not that cold but it was pitch dark. No traffic appeared on the road. I hoped none would show

<u>Area Manager Newton Abbot</u> to arrange

(vi) <u>Departure from the Stabling Point</u>

After the rearmost locomotive has been detached protecting detonators lifted, and the route set with points clipped as required, the train will depart at 09.28 and proceed from the Heathfield Branch, ~~via the Up Main line at Newton Abbot under Single Line Working conditions~~ thence onto the Down Main Line towards Aller Jct.

	Arr	AIR	Dep
HEATHFIELD BRANCH STABLING POINT	02.55		09.28
Newton Abbot East	09.39	UP MAIN	09.40
Newton Abbot		09/42	
Aller Jct		09/45	
TORRE	09.55		

<u>Load</u> 4 = 161 Tonnes

<u>Locomotive</u> - Class 47 E.T.H.

<u>Special Light Diesel : 0E37 : 09.41 Heathfield Branch (2 milepost)to Newton Abbot</u>

	Arr		Dep
Heathfield Branch Stabling Point			09//41
Newton Abbot East		09/51*	
Newton Abbot	09//53*		

* - via Up Main Line

<u>Locomotive</u> - Class 45/46

<u>Notes on Other Trains Concerned</u>

6081 : 08.50 Plymouth Friary to Fawley - To be regulated

5E37 : 09.52 ECS Newton Abbot to Paignton - <u>RETIMED</u>

Newton Abbot			10/06
Aller Jn.		10/08	
Paignton	10/20		

2B17 : 09.10 Plymouth to Paignton - <u>RETIMED</u>
<u>a.b.t.</u>

Newton Abbot			10.13
Aller Jct.		10/15	
Torquay	10.23		10.25
Paignton	10.29		

/Continued.........

Part of page 8 of the same Royal Train notice which shows the movements from the Heathfield Branch as described in the text.

whilst the gates were closed as this would be a surprise to any motorist in the middle of the night with the only warning being a pair of tail lamps placed in the road, one to shine in each direction. From one direction the crossing was approached over a narrow, humped bridge so I placed the tail lamp up on the bridge for good sighting when it was time to close the gates. This had to be done before giving "Line Clear" on the telephone to East box in order to ensure a clear run for the train over the crossing to its stopping point about a quarter of a mile away on the Heathfield side at 2 miles 10 chains. The gates were closed for a good ten minutes therefore before the train which had departed Paddington at 23.03 showed up at 02.50 in the morning.

Displaying a green hand signal from my bardic I watched the "Peak" that had been attached to the rear of the train at Newton Abbot draw the Royal formation of varnished claret coaches, together with the pristine Brush type '4' train engine, over the crossing and come to a stand a little way further on alongside the SW (Sound Whistle) board that had been designated as the stopping point, just short of the defunct Teigngrace halt. Fortunately the road remained silent. I opened the gates, withdrew the red lights but placed one of these in the track alongwith three detonators on one rail then gave the "Train out of Section" signal over the 'phone to East box.

Job done I could relax now until later in the morning. A visit from the local British Transport Police Sergeant was the only punctuation for the rest of the night before Traffic Assistant Bob Yabsley arrived shortly after dawn with the requisite number of newspapers for the Royal party, including the obligatory copy of Sporting Life. After a chat he let himself through the gate and strode down the line to deliver these to the Chief Guards Inspector on the train.

The departure procedure was a little more complicated as the "Peak" which had towed the train down the branch was to detach, remaining at the overnight stabling point whilst the Royal Train proceeded direct to Torre for its rendezvous with the red carpet on the platform there at precisely 09.55.

At 09.28 a toot from the train locomotive was my signal that departure time had arrived. I got the road from East by telephone, lifted the detonators and red flag that had replaced the lamp once dawn had arrived, closed the gates and held up a green flag to the driver. A second toot signified the train was on the move. There was no sign of Royalty, all the curtains were still drawn but the driver of the car that had turned up at the gates was doubly surprised. Firstly to be stopped for a train and secondly to see what train it was, the Royal crests on the coach body sides revealing its unique status.

Having replaced the det's and red flag I opened the gates then advised East box the train was on its way. The Newton Abbot engine trickled up towards the crossing to await its turn once the Royal Train had cleared the branch at East box. It would not be going back to shed however as its next working was 5E37, the slightly retimed empty coaching stock from Newton Abbot to Paignton that would follow the Royal Train down the Paignton branch to form 1E37, the 10.50 to Leeds. I wonder if the Royal family ever knew the logistics of what went on to safely ferry them around the country?

Despite British Railways having been in existence since 1948 and everyone working to a common rule book after 1950, a variety of regional practises, left over from the days of the constituent companies, continued around the country. On the Western Region the men in most areas continued to disregard the stipulation in the regulations requiring that the "Train out of Section" signal be both preceded by the "Call Attention" signal and that it be repeated back by the receiving signalman. This had never been a feature of the Great Western Railway, nor of the Western Region in its early days and so was seen by the stalwarts as unnecessary standardisation that was inconvenient and without benefit to the safe operation of the railway.

I sympathised with this view and was happy to continue in the time honoured Great Western fashion. However, inspectors and other managers thought differently and were always consistent in checking that the full procedure was adhered to. Often we thought it the only operation they recognised as being incorrect to the book. The simplicity made it obvious to them, yet there were many other things that went unnoticed. It was as if attention was being paid to something insignificant, yet easily spotted. If caught, a warning would follow, with persistent offenders courting the possibility of being placed on a charge. Care had to be exercised not to be heard working slack over the telephone or to fail to warn adjacent boxes if officialdom arrived at your box.

I had been caught from time to time, as had most signalmen, but whilst at Newton Abbot had received a couple of successive warnings. I can still hear the words that our Divisional Chief Inspector, Mr Forrestor from Bristol always used to make his point: "There's only one way to give the "Train out of Section" signal lad and that's to precede it on every occasion with the "Call Attention" signal." These words he spoke clearly and concisely with his Shropshire accent. Having had the ultimate verbal warning I decided that I had no choice but to "play it straight" for a while, at least during daytime when the risk of being caught was greatest. Some of the other signalmen in the area were pleased to co-operate as it allowed them to relax their guard too. Others were indifferent but went along with the idea to keep me happy. One or two were a little more hostile, refusing point blank to compromise their GW integrity. Inevitably, this created a little friction that eventually came to a head one afternoon.

Booked to cover for Arthur Davies on late turn in Newton Abbot West one day I duly relieved Charlie Hammacott at ten to two. Changeover time usually saw a lull in traffic and so it was on this day. Charlie Lloyd, as booking boy, was not far behind me which meant both Charlie Hammacott and Stan Rowe were away home just before two o'clock leaving us to settle in for the afternoon. The kettle was simmering on the stove as I unpacked my bag and Charlie opened his locker to take out his cup and tea bags. "Call Attention" rang out on the main line bell from East box. I answered it and the following 4 bells for the 10.40 Paddington to Plymouth, placed the commutator at "Line Clear" then waited for the train to be put "On Line" and arrive. Collecting the cloth from a facing point lock lever on the way I pulled off the home signal by reversing lever 2. As the train departed I got the road from Aller Junction, reversed the starting signal (No. 8) and sent "On Line" to Aller before going to the window to watch it pass. The driver exchanged a wave as the train tipped into the curve at the platform end and headed west out under the Torquay Road bridge on the final leg of its journey.

Having replaced the signals behind the train I gave "Call Attention" to East, as per the book. When East answered I sent 2-1 "Train out of Section" but received no reply. A moment later the direct line box to box 'phone from East rang. Charlie leant across from his stool to pick up the receiver. "They want you" he said in a concerned voice, passing me the handset. Willy Vowden spoke down the 'phone in his broad Devon accent. "We don't work like that round 'ere" he said. Explaining my current practise of "working straight" once again, did nothing to mellow Willy. He ended the conversation with a little swearing before hanging up the 'phone.

Charlie advised that George Dennis was on with Willy at East which meant neither of them would "work straight" in front of the other. Both men regarded themselves senior to me, and so they were but I was not going to let them think they were superior too. I left the block pegged at "Train on Line".

Meanwhile Aller "knocked out" so I answered his 2-1 to let him know I wanted to work by the book. Looking at the roster pinned on the wall I saw that it was Peter Davis at Aller rather than one of the resident men like Sid Medland, John Congdon or John Haycock. That was unusual as Peter was a Dawlish Rest Day Reliefman who only worked Aller when he was spare or off his normal roster. Peter was a nice bloke and a dedicated railwayman, having spent many years as a regular man at Dawlish before the box became part-time and he went on the relief. I think he probably found Aller a bit more of a challenge than Exminster, Dawlish Warren and Teignmouth where he normally relieved. In the up direction the 13.45 Plymouth to Paddington passed. Peter obliged me by acknowledging my "Call Attention" and "Train out of Section" but when the train left the station and passed East all I got was 2-1 on the bell and the block dropped to Normal. I answered the 2-1 to enforce my position.

The Down Main block was still resolutely sitting at "Train on Line" when its associated bell rang out "Call Attention" again. I answered it to be offered the "Limited" - a runner. With the block needle in its current position I could not accept the train and so ignored the 3-3-3. After a minute or so the two men in East became anxious, offering the "Limited" down the Through line this time so I set the trailing points from the Through towards the Relief to establish the requisite clearing point, accepted the train and offered it straight on to Aller. Peter answered the "Call Attention" promptly but there was a visible pause while he comprehended the fact that he was being asked the "Limited" down the Relief line. However, he had no reason to refuse it so he set his points from Relief to Main and accepted the train. Having offered the train on down the Relief, rather than turn it out main line again myself I was able to pull the Down Through Distant (No. 18) and watch each of the three arm indicators A, B and C stacked one above the other on the block shelf flick from "on" to "off" one at a time signifying that the inner, intermediate and outer distant arms under East's signals had all motored to the clear position. East had not been able to clear his distant for the move, nor could Aller but for West box all the flags were flying!

The box to box 'phone rang again. Charlie left it for me to answer this time. Willy explained how the crack train of the day would be slowed as it approached East to be switched to the Through line and how it would run slowly through the station looking to be switched back again at West. All because I insisted on using the correct procedure rather than doing things the Western way. I suggested that if he looked out of the window he would see that all my backboards were "off" and so the train would experience no delay at West. Willy completed the discourse berating me with a tirade of strong language before abruptly hanging up.

When the "Limited" finally drifted past on the Down Through line, between the station and Carriage Sidings, the driver surveyed the scene, turning his head from side to side in a bemused fashion to see if he could ascertain why he had not been routed along the Main line as normal. This time my "Call Attention" was answered by one of the men in East with a firm single beat and the 2-1 with a deliberately heavy, slow reply that held the hammer against the bell at each beat, dulling the tone. I unpegged, repeating the procedure on the Main line where a similar response allowed me to normalise the block some twenty minutes after the previous London had gone. The rest of the shift was spent working with two very disgruntled reliefmen at East box who rang the bells with continual sarcasm.

Some twenty minutes or so after the "Limited" had passed the Control 'phone rang. I told Charlie to leave it for me. The controller at Plymouth was looking to find a reason why the "Limited" was right time at Dawlish Warren but had lost a couple of minutes by Totnes. I advised that she had had a clear run at West but that East might know why. What story Willy and George spun to Control I never knew.

George was always curt if ever we relieved one another somewhere thereafter. Willy was more easy going and, being a practical joker, knew he could get his own back when the time was right. Many years later when I visited Exeter Panel he was on duty. The first thing he did was loudly chastise me in front of his colleagues over that afternoon shift at Newton Abbot.

CHAPTER NINE

READY AND ON

The strange thing about the methods of working at Newton Abbot was that whilst some corner cutting, or what I like to call simplifying went on, the old hands played other moves exactly to the book, even though this created more work for them. A typical example was the "ready and on" procedure when a train was offered forward on the block and put straight "on line", as would happen at East or West for a loco' from shed, empty stock from the carriage sidings or for a passenger train which had stopped in the station.

In many places, when exchanging bells for such a departing move the "Train Entering Section" signal would be sent immediately the "Is Line Clear" was acknowledged. The forward signalman would wait a few seconds, usually whilst getting the road himself and entering the times in the train register book, before pegging the block across from "Line Clear" to "Train on Line" in order that the sending signalman could operate his section signal lever. This saved time and walking but had never been embraced in the Newton Abbot area. So at East and West boxes, dozens of times a day, the signalmen would stick rigidly to the full procedure. For a departing passenger train on the Down Main for example this would mean reversing lever 2 at West box to lower the Down Main Home just before departure time, watching for the guard to give right away and, when seeing this, walking along to the Aller Junction main line bell to get the road. This bell sat on the shelf above lever 100! Having obtained a "Line Clear" the signalman would walk back to pull lever 8, the Down Main Starting, then return all the way back to the Aller bell to send the two beats of "Train Entering Section" followed by walking back to lever 2 again to replace this behind the train, perhaps pausing in the window to watch the train as it passed the box. This ritual, equivalent to walking 42 yards past 380 levers, was completely at odds with the culture of making the job easy and even more bizarre when one of the reasons cited for not using the "Call Attention" with the "Train Out of Section" signal was that it created unnecessary walking to and from the bells.

Not "asking on" until trains were ready to leave or leaving made little difference to the working between Newton Abbot East and Teignmouth but in the other direction, from West, it dictated the entire method of operation at Aller Junction. A down train being "asked out" as it was departing in the "ready and on" fashion required the signalman at Aller to respond very quickly, not only in giving the road to West box, but in getting the road ahead in order to pull off smartly so that the driver would see the distant drop beneath West's starter before he passed it. Both the main and relief line distants were mechanically worked slots that provided challenging pulls. It was especially important to get the Down Main Distant "off" so that trains got the best run possible at Dainton bank, which effectively started immediately beyond the junction. Sitting in the box at Aller, the signalman would have no idea where the next down stopper was until it was "asked out". This made regulation of the junction quite difficult, especially when running a train from the up branch at a time when a down train for the Plymouth direction was expected. In years gone by trains had been "wired" from Exeter but this practise had ceased. When conflict arose between getting an up train off the branch or giving a down train a run at Dainton then preference was invariably given to the down train.

Quite often a down Plymouth or Cornish train stopping at Newton Abbot would have a branch connection waiting for it. In Aller box the expectant silence would suddenly be punctuated by "Call Attention" signals from West box on both the Main and Relief line bells, followed by 4 beats on the Main and 1 pause 3 immediately on the Relief heralding that both trains were departing the station together. Once answered these were shortly followed by "Train Entering Section" for the pair. This meant quickly getting the road from Dainton and Torre, calling their attention before answering West to save vital seconds, then quickly pulling off the Down Main and Down Relief line signals. Seconds later both trains would hove into view racing alongside one another in a seeming attempt to pass the box first as if it were some winning post. As they came under the bridge between the home gantry and the box, they would part company alongside the allotments on the bank, the branch train shooting straight on beneath the box windows towards Kingskerswell whilst the main line train peeled away through the switch-diamonds in the middle of the junction, tilting into the curve and digging in for the climb to Dainton. Its coaches would send out a thrilling staccato sound as the wheels of each bogie hit the ironwork of the diamonds; bash-bash-bash-bash, bash-bash-bash-bash. Once the locomotive was through the diamonds the driver would notch up on the power in an effort to maintain speed climbing the bank. From accepting the two trains to the replacement of the signals behind them would be little more than two minutes - a spurt of activity that could be triggered at any time.

Moves in the up direction didn't quite coincide in the same way. Those Paignton services which connected with trains from farther west were timed to arrive at Newton Abbot five or ten minutes beforehand. This meant they would be through the junction and often waiting in the station before the connecting train was heralded on line from Dainton. With four tracks into Newton Abbot and crossovers between them all it was possible to route trains in a number of ways so as to assist the working in the station. An up runner from Paignton might, for example, be turned onto the Up Main at Aller so that it could be routed up the Through line at West box without conflicting with moves taking place to and from the platform lines. In the down direction branch trains were sometimes sent out down the Main line whilst those from the Down Through were sent on down the Relief. The Hackney trips to Stoneycombe usually came down the Relief so that the Aller man could decide whether to hold them there, turn them into the Loop or run them straight up the hill to Stoneycombe if there was a margin.

Care was needed when accepting down trains as, with only one home signal on each of the two lines, the clearing points extended beyond the junction. Thus a number of combinations of moves were restricted: Running a train off the branch meant that only one down train could be accepted, with the clearance point established towards Torre; If two down trains were accepted, then a move from the Up Branch would have to wait. Should a down train for the branch be accepted on the Down Main then nothing could be accepted down the relief, but if a train had already been accepted on the Down Relief, then it would first have to arrive at a stand at the Home signal before the points could be turned for the train on the main to run down the branch. The opposite situation applied for relief line to main line moves.

Although the layout had been track circuited, the mechanical locking retained its original facing point lock route holding whereby each FPL lever was locked by the previous one in the route. This meant that to move the switch-diamonds, its FPL lever (No. 21) had to be released by normalising the FPL lever associated with either the Down Main (No. 33) or Down Relief (No. 31) facing points, depending which way the relief line points were set. Moving the loop entry points was even worsc as the FPL for these (No. 15) required the switch-diamond FPL lever normalised which, of course, in turn first needed the relevant down facer FPL normalised. Once the points were moved, these three FPLs then all had to be pulled again to lock their respective points and so release the relevant signal for the move.

The Down Home signals at Aller Junction straddle the Down Relief and Down Main lines on a gantry. The arms read to the Down Branch, the Down Goods Loop and the Down Main from each of the two lines. *(Author)*

The box was quite narrow, set into the bank below the main Newton Abbot to Torquay road which ran behind. There were only two spare levers in the 46 lever frame. These had once operated a trailing connection to a siding alongside the Down Branch and its associated exit signal. These had been recovered in 1964. A plethora of arm and lamp indicators, plungers, switches and sealed releases filled the block shelf alongwith the four blocks, their associated bells, a row of Nalders and a timer relay. This resulted in some of the indicators having to be located on the window ledge behind their respective levers. With an inside staircase, separate two lever detonator frames at each end and newly plumbed in sink with hot water geyser above, there was not a lot of room in which to manoeuvre. But it was a very enjoyable box to work and a great location, looking out across the junction onto fields where cattle grazed.

It would be wrong to say that I had a favourite signal box out of those on the district, as each one provided unique attractions. There was the obvious appeal of the Newton Abbot boxes, with their impressive number of working levers and constant activity and of Aller with its busy junction but as mentioned earlier a shift at Dainton Tunnel box in the heart of the Devon countryside, just passing trains, was equally rewarding in its own way, although the long dark winter evenings in the quieter boxes could sometimes drag without a book or newspaper to read.

Dainton reminded me of my earlier days at Whiteball as it shared a similar situation, at the top of a bank adjacent to a nearby tunnel. It was here that the signalman converted the 4 beats of an up class 1 into 3-3-3 going forward if the train was a runner at Newton Abbot. The location differed though in a number of ways; the box was much nearer to the tunnel mouth and was a modern Western Region replacement for the original 'Saxby and Farmer' box. And, in this instance, the box name included the word Tunnel unlike Whiteball. The bank was a little steeper on the Newton Abbot side with the worst gradient a mountainous 1 in 36 whilst on the Plymouth side it varied from 1 in 55 up to 1 in 37 outside the box, a legacy of Brunel's atmospheric experiment. There was the added hindrance of some very tight curvature too. This severe gradient was reflected in the short distance between the distant signals and their respective homes. The Up Distant was positioned only 764 yards from the Up Home whilst the Down Distant, situated to the east of the tunnel, was a mere 573 yards from the Down Home. Trains would growl up past the box, even the expresses reduced to less than 50 mph. To assist driver's approaching from the east in handling their trains, particularly those with a banker on, a banner repeater for the Down Home signal was provided before the entrancc to the tunnel. Once over the summit trains would squeal down around the curves, brakes on to control speed, wheel flanges singing against the rails.

The box derived its name of course from the tunnel but the village of Dainton was on the other side of the hill, similar to Whiteball where the village there is on the Somerset side of the tunnel. Access required a quarter mile walk up the line from an overbridge at the end of one of those narrow Devon lanes characterised by high hedges and the occasional passing place. This lane left the A381 Newton Abbot to Totnes road and passed through the small habitation of Wrigwell before expiring into a bridle path alongside a farm perched adjacent to the bridge.

Banking up to Dainton, whilst still permitted, rarely took place by now and so the sidings here had been removed but as mentioned earlier some of the heavier trains regularly enjoyed the assistance of a pilot locomotive over the line between Newton Abbot and Plymouth. The box retained a crossover which found occasional use but otherwise it's purpose was to split the section between Aller Junction and Totnes. Being a fairly new structure, dating from 1965, the design, dubbed "Plywood Wonder" was modular and made of wood with a flat roof. Floor to ceiling glass panels in the end walls gave exceptional vision but the electric bar heaters suspended from the ceiling did not provide adequate warmth in winter, most of the heat escaping straight out through the roof and glass. The heat they did give out was dry and one was always in danger of receiving a singed head from standing underneath them. The lever frame was positioned to the rear of the box, an unusual arrangement on the Western but standard for the "Plywood Wonder" design.

Locomotive failures were a weekly occurrence on the South Devon banks between Newton Abbot and Plymouth providing myself and other signalmen at Dainton and Totnes with plenty of practice in the application of the relevant rules and regulations pertaining to the rescue of failed trains. The "Western" hydraulics had gradually been phased out now to be replaced by the 50s. The availability of these locomotives was poor to begin with but the Devon banks were not fussy as to which class of loco' they helped to flounder.

One morning when enjoying a week of early turn at Dainton, the 07.25 Plymouth to Edinburgh came up past the box with a wheel skidding on one of its coaches, the brakes locked on hard. The train could well have come all the way from Plymouth like it, the tyre being worn flat. After having stopped the train at the Up Starter, on the far side of the tunnel, for examination it was allowed to proceed at reduced speed to Newton Abbot where the errant coach was shunted out of the train. Amazingly, by some improbable coincidence, the same train, although of course a different set of stock, fell victim to the same problem the very next morning. I couldn't believe my eyes as the train struggled up past the box. My mates at Totnes, Aller and Newton Abbot didn't believe me either, nor did the controller at Plymouth. The next morning everyone wondered if I would make it a hat trick but the train was in perfect order as it went by that day.

Catch points were provided at various places in the main line to derail any vehicles that might run back if detached from a train and loose coupled freights would stop outside the box to enable the guard to pin down brakes before the descent to Totnes. Indeed alongside the Down Home signal was a cast sign bearing the words "ALL DOWN GOODS AND MINERAL TRAINS WITH 35 WAGONS OR LESS MUST STOP DEAD HERE". This instruction was designed to ensure trains descended the bank under full brake control, having first been brought to a stand at the top. Unfitted, or partly fitted trains would have their hand brakes pinned down by the guard here to ensure the locomotive could hold the train on the descent.

With the crossover being located virtually at the top of the bank, necessitating trains to stop or shunt on the severe gradients, and a tunnel to complicate manoeuvres further it was usual that any planned single line working was introduced between Totnes and Aller Junction and even extended to Newton Abbot on occasions. Dainton then became an intermediate box on the single line with the added complication that its crossover had to be clipped and padlocked but so too did the catchpoints on one side or other of the bank every time depending which line was the one designated as the single line and the points at Stoneycombe had to be clipped as well together with the loop exit points at Aller. On the up line there were catch points at Combe Fishacre on the 1 in 38 grade about ¾ mile before Dainton box. On the down line there were two sets; one 347 yards before Stoneycombe's Down Home signal where the line rises at 1 in 46 and the other at the 217½ mile post on the 1 in 39 just before the tunnel at Dainton.

Setting up single line working on a typical Saturday night would therefore be quite a rigmarole for the pilotman. Before being able to deliver the single line working forms to the signal boxes involved I can remember having to be driven out in the darkness in a railway van by the Responsible Officer, usually Frank Williams from Exeter who always volunteered as RO. Frank was a seasoned railwayman having started his career in Cornwall, served in the Royal Engineers during World War 2 and become an Inspector at Exeter in 1955. He enjoyed organising the night's activities, together with the opportunity this gave for camaraderie with the signalmen and some story telling. At each of the nearest access points it was a case of scrambling up the bank to each of the catch points, clipping and padlocking them and leaving an oil handlamp shining a green light towards traffic that would approach in the facing direction. Come the morning, the whole palaver would have to be repeated in reverse before normal working could be resumed.

After a few instances of this Frank and I decided on a more sophisticated approach arranging for a light engine and crew to travel up from Laira shed to Totnes to act as a taxi for us. This made the setting up both faster and safer. We would travel through on the engine in one direction with all the clips, padlocks and lamps we required stowed on the footplate, stopping exactly where we needed and then travel back to deliver the forms to the signalmen and open up single line working once the possession had been taken on the other line.

The enjoyment of being a pilotman over this switchback stretch of railway was no less than that of performing the same role around the sea wall but the countryside was dark at night and the mist often rose above the river Dart at Totnes hampering the crossing over of trains there. I found it preferable to be on the locomotives rather than on the ground clipping up the crossover at one end or the other of the single line to handsignal the trains "through the road". Many of the older reliefmen preferred the groundman's duties, being able to take refuge in the warmth of the signal box between trains and avoid the climbing up and down on locomotives and to-ing and fro-ing between each end of the section. This allowed me to undertake the Pilotman's role a little more often than seniority might otherwise have allowed. The Pilotman always assisted with the shunting of the trains but did not have to handle the greasy point clips.

Whilst the summit of the incline was recognisable outside Dainton box, back down around Stoneycombe Sidings signal box the severity of the bank, with its 1 in 46, reducing to 1 in 56 by the box and then shortly rising again to 1 in 41, was starkly apparent to the eye, both in terms of the visual comparison between the heights of the railway looking in each direction and the relative slope of the formation compared to the surrounding countryside.

The stone quarry was opposite the box on the down side of the line with the sidings and loading hopper beyond the main lines. Empty wagons would be left at the top end of the loading siding beyond the hopper. From here the loading foreman would uncouple a pair of wagons at a time, walking them down the incline, under the control of the hand brake, below the chute to be loaded before then allowing them to gravitate to the bottom end of the sidings. It was the guard who arrived with the next trip or engine who would recouple all the wagons before attaching the engine. The loco' was often required to buffer up the wagons as they would not always have come to rest together.

Exeter area trip No. 9 (B77) was assigned to servicing Stoneycombe, usually with short rakes of 'Dogfish' or 'Salmon' wagons, the loads having to be fairly light. Movements varied according to demand but there was generally a trip from Hackney Yard in the morning and another one in the afternoon, the crew and loco' coming off Newton Abbot shed. Loaded traffic was either taken back to Hackney or onward to Tavistock Junction, or Tavy Junction as it was colloquially known, near Plymouth for the civil engineer. Besides the characteristic pink ballast, used all over the Western, a train of crushed stone ran every week for the railway concrete works at Taunton, to be used in the manufacture of such things as cable troughing and drainage pits.

The signalman's view of a train being loaded at Stoneycombe. Here a rake of wagons are being filled with aggregate for Taunton concrete works. *(Author)*

The trips going back to Hackney required the locomotive to draw the vehicles back up the sidings so as to be able to run round them before taking the train out through a slip connection straight onto the Up Main. For trips heading west the locomotive would start the train from the bottom end of the sidings on the level so as to have a chance of hauling the load out onto the 1 in 41 rising gradient. This could often prove a spectacular sight, especially in damp or wet weather, when the locomotive would lose its feet. All engine wheels would spin with the train at a stand or even drifting backwards. It was not uncommon for the crew to split the train and take the load out in two separate trips. There were even times when the crew would give up altogether, taking their locomotive back light to shed. The rails in the siding were burnt in many places with flat crowns and a blue tinge to the steel from years of slipping ballast trains.

Paid for by English China Clays Ltd, owners of the quarry, the box was only manned for a day shift from 08.45 to 16.45 Mondays to Fridays and hence there was only one regular signalman based there. The job suited a particular kind of person as, although it was effectively "office hours", there was no overtime and no shift enhancement. It therefore only paid a basic week's wages. Having said this, Phil Wain, the signalman at Stoneycombe, who had moved there on promotion from Dainton, managed to supplement his income by getting himself rostered for groundman turns at the weekend from time to time when there was engineering works between Newton Abbot and Totnes. The box had no running water, no toilet facilities and no electricity. Water was collected from the quarrymen's mess hut whilst a tilley lamp afforded light on winter afternoons. Being manned for just a single shift and only scored for the brief periods it was switched in, the box achieved sufficient marks to attain class B, a grade higher than Dainton and the same as many busier boxes.

For us reliefmen a shift at Stoneycombe was a rarity. Only if Phil was on annual leave or off due to sickness would one of us be required to cover the box. I was rostered to do this on a few occasions including a week of Phil's annual leave one summer. The day shift made a pleasant change but five consecutive days was quite enough because another difference about Stoneycombe was that the box spent most of its time switched out with all the signals at clear. The box would have only been a hindrance switched in anyhow, as the gradient and closeness to the adjacent boxes meant that it was not really expedient to potentially stop trains there in either direction, up hill or down hill. The footnote instructions therefore stated that the box was to remain switched out until required. This meant either when a trip was on its way for the quarry or when blasting was to take place. So, during the eight hour shift period the box might switch-in perhaps three times, once each for the morning and afternoon trips and once for blasting. A total period of time of probably little more than an hour.

To avoid the possibility of stopping a train on the gradient the footnotes mandated that "Line Clear" had to be obtained from the box in advance before a train could be accepted from the box in rear, except for light engines and trains destined for the quarry sidings. Even before a train for the sidings was accepted the section ahead had to be unoccupied. This was to guard against the possibility

Spoilt GWR - the 1894 Stoneycombe Sidings signal box with its ugly flat roof of reinforced concrete to protect against falling rocks and wire mesh on the front windows. Note my pushbike leant against the box steps. *(Author)*

of vehicles running back in the wrong direction on the down line towards a trip, or a trip failing to be able to stop on the Up. Due to the shortness of the sections the "Train Approaching" bell signal was authorised between Stoneycombe, Aller Junction and Dainton in both directions when Stoneycombe was open.

The trailing crossover and slip connection eventually became life expired and were removed. This left five additional spare levers in the frame and meant the only access to the sidings was via the trailing connection from the Down Main line. All departures, even for Hackney and Taunton, had to then travel to Totnes where the locomotive would run round its train. Light engines were however able to cross over at Dainton. The distant signals remained as stand alone semaphores, never being converted to colour lights, which was unusual for this stretch of the main line. The box was only ever fitted with a short block shelf. This meant it was not possible to fit an economiser plunger above the Up Starter lever for its electric lock and so a sprung contact, released by the lever catch block, was fixed to the quadrant plate of the relevant lever. Although both section signals were released by "Line Clear" there was an unusual arrangement whereby a permanent feed to the economisers was established when the block switch was turned to the switched-out position. Hence it was possible to clear these signals by turning the switch regardless of the state of the block. This may well have been a feature to make it easy for the signalman to protect an incident and then reclear his signals whilst in the switched-out mode.

When blasting was to take place, the quarry Foreman would first seek permission from the signalman. The box would then be switched-in and, providing there was a margin between trains, the line would be protected by sending the special bell signal "May blasting be permitted" 6 pause 3 to Aller and Dainton. Once repeated back, the block indicators would be placed to "Train on Line" and the Foreman given permission to blast. The hooter would then sound in the quarry followed by what always seemed a long silent wait before the dynamite exploded and the ground reverberated to the blast. It was rare for debris to fall on the line but the signalman had to ensure the track was unobstructed once the Foreman returned to signal the all clear. The exchange of information with the quarry Foreman was all done by whistles and hand gestures from a distance. The roof of the signal box was constructed of reinforced concrete just in case a stray rock should land on it. Once blasting was finished the "Obstruction Removed" bell signal was sent and the block indicators returned to "Normal" before the switching-out process was undertaken. Interestingly, 6 pause 3 had not always been the designated bell signal for this situation. Both 5 pause 3 and 4 pause 3 had been used previously at Stoneycombe at different times in history.

The 6 pause 3 bell signal was not unique to Stoneycombe. It was employed at two other Newton Abbot area boxes but carried completely different meanings at these. At Newton Abbot West it added to the variety of codes by being used to request the signalman at East box to reverse his interlocking lever for the trailing crossover in the middle of the station between the Up Relief and Down Main lines referred to in the previous chapter. At Paignton North the same bell signal was used to ask the signalman at South box to normalise his interlocking lever (No. 51) for the reversible working on the up platform line to allow a shunting movement onto a train already occupying the line. Once the move was complete the special bell of 3-6 beats was sent.

Besides this little peculiarity, the working at Paignton North was even more interesting in as much as trains were allowed quite normally into the section to Paignton South when South box was closed. There were two lines through the section, each with a platform - the Down Main and the "Up and Down Main" which was reversible. The Down Main was worked in accordance with the normal double line absolute block regulations using a bell and half a double line instrument. The pegging half was of course in South box, the non-pegger in North. The "Up and Down Main" was fully track circuited being worked as a single line with interlocking levers and a separate bell with a complete double line instrument in both boxes. The two block indicators applied to opposite directions of travel over this one line rather than to separate Up and Down lines. To route a train into this line from one end or the other required a "Line Clear" on the correct indicator and the relevant interlocking lever reverse. The interlocking lever could only be operated if its counterpart in the other box was normal. So when reversing No. 8 in North box in order to send a train towards South, No. 51 in South was required to be normal and vice-versa.

With the station buildings and way-out being on the up side of the line it was preferable to terminate trains in the "Up and Down Main" whenever possible. If the terminating train was a diesel multiple unit (dmu) and it formed the next working back then all the signalman at South box had to do was accept it, take it "on line" and then receive a cancel when it had departed again. The last three trains on weekday evenings and the first five on Sunday mornings were all dmu workings. To economise on signalmen's hours, reducing the establishment to just two men, South box could be switched out and the dmus still admitted onto the reversible line at North. It was a unique arrangement as South still left all his signals at danger, indeed the level crossing gates remained closed across the railway. The switch, when turned, allowed lever number 3 in North box, which operated the Down Main to Up and Down Home signal, to be pulled without a "Line Clear" being obtained provided the track circuits were all clear and the respective interlocking levers in the two boxes were in their correct positions.

The reversible working at Paignton had first been provided in 1925. A crossover towards the south end of the up platform allowed South box to signal through trains on to Goodrington. This facility had been provided to allow greater flexibility at what was otherwise a very constrained station. Indeed the arrangement was not unique to Paignton as, at one time, both Torre and Torquay stations had a similar feature until the 1960s. Torre's Down Inner Home still retained its defunct right hand doll whilst in the lever frame, spare levers 8 and 34, which had once worked the facing point locks on the facing crossover No. 9 at the north end of the layout, were bolted reverse to release the locking.

With no traffic at night the branch boxes would close. The Paignton South signalman was able to take advantage of the switch and get away after the last loco' hauled train at around 21.15. This was a far cry from the days when South had been a three shift box. With Torre closing late evening too, only Paignton North had to remain open whenever there was a train on the branch. This meant a very early start for the early turn shift of 04.20 in order to accept the first train from Aller, which conveyed the newspaper van from Paddington. Whenever I was caught for this shift I preferred to travel down the night before, kipping in the box until the due time. I would catch the next to last branch train from Newton Abbot as this connected with the Leeds - Plymouth which called at Teignmouth. This had the advantage for the late turn man in that I could let him get away early by seeing the last passenger train down and its empty unit away on his behalf, closing out around 23.30, once it had passed Aller. Jim Benham, Tom Way or Reg Peacock were always pleased to get off home that little bit early but probably thought I was just a bit mad to bed down in the box. By letting the night turn man at Aller know I was there he could wake me as soon as I was required to open up and, if the Paper train was late, be allowed to rest a while longer. Having switched in and taken the first train on, there was always time for a bit more of a doze as the Papers called at Torre to unload newspapers and at Torquay to set down mail before eventually arriving at Paignton.

South box would open at 04.55 when Herbie James or Dave Bright would arrive so that the Papers could run into the down platform for unloading. Sometimes it might be Mervyn Jeans, one of the Paignton Rest Day Reliefmen. Mervyn was the brother of my old mate Eric at Wellington from my Whiteball days. If the man coming on at South was late it was incumbent upon the North signalman to walk down to South box to deal with the run-round move. The Down Main Home at North was not locked by the block and so the train could be let into the platform without obtaining a "Line Clear". Similarly, if the South signalman arrived to find his mate at North had failed to show and the Papers were still stuck at Aller, he was obliged to walk to North box and open up.

With opening hours from 04.20 to 23.30 or so, the shifts at North box were split between early, middle and late turns. The early turn finished at 12.20 whilst the late turn commenced at 15.20. The intervening three hours were covered by the middle turn but the man on duty for this started at 07.20, spending the first five hours of his shift manning the ticket barrier on the station. This was an activity I found little pleasure in so was pleased to be rarely rostered for middle turn at Paignton North.

To allow for movements on and off both platform lines at North a scissors crossover was provided. The facing half of these, operated by lever number 4, was fitted with a Prince's economical point and facing lock movement whereby both functions were combined onto the one lever which, consequently, was painted half blue and half black. The drive to the Prince's lock was taken via a lifting bar that had to be raised above rail level and then dropped to unbolt the points, move them, and then bolt them again. This prevented the points from being moved if a train was stood on them or was moving across them. Lifting bars had once been common before the use of track circuits. With all this apparatus to move, lever 4 was particularly heavy.

Lever colours are an interesting subject in their own right. Apart from the familiar colours of red for stop signals, yellow for distant signals, black for points and blue for facing point locks, other colours and combinations of colours added to the variety found in many of the boxes. Brown was used for levers associated with mechanical releases such as those fitted to a level crossing whilst half blue, half brown was used for electrical releases such as those applying to a ground frame or, as in the case at Paignton, to the interlocking levers for the reversible line.

A white stripe was applied in the middle of those levers released by an adjacent signal box. So section signal levers commonly had a white stripe to show they required a "Line Clear" release. Detonator placer levers were painted with alternate black and white chevrons. The chevrons pointed up for up line placers and down for down line placers. Sometimes these levers were accommodated in the main lever frame with all the other levers but often they were provided as separate small frames to one side of the main frame. At Newton Abbot West the six detonator levers were split unusually between the main frame and a separate one. The three up line placers, one each for the Up Relief, Up Main and Up Through lines, were worked by levers 129, 130 and 131 respectively in the main frame whereas the three down line placers were worked from a separate three lever frame located to the left of the main frame. These were numbered 1, 2 and 3 looking incongruous alongside the full size real levers 1, 2 and 3 of the main frame. Arguably one could say that although the main frame was 153 levers in length the box was actually equivalent to 156 by virtue of the additional three detonator levers. A similar anomaly existed at Torre where the down line placer had its own separate small lever whilst the up line apparatus was connected to a lever in the main frame.

A colouring feature unique to the Western was that goods line signal levers were provided with a black stripe half way down their length and that relief line signal levers had their entire lower half painted black. Examples of these could be found in the area, indeed with relief lines running through Newton Abbot and on to Aller Junction significant numbers of levers in the three boxes concerned were painted half black giving a unique dark appearance to these frames. This twin colouring was an exception to the norm which dictated dual coloured levers performed two functions, e.g. blue and black performed both the operation and locking of points, as in the Prince's economical movement at Paignton North or motor operated points on a passenger line. At Aller Junction the Down Goods Loop Starting gave access into the section to Dainton and so was released by "Line Clear". The controlling red lever complied with the colouring conventions by having a deep black stripe half way down in the middle of which was a smaller white stripe.

Digressing away from the Newton Abbot area for a moment, I remember a unique lever at Cogload box, to the east of Taunton where both colouring techniques had to be applied. There was only one stop signal controlled by Cogload on the Down Relief line (after the box became the fringe to Bristol panel) the Down Relief Home. This acted therefore as the section signal also, released by "Line Clear" from Taunton East Junction. The last automatic three aspect signal on Bristol (DM157) performed the distant function for this home signal, the yellow aspect automatically changing to green upon operation of the home. To represent this combination the lever (No. 7) was painted, in order of descent, red, white stripe, yellow, black!

Separate small frames were also favoured by the Great Western to lock the pedestrian wicket gates of level crossings. Paignton South had one of these frames placed under the end windows, the levers of which were still painted light blue, harking back to GW days before the Railway Executive standardised on brown for mechanical locking levers. The gate stop and lock levers in the main frame had however been over-painted in brown. Evidence of earlier colouring would appear on some levers through wear and tear. Most commonly green could be found under the yellow on distant signal levers from the days before the late 1920s when the fishtailed arms had been painted red rather than yellow and the spectacles had carried red and green lenses instead of yellow and green. The wicket and detonator placer levers often remained adorned with their original ornate brass plates which were oval in shape and hence wider than their counterparts on other levers.

The two level crossings at Paignton could not have been more different. That at the South, across Sands Road, comprised four wooden gates operated by a gate wheel at the right hand end of the frame, together with pedestrian wickets. The road was not particularly busy and had been made a one way street at some stage so traffic only approached from behind the box. By contrast the crossing at the North had been converted to electro-hydraulic barriers within a short time of my arrival at Newton Abbot, as mentioned earlier in chapter 7.

There were four booms and, like all manually controlled barriers, these were fitted with skirts which opened out under gravity to fill the space between the boom arm and the ground, thereby fencing off the railway completely. To give a degree of protection to each skirt to prevent deformation the end struts at the tip of each barrier were made longer, from a higher weight steel and fitted with a stud designed to come to rest on the road surface. These were known as Pogos as they were like a miniature version of the child's Pogo stick, even down to the fact that they bounced on the road. Invariably this bouncing drilled a hole in the tarmac, as maintaining accurate adjustment over a period of time is quite difficult. The barriers at Paignton had this propensity.

The station platforms were immediately beyond the North crossing on the opposite side of Torbay Road from the box. Up trains would draw right up to the home signal only a few feet short of the level crossing, menacingly close to the pedestrians and cars crossing in front. The road was extremely busy, not only with motor vehicles, but with pedestrians too, especially in summer for this was the main drag from the railway and bus stations and the town centre down to the sea front. In fact Woolworths was just behind the box. Most of the shops in the road were tacky gift and clothes outlets interspersed with cafés, ice cream parlours and amusement arcades, many having veranda awnings sheltering the pavement. The Cinema was located diagonally across the crossing from the box, alongside the entrance to the Torbay Steam Railway whilst directly opposite the box, alongside the down line was May's Café. With a number of nearby night clubs too, the area was never quiet, whatever time of day or night.

There was a constant scene of passing traffic and people to idle away the minutes between trains. Closing the crossing, in order to signal a movement in or out of the station meant bringing this momentum to a halt. Car drivers would often disregard the warning lights and continue to cross. So too would the pedestrians, many oblivious to the sound of the warning bell and lowering of the barriers. Others would quicken their pace or run to beat the barriers such was their urgency to cross the line, despite the alternative footbridge. Once the flow of humans had been brought to a stand they would congregate along the length of the barriers, some leaning on the wooden boom arms to watch the spectacle of an arriving or departing train.

When in the raised position the wind would catch the booms, rattling the folded skirts from time to time, causing surprise and often alarm to the passing pedestrians. There was no danger that the booms were about to lower on their heads but if I was stood at the window spectating the scene I am sure they were convinced I had taken some specific action to rattle the booms and engage in the sport of striking panic into harmless locals and holidaymakers. There were times when such holidaymakers were too engrossed in their vacation and, being unfamiliar with such a level crossing, failed to see the lights, hear the bells or register that a boom was falling towards them. Control of the crossing had been far easier with the wheel operated gates as it still was at South. Neither pedestrians nor vehicle drivers could fail to see the large white wooden gates with their red target start to swing. Their sheer bulk resisted any argument as they swept across the road, their speed of movement being regulated by the signalman at his wheel.

There was one particular motorist who drove the length of Torbay Road a number of times a day. He was the local landlord, reputedly owning many of the shops on the street. He obviously viewed the level crossing as an impediment to free movement as the regular signalmen and other reliefmen had all experienced his indifference to the road lights and even the lowering barriers. I too had been subject to his self extolled status, with him running the gauntlet of the lights and causing interruption to the lowering sequence on more than one occasion.

One morning a down train had passed Torre a few minutes when I went across to the window to activate the lowering sequence ready for its arrival. Having checked the scene, and waited for a gap in the traffic, I pressed the lower button. The yellow lights came on and the warning bells began to sound. With this I spotted our friend in his brown Rover 2000 coming up the street from the sea front. The yellow lights extinguished to be replaced by the twin red flashing lights which were now sending out their unambiguous stop message. The Rover kept coming, the nearside barriers began to lower, their skirts unfurling. I kept my finger on the lower button, I was determined he should obey the road lights, he was determined to exert his self appointed status and have me halt the barriers so he could pass. He approached the crossing in the middle of the carriageway to gain maximum clearance below the nearside barrier but realised it was not going to stop and that he was not going to pass through underneath.

As the car halted, with its front well past the white stop line marking in the

The neat little box at Paignton North shortly after the crossing gates had been replaced with barriers and the footbridge renewed in a new position behind the box. The barrier arm nearest the box has already been broken off by an unfamiliar motorist, its jagged remains pointing forlornly skyward. *(Author)*

road, the Pogo punctured its way through the bonnet of the Rover and into its engine compartment. I released the pressure on the lower button and the movement stopped. I then momentarily pressed the raise button. The barriers rose a few degrees and the Pogo extracted itself, accompanied by the sound of sheet metal being damaged as the stud re-emerged from the bonnet. Having conceded the situation our friend reversed behind the stop line and I completed the lower sequence before clearing the signals for the approaching train. For the next few minutes I expected a confrontation but at no time did the driver leave his car nor did he even look up at the signal box when he eventually drove away. He obviously was fully aware of the illegal position in which he had placed himself and had no desire to compound his situation. From that day onwards he became the very model of a driver when cruising Torbay Road and respected the level crossing on all occasions. The regular signalmen at Paignton North were forever grateful of my encounter that day.

The Paignton boxes were of course busier for the duration of the summer timetable compared with the winter. South box enjoyed the added bonus of the Torbay Steam Railway shuttles to and from Kingswear, hauled by ex Great Western steam locomotives like Prairie No. 4588 and Lydham Manor No. 7827 resplendent in their green livery with copper top chimneys. Occasionally a through train might travel between the BR system and the Torbay railway resulting in engine changing at South box. Some terminating trains ran empty stock out to Goodrington sidings to be watered and cleaned by seasonal staff. On Saturdays nearly all trains ran out to Goodrington. Access to and from the sidings was over the former Up Main line. A handy set of trap points enabled locomotives to run round without the need to close the level crossing. The same set of traps allowed the signalman to get empty trains moving up towards the crossing as soon as the previous train could be seen to be ready to depart the up platform. The gates would then be swung, the traps closed and the disc operated to allow the train to trickle across the road towards the starting signal just as the platform became clear and North was able to accept it in. In earlier years, until BR abandoned the line to Kingswear, South box had been provided with a relief signalman between 08.15 and 16.15 on summer Saturdays to act as an assistant such was the workload of the box.

The Warning Arrangement was authorised at South box for the acceptance of trains on the Down Main. This was handy, if not essential, enabling stock and loco' movements to continue whilst allowing down trains to arrive in the station. With North's section signal being in rear of the box, the signalman there could not use the green flag routine to "warn" a driver that he had been accepted under regulation 5 but instead had to bring the train nearly to a stand before lowering the signal, the driver taking this as intimation that the clearing point was fouled at South.

During quieter periods of the day some of the loco' hauled arrivals would terminate in the up platform and then form the next departure back. In these instances the locomotive would run round its stock by travelling "wrong road" from South to North over the Down Main. The shunter would couple the engine on and connect the brake pipe to the first coach at the north end of the station, often watched by people on the platform. On one occasion when I was in North box the shunter connected up the vacuum pipe but forgot to sling the coupling over the hook. Upon departure the locomotive began to haul its train forward with only the vacuum pipe for drawgear. It only made it on to the level crossing before the pipe was torn away with a bang and, with an in-rush of air, the brakes automatically applied, bringing the train to a sudden stand, the loco' and first coach straddling the crossing. There was a massive traffic jam in Paignton that afternoon as all road traffic was compelled to wait while the shunter found a spare pipe in his cabin with which to effect a hasty repair and so get the train on the move again.

CHAPTER TEN

THE TAIL END

One of the last boxes I learnt on the district was Totnes, spending a couple of spare afternoons there sometime after I had "taken on" at the others. I had intended to spend a bit more time learning there but a couple of weeks after those initial afternoons the roster clerk was having difficulty arranging cover for sickness and asked me if I would go to Totnes to work the early turn for four days. Although one of the Newton Abbot district boxes, Totnes did not fall under the responsibility of the District Inspector at Exeter but rather under his counterpart, Arthur Thornton, at Plymouth. I had not been formally examined by the Plymouth DI but agreed with the roster clerk that I should go to Totnes on the Monday. The four shifts passed without event and it was a further two months before I was rostered back, this time for a single late turn on a Wednesday afternoon.

Taking over the box just before 2pm, I settled in for the shift. The first up train was the 13.45 Plymouth to Paddington which was booked to call at Totnes at 14.14. I looked down from the vantage point of the bay window as the train arrived in the up platform, watching the passengers board, some with luggage, some being seen off by relatives. From the front carriage a solitary person alighted. Wearing a black railway greatcoat and looking rather "inspectorish" he made his way towards the box, entered the door at platform level and climbed the stairs to the operating floor. From the blue socks he was wearing and the blue and white striped Marks and Spencer shirt I surmised that this was Harold Joiner, Arthur's assistant at Plymouth, whom I had heard all about, out on a casual afternoon visit. As soon as he spoke in his Yorkshire accent my suspicion was confirmed. After expressing surprise at meeting a new reliefman he enquired as to when I had seen Mr Thornton for my examination. Guardedly I revealed that no official exam had taken place to which Harold took off his coat, sat down on the wide ledge of the bay window and declared that he should therefore stay and watch me a while, finishing with the suggestion "why don't ye make a mash".

So I put the kettle on to make tea whilst exchanging conversation and going about the working of the box. Being a forthright Yorkshireman who had moved to Plymouth from Wath near Sheffield, Harold was not fully accepted by the Devonian and Cornish signalmen he supervised, nevertheless he never created a fuss about the fact that I hadn't "signed" for Totnes. Indeed I never did actually sign a competence slip for Totnes but worked it many times. After a good old chinwag he caught the 10.23 Manchester back to Plymouth at 15.50, just right for a four thirty finish!

I was to meet Harold on two subsequent occasions years later, confounding him again both times. The first was in Plymouth panel when I was there from Reading as a Tester with the S&T testing the signalling alterations for the new High Speed Train depot at Laira. The second was when he entered the box at Par in Cornwall to find I was back in the traffic department as one of the regular signalmen there and he had not known of my appointment. Nor had Arthur told him that, in this instance, he had come and passed me out for the box. But these are both stories for another occasion.

Sitting on the up platform looking out on the station, passenger loops and centre through lines Totnes was a pleasant box to work. The station's down side buildings and canopy looked a little forlorn, being the remnants from a fire that had claimed the rest of the structure in 1962. Behind the box the busy creamery, which had opened in 1934, was housed in the former Engine House originally built for Brunel's abortive South Devon atmospheric railway. Atmospheric operation never reached Totnes, the Italianate design engine house not actually ever being fitted out with an engine. The creamery could be noisy but it generated traffic for the railway and therefore shunting for the signalman. Whilst the loaded six-wheeler milk tanks were picked up by 6A21 around eight o'clock every evening, on its way from St Erth to London, the empties were detached from the down Acton at Hackney at around 01.15 in the morning. These were then tripped out to Totnes by Exeter trip No. 7 (7B74) which departed Riverside Yard at 04.35, arriving Totnes at 05.50 after dropping any other local traffic at Hackney Yard on the way and having picked up the milk tanks. There was thus plenty of activity for the early turn signalman shunting this trip as soon as he relieved the night man. Following shunting at Totnes the engine, either a class 46 (Peak) or 50 (Hoover), would then return light to Exeter leaving the signalman to get breakfast underway.

Early and late turn Chargemen were provided at Totnes to deal with shunting the tanks. This activity only took up a small proportion of their shifts which were otherwise spent assisting with the despatch of passenger trains. One of these Chargemen was Colin Harmes who had rejoined the railway at Totnes following redundancy from the nearby Dart Valley Railway during a downturn in that line's fortunes. Colin had started his career as a fireman at Nine Elms on the Southern. Like myself he was therefore a "Green Badger", as the Western men liked to call anyone that had moved onto the "Chocolate and Cream" railway from the Southern. The nickname alluded to the colour of the cap badge following nationalisation when each Region retained its own colour. Colin sported a moustache and mutton chop sideburns that suited the appearance of a Victorian steam driver. In the evenings he would come across to the box to share a pot of tea and reminisce whilst waiting for the St Erth to arrive, setting himself down on the wide ledge of the bay window where most visitors enjoyed to sit.

One morning when Colin was on duty an up northern train hauled by "Peak" 46 004 failed in-section at Brent. Following behind was an empty continuous welded rail (CWR) train on its way back to Hookagate. Arrangements were made for the rail train to push the passenger through to Totnes where a fresh engine would be waiting, sent down from Newton Abbot. I had my camera with

46 007 with an ex GWR Toad brake van behind and empty CWR train propels a failed passenger train into the up platform line at Totnes. Sister locomotive No. 46 004 had failed at Brent whilst hauling the passenger train. *(C. Harmes)*

me that day so called across to Colin that he might like to snap a couple of shots for me of the failed train being assisted in by the CWR. Colin came over and borrowed the camera. In due course the passenger arrived in the platform with sister "Peak" 46 007 providing power from behind whilst still towing its own train. When Colin came bounding back to the box I asked him if he had got any good shots. "Plenty mate" he said enthusiastically "I've used the whole film up".

On a future occasion the 10.20 Penzance to Leeds developed engine trouble. Having coasted down from Marley Tunnel the loco' expired before passing the advanced starter into the section towards Dainton. It was a beautifully sunny day following a cold start. Frost still lay in the shadows where the sun had not reached. The hour was not long after 1pm, so by the time I had organised for a rescue engine to come down from Newton Abbot and cross over to go onto the rear of the train, so as to drag it back into the four track section of the station, Guy Hill had arrived to relieve me. He was none too pleased to have to pick up sorting out the rest of the rescue and to deal with the stack of trains building up behind, including the Up "Limited" (10.55 ex Penzance) which I had turned into the up platform to wait events some half hour earlier. Having travelled down from Teignmouth that morning on the "Owl" I had planned to return home on the 14.14 from Totnes but seeing as how the failed train had still not been dragged back into the station by twenty past two I decided to catch the 10.40 Paddington and head west to Plymouth to go shopping instead. By the time I returned on the 13.55 Penzance the up line was back to normal. We sailed through the centre Up Main at Totnes. Guy was looking out from the box so I waved to him in recognition.

Locomotives that had been repaired at Laira were often first tested out on the main line before being returned to traffic. A run up to Totnes and back, over Hemerdon and Rattery banks, provided a good test. Light engines would therefore be sent through on a regular basis for the Totnes signalman to cross them over and send them back towards Plymouth. Accompanying the driver would often be a group of fitters to ensure their handiwork had been successful and to be available to make further running repairs should the need arise. It could sometimes be a comical sight to see an engine arrive in the through road, its cab crammed full of overall clad railwaymen who might mill around the engine before climbing aboard again and disappearing back from whence they had come. Passengers, gathered on the platform, must have been quite bemused by the sight.

With a frame of 111 levers Totnes box was quite large. It had been extended in 1943 when a new up loop had been brought into use. This addition, on top of having taken over the work of nearby Ashburton Junction in 1933, precipitating the extension. A new frame had been placed in the back of the box leaving access to the windows at the front, one pair of which had been built out to form a bay over the platform. Following the extension, clearly visible in newer brick, this bay was no longer central but it continued to be very useful to see under the footbridge and along the up platform to the west end of the station. The end windows nearest the footbridge were whitewashed to provide privacy from anyone who might gaze in. With the stove unusually located against the end wall of the box nearest the footbridge, an extended pipe, with cowl on top, protruded from the roof to take the smoke away above the footbridge. There was a logical reason for this. The original lever frame had been in the front of the box and therefore the stove, train register desk, lockers, telephones, etc., had all been positioned against the back wall. These had to be moved to allow the new lever frame to be installed whilst the old frame was still in use. They were thus relocated to the front and end of the extension, the only place available for them at the time.

With only the one coal stove in such a large box, the train register desk, table, chair and armchair were all clustered close by, at the low numbered end of the frame. There was an inside toilet here and also a sink. The block instrument with its attendant bell to Dainton and the train describer unit and bell to Plymouth panel were positioned at the extreme left hand end of the block shelf too. There was a massively long illuminated diagram depicting the layout which used twin red lights to show when track circuits were occupied.

The method of working to Plymouth was by track circuit block. This did not require the same co-operative action as demanded by absolute block. If the track circuits to the overlap of the first Plymouth signal showed clear then the Totnes signalman was free to send the next train forward. Similarly once an up train had passed beyond the overlap of the Totnes home signal the next train could be sent forward from Brent by Plymouth. The Down Advanced Starting signal did not therefore have a white stripe on its lever. The lever itself could be pulled at any time, even if the section was occupied.

Once the track circuits cleared the signal would change to green. All of the individual track circuits on each of the two lines through the section to Brent were summated into single indications on the diagram so it was not possible to determine the progress of a train at any particular time. The section also included the twin bores of Marley Tunnel. As an afterthought an electric indicator had been fitted to the block shelf which showed either tunnel clear or tunnel occupied, worked by the two individual track circuits through the tunnel, one on each road. This was a useful addition as in the event of a track circuit failure at least we could determine whether or not it was a track circuit in the tunnel at fault. This helped when carrying out Regulation 15 (Examination of the Line) as tunnels had to be dealt with in a particular way that was different from the rest of the line. Being twin bores was a bonus as a problem on one line meant we could still operate the other normally.

The indicator of course pointed to occupied whenever a train was in the tunnel, whichever line it was on. With careful attention to timing and in combination with the illuminated diagram it was usually possible to work out which train was in the tunnel, even when there were trains travelling in both directions. In the case of a down train this gave the Totnes signalman some comfort that it had reached the tunnel and so conquered Rattery, the remaining uphill stretch to Wrangaton being far less onerous.

A train describer at Plymouth tracked train movements, displaying the headcode of each train in berths on the panel, relevant to their position shown by the illuminated red track lights. This standard Western Region system was electro-mechanical, using relay and uniselector technology copied from post office telephone exchanges. Indeed the headcodes (or descriptions) were input by the signalman using a telephone type rotating dial. This limited the second (alpha) digit to just ten letters restricting the variety of codes which could be displayed (only A, B, C, E, F, M, O, V, X and Z were available - see Appendix C). With no S, trains destined for the Southern Region were assigned the letter O but this left no letter for the Scottish Region. Trains for Scotland were described using M as they first had to travel onto the London Midland Region. Thus 1S27, the 07.30 Plymouth to Edinburgh, masqueraded as 1M27. The visual displays on the panel comprised four back lit rotating counters driven by the relay circuitry. As trains stepped along the panel each display would count out as the next counted up. The sound of this activity was a useful stimulus to the signalman to draw his attention to dealing further with the train, although at busy times this added to the noise level in the panel. The mechanical nature of this stepping operation sometimes meant the code would corrupt during its transfer along the panel by occasionally missing a step or two.

Modern technology in the form of a device known as a fringe unit was provided at Totnes to allow the transfer of descriptions between there and Plymouth. This comprised the relay equipment housed in a cabinet downstairs in the locking room and a set-up and display unit on the block shelf for the signalman. This unit contained the telephone type dial, set-up, clear out and cancel keys plus a number of description display windows made up of the rotating counters covering set-up, last sent, arrived, first and second trains approaching. For down trains the description was set up with the dial and then transmitted forward to Plymouth by pressing a button when trains entered the section from Dainton. In the up direction, descriptions were received automatically as trains passed Ivybridge. Providing the ambient noise level was not too great, it was possible, if you knew what to listen for, to hear the faint tick, tick of the relay equipment downstairs receiving and storing the pulses of an incoming description from Plymouth before it was then counted up onto the fringe unit for display to the signalman. Thus it was possible to move across to the unit to acknowledge the receipt and silence the alarm buzzer just as it sprang into life. This apparent clairvoyant ability would bemuse any visitor who might be in the box at the time!

The ability of the apparatus to corrupt numbers sometimes meant that the description of an approaching train displayed in the fringe unit required interpretation to attribute it to the correct train or a telephone call to Plymouth to confirm its identity. At other times the equipment would just lock up completely, at which point the describing would have to revert to using the emergency block bell. Maintenance and fault rectification on the fringe describer was the responsibility of the Totnes lineman, Roy Tucker and his assistant, Roy Andrews. Roy Tucker was a gentleman, always helpful and cheerful. He and his mate had a split patch, looking after the Totnes and

The fringe train describer unit and emergency block bell at Totnes. These provided communication to Plymouth Panel for the describing of trains and the exchange of bells. Codes for transmitting are set up using the telephone type dial. These then appear in the windows directly above. On transmission to Plymouth the code moves to the Last Sent display at the top right. On the left are displays for an arriving up train and two approaching trains. *(Author)*

Dainton areas and down the Paignton branch. I would see a fair bit of them therefore in their pressed blue overalls going about routine maintenance activities during which they would always call at the box for a cup of tea and sometimes rest to partake of their lunch. The equipment was so well looked after that it was rare to need to call Roy to a problem, except perhaps to the temperamental train describer that needed his special touch. Roy's base was a cabin on the down side dock at Totnes. In common with most lineman's huts on the Western it was built from signal box parts, looking like the top half of a small box placed directly on the ground. Entering this building was like arriving in Aladdin's cave. All manner of signalling spare parts and recovered equipment adorned shelves, sat on benches or hung from the walls and ceiling.

Roy and his mate normally worked a day shift but were on-call outside of these hours. Before going about their business Roy would telephone across to Totnes box to leave details of their whereabouts for the day with Guy Hill or Keith Down or whoever was on duty. Thus if anyone needed to get in touch with them in a hurry, the signalman at Totnes would be able to advise their likely location at any time. When across at Paignton they availed themselves of a small cabin alongside North box where they kept a few more of their stores and a working area.

The one Rest Day Reliefman based at Totnes had a unique job. Since 1973 when Plymouth Panel had assumed control west of Totnes and the old boxes at Brent, Ivybridge, Hemerdon, Tavistock Junction and Laira Junction shut, only one rest day post had been retained and this covered just Totnes. The incumbent, Len Kent, was therefore only rostered for three shifts a week, one early turn, one late turn and one night turn, giving each of the three resident men their day off. With the gap for rest in between, these three disparate shifts were often the sum total of his week's work.

It was quite an envied job which Len had landed for himself. He was an experienced signalman, having been a special class reliefman in Bristol before the new panel there had swept all the old boxes away. He boasted of being the only Bristol man who was qualified as a north side and a south side reliefman. Apparently it was usual to stay one side or the other of Temple Meads. His knowledge had extended not only to the large mechanical boxes in and around Bristol but to the two big power boxes of Bristol East and West. Rather than go into the new panel when it opened he opted for redundancy which meant he could select a job from whatever vacancies were available at the time.

He chose Torre, moving to what would become his eventual retirement home in Torquay. When the plum Rest Day job at Totnes subsequently fell vacant no one in the division could touch him for seniority. The position at Totnes only took Len one step closer to his substantive grade but of course he continued to be paid at his pre-redundancy special class rate. Not bad for working three days a week. Occasionally he would be taken off his roster to cover holidays or sickness at Totnes and once in a while would work a turn back at Torre on a spare day.

He was put under pressure to learn other boxes in the Newton Abbot area based on his relief position and his evident abilities. He always stood his ground, maintaining that as a Rest Day man with only one box on his roster he could not be compelled to learn anywhere else. He was of course absolutely right. Further pressure was brought to bear that he should apply for more senior roles closer to his substantive grade as and when they became available but Len always resisted, having made up his mind that Totnes was just fine and that retirement was not that far off. The railway might have saved money if he had taken on a higher grade role but there would have been no benefit for Len himself.

He was a great big bloke with a mass of curly unkempt hair like a giant brillo pad. He would run his hands through to brush it - all sorts would fall out. He wore braces and a leather belt to keep his uniform trousers up, making him look more like a farmer than a signalman. The belt was the sort with which you might expect a strict father to tan the hide of his errant children. He brought his snap (food) and belongings in an ex-army rucksack that had seen a lot of service, carrying it under his arm because the straps had long since broken. His snap usually comprised thick slices of bread, cheese and pickle, a proper ploughman's meal. Working the box was effortless for him, the levers were like twigs in his hands. What a character he was, a cartoonist's dream, and what stories he could tell for his 40 plus years of railway service. I can remember a night when Len was on duty and I was next door at Dainton box. He didn't let me away from the telephone until the early hours, telling me about his days in and around Bristol!

Having dropped down from Dainton through Combe Fishacre and Littlehempston on its way west the line ran on the level across the river Dart and

Totnes box with its double bay window sat imposingly on the up platform. The left hand extension, in newer brick gives a lop-sided impression to the whole structure. Even without the bay, the other windows are vaulted forward and there is a nice angled piece at the right hand end. The extra tall stove pipe is visible plus the additional roof vent. Milk churns are being unloaded in the dairy behind. (Author)

through Totnes station before immediately hitting the 1 in 66 rising gradient at the start of Rattery Bank. The Down Advanced Starting signal, a colour light plated T100, was positioned well beyond the station, being planted right in the middle of the 1 in 66 grade. It was local practise never to let trains run up to this signal to wait the road to Brent as they would struggle to get moving again. Instead they would be held back on level ground in the Down Platform or on the Down Main so at least they were able to build some momentum before the whole weight of the train came under the negative influence of gravity. It was not unusual for down trains to be delayed at Totnes, especially if the previous train had called at the station whilst the second approached from Dainton. The block sections on Plymouth panel were no shorter than those that had latterly existed when the few remaining mechanical boxes at Brent, Ivybridge and Hemerdon were closed which meant trains could often get checked or stopped at Totnes. The Up and Down Passenger Loops held 60 and 55 SLUs respectively but longer trains could fit on the Main lines.

At their exit ends the two passenger loops trailed into the main line. A series of three mechanically operated detonator placers were attached to each line prior to the convergence and beyond the respective protecting signals. These worked in unison with the movement of the points such that one set placed detonators on the rail of one line whilst the other removed detonators from the adjacent line. Thus if a train incorrectly passed the protecting signal and moved towards these points when laying in the wrong position, the driver would be alerted to stop by the exploding detonators.

I was on duty one Saturday night at Totnes when engineering work was published to take place between Brent and Ivybridge. A tamping machine had been stabled in the Down Siding ready to take part in the work once the last down train had passed and the engineer had taken possession of the line. The machine operator came to the box to enquire when he would be allowed to proceed forward to Brent. I explained that he would have to wait for the 21.20 Bristol and the 18.30 Paddington, which called at Totnes but which was running late, before I could give him the road out of the siding and let him on to Plymouth Panel's area.

The signals were "off" through the middle for the first of these two trains when the operator sauntered back across to his machine out of sight at the other end of the station. Sometime after the Bristol had hurried through the London, which was well late, was belled off Aller Junction so I pulled off for it via the Down Platform. A moment or two later the piercing klaxon of the tamper sounded, followed by the high revving noise of its engine as the machine moved off. Then came the thudding sound of its wheels landing on mother earth as the machine ran off the end of the trap points in the siding. I replaced the platform starting signal to danger to protect the scene, just in case the tamper had fouled the line and waited for advice as to what had happened. The track circuit through the points showed occupied on the box diagram signifying that the interrupter in the traps had been run through. The operator had mistaken the platform Starting signal, positioned between the siding and Down Platform line, as applying to him rather than the ground disc to the left of the trap points. Once it was ascertained that the Platform line was clear I was able to instruct the driver of the now arrived London to proceed. Needless to say there was no engineering work done that night!

My very first turn alone at Aller Junction was on one Monday night. The car journey from Teignmouth would normally take around fifteen minutes so, on being ready to leave home at 9.30pm, I decided to take a leisurely drive. A light drizzle was falling that evening after a prolonged dry spell. I really did take it deliberately slowly out of Teignmouth so as not to arrive at Aller much before ten to ten. However, for some unexplainable reason which baffled me then and has baffled me ever since the car skidded just out of town on Bishopsteignton Road, hit the bank and rolled over 360 degrees thus sustaining serious damage. Needless to say I was a little late in relieving John Congdon that night, eventually being dropped off at the box by the tow truck. Fortunately I was not injured but had to manage without the car for quite a few weeks whilst it was repaired.

Aller I reached by train and foot for the rest of the week before I then collected a bicycle to assist in getting about. Some boxes were relatively easy to reach others, like Exminster, were more difficult, especially for early turn. The 15 mile ride took around 90 minutes, largely due to the long slog up hill out of Teignmouth followed, after the brief but welcome free wheel down into Dawlish, by an even harder climb back out. So early turn meant a 4.15am start from my digs. Coming home in the afternoon I found it preferable to cycle the level shorter distance into Exeter along the side of the canal and catch the train back to Teignmouth from there.

One morning the rain was teeming down when I left to go to Exminster. I was soaked to the skin long before reaching the box. How glad I was of the coal stove by which to dry both myself and my clothes. It was a good job the box was well elevated so that no one could see in! Stuck out on the flat ground of the Exe Estuary, the lofty box could be a draughty place with the wind finding its way between the timbers of the weatherboard walls. The lights and sound from the Swan's Nest public house at the entrance to the old station beckoned but were out of bounds. Out across the river behind the box could be seen Topsham, Exton, Lympstone and Exmouth. The modern blocks of accommodation at the Lympstone commando camp looking incongruous in contrast to Peter's Tower standing on Lympstone's picturesque quay side. Away to the south, on the western bank of the estuary, down towards Powderham, was the isolated slate-hung Turf Hotel. Perched on a spit of land that formed the river side of Turf Lock, at the entrance to the six mile long Exeter Canal, it dated from 1820 when the canal had been built, some 26 years before the railway opened. There was no public road to this hotel but it was a popular venue with sailors and walkers. Turf Lock accommodation crossing gave access across the line not far from the hotel and this was subject to a special instruction in respect of usage by the fire brigade, probably precipitated by an incident in the past. The Fire Brigade Control would advise the Railway Control in the event of them having to attend. Railway Control would then contact the signalman at Exminster so that trains could be cautioned until the all clear was given.

Following some heavy overnight snow, some fourteen inches having fallen, I had another interesting journey out to Exminster. This time it was by passenger train. The late turn signalman the previous evening had switched out and escaped before the roads became impassable. The night turn man had not been able to make it through. I was "waiting orders" the next morning and so was asked to catch a train at Teignmouth that would make a special stop at Exminster to drop me off. The blizzards had blocked many roads, even the railway between Bristol and Taunton had been blocked by drifts so the service was in disarray. A Deltic railtour was booked to run from Paddington to Kingswear but this only made it as far as Temple Meads before being turned back. The Newton Abbot and Exeter snow ploughs had been busy during the night successfully keeping the main line through Devon open.

I travelled up to Exminster on the footplate, the driver halting his train on the Up Main opposite the signal box. With the collar of my greatcoat turned up and cap pulled down tight on my head I climbed down off the locomotive, slamming the cab door closed behind me. Now Exminster had once had a station far more lavish than its needs. It had closed in 1964 and where its two wide island platforms had once been there were now voids between the main and loop lines, the straight main lines having been raised and ballasted for speed. My feet dropped off the last step and into the snow on the ballast shoulder. I then stepped back into the void and found myself waist high in snow. The train moved off, drawing powdery snow up behind it, and there I was, a black speck marooned in the middle of a white landscape like a button on the front of a snowman.

Opposite, on the down side of the line stood the signal box. The wind had blown from the north depositing snow against the wooden walls and windows of the box which had then frozen. Formed against the north side of the building was a massive drift sculpted such that it tapered to a point at window level. Somewhere within it, at ground level, was the box door. I felt like I was not really equipped to be here.

Heaving myself back up on to the ballast shoulder I crossed the two main lines before dropping into the other void, over the Down Goods Loop and across to the box. With gloved hands I scooped away at the snow to find the door, unlocked it and pushed it with my shoulder to break the frozen seal. The door opened and much of the remaining drift fell in behind it. I would need the coal shovel to help me clear it but the first priority was to get the stove lit. Upstairs I was met with a strange sight. The impression was as if almost every window had been fitted with panes of frosted glass. There was light coming in but no view out, except through the southerly end of the box. With damp paper and plenty of ash and clinker in the bottom the fire was slow to take.

After telephoning Dawlish Warren I went through the opening procedure but only the colour light distants responded to their levers. All the semaphore running signals remained stubbornly frozen "off". I switched out again, collected the coal shovel and a brush and set out into the white world to try and free up the signals. I scraped and brushed around the wheels and pulled at the wires to get them running through the pulleys. A bitter, icy wind was blowing down across the estuary which continued to stir up more snow and bank up the drifts. More alarmingly it blocked out what muffled sounds there were such that trains approached in silence, surprising me with their closeness before I spotted them. It was not really safe for me to be out alone in the prevailing conditions, besides I was making little headway. It would take hours to get all the main line signals free.

Back up the line, the signal box stood amidst the temporary wilderness, a thin line of smoke being sucked from its stove pipe and played with by the wind. Returning to the box I was pleased to find the fire well taken. It was good to get inside and start to thaw out. The warmth was relative, the box thermometer showed only a few degrees above freezing. It would be some time before the fire had any real impact on the big draughty wooden signal box. Appraising the controller at Plymouth of the situation we both reluctantly agreed I should abandon any attempt to get Exminster open at this stage. He arranged with Exeter for the next down train to stop and pick me up. Before leaving I banked up the fire and closed the damper. It would take hours to burn through but add a little warmth ready for whoever ventured there next. In fact the service had to contend with Exminster being closed for a further three days before the freezing conditions abated sufficiently for a gang of men to get all the signals and points working again.

A blanket of snow at Exminster was not an annual occurrence but flooding often was on the low lying estuary fields, especially in the Spring. The slightly elevated level of the railway meant that it usually escaped the floods, the resultant scene appearing as if the route was built on a causeway across some inland lake. There were times when the water rose above the sleepers in one or two spots and even above the rails but the railway continued to operate under caution.

Another perennial problem here in the Spring but by no means restricted to Exminster was that of lambs and sheep finding their way through the fence to graze alongside the line. Trains would have to be cautioned through the section under Regulation 13 (Animals on Line) until the permanent way men could attend to usher the errant creatures back through the fence and make repairs. One day, with sheep on the line, a "Western" running light to Laira was cautioned forward by the signalman at City Basin box. It was sometime before the engine came into view at Exminster, travelling at walking pace with a small herd of sheep ambling along in front, ignoring the secondman's comical efforts to shoo them from the line as he strode in front of the loco' wildly gesticulating with his arms. We had to corral the animals near the box to await the farmer to come and collect them.

I have mentioned fish specials earlier. Surprisingly these still ran from time to time, usually employing open wagons which were not always sheeted. Arriving for late turn at Exminster one Saturday a train of mackerel, up from Cornwall, was stabled in the Up Siding, Riverside Yard having been full that morning, Being the weekend, the train remained in the siding until an engine and crew came to collect it on Monday morning. The wagons, in this instance, were sheeted, fortunately, as otherwise the gulls would have picked the contents clean. Nevertheless they were driven to distraction by the taunting smell, as was I all afternoon and evening Saturday, all twelve hours of Sunday when I came back, and again on Monday. The wagons stank of salty fish, as did the whole area from the melting ice that drained out of the wagons all Saturday afternoon to contaminate the siding. The box windows stayed firmly shut that weekend.

Getting my car back from the garage made life easier again but, as is often the case after major repair, the car did not feel or handle the same. Dipping into my savings and with the help of a small loan from the bank I traded in the Wolseley for a brand new Volkswagen Polo from Renwicks in Newton Abbot. Appropriately it was mint green in colour. Being seen driving a new car soon brought ribald comments from other signalmen about the monetary benefit of life on the relief. The extra money may well have been a bonus but the role required the ability to go anywhere, any time, thus a reliable car was essential. Whether collecting my thoughts, at being woken at 5am, to remember that today was to be an early turn at Dawlish Warren or looking forward expectantly throughout the morning to 2pm and a busy late turn at Newton Abbot, the variety that the job produced was a bonus in itself, even if there were more late and night turns rather than earlies. But early turns there were and how enjoyable they could be in the summer months at a place like Dawlish Warren, with the sun blazing down, extra trains in the timetable and the expectation of a pleasant afternoon and evening off.

Dawlish Warren was a strange place, a caravan and arcade city. In the summer it was alive with holidaymakers, in the winter it was a ghost town frequented only by local hardy dog walkers or couples out for a bracing constitutional. The golf course, which extended out onto the wind blown spit, was popular all year, not just with golfers but with bird life that frequented the estuary. Behind the course, extending upstream beyond Starcross were mud flats and wetlands subject to the rise and fall of the tides. At low tide the wading birds

The interior of Dawlish Warren box with polished lino' and almost a full complement of levers in the 58 lever frame. The cloth can be seen draped over an F.P.L. lever.
(Author)

would feed from the waters edge whilst men dug worms for bait or collected peeler crabs. At night a high tide would bring fishermen in flat bottom boats, each equipped with a single lantern on a pole to mark their position. The spectacle of these lanterns on the water presented an eerie sight in the small hours when viewed from the solitude of the signal box.

A few trains called at the Warren for holidaymakers and day trippers, otherwise most rushed through on the main lines in the centre of the four track stretch that the box controlled. The platform lines were sometimes used to loop a freight. The Down Platform could hold 75 SLUs plus engine and brake van. On the up side the platform line was shorter but extended into a goods loop which benefited from a spur up to a set of buffer stops. This unusual arrangement allowed a freight of 74 SLUs to be sidetracked and, if needs be, drawn into the spur extension to allow an up passenger train to call at the platform. The afternoon all stations unit from Exeter that called on the down sometimes brought notices or vital stores like soap and toilet rolls. At other times notices were sent by post to the Warren Golf Club behind the box necessitating a visit to the club house for the signalman.

The railway runs north to south here alongside the Exe. Down trains could be spotted two miles away as they rounded the curve at Starcross heading for Cockwood harbour, long before they passed the Distant signal. By contrast, the view in the opposite direction was only as far as Langstone Rock where the line turns south westerly striking out along the famous sea wall. Up trains would round the corner, leaning into the curve, before passing the chocolate and cream camping coaches parked in the up sidings which, like the caravans, were only occupied during the season.

Dawlish Warren box conveyed a rustic charm inside. The levers had not been painted for decades and many retained polished brass leads, rather than the newer engraved ivorine version, bearing the lever number, its function and those levers that had to be pulled first to release the lever in question. The facing points had short track circuits installed through them to lock the facing point lock levers but these were indicated by "locked/free" needle indicators on the shelf rather than track circuit indicators or an illuminated diagram. Indeed many of the boxes in the area did not have illuminated diagrams, most retaining red banner indicators mounted on the shelf. Sheets of yellowed newspaper, their old stories bleached by the light, were pinned to the window frames around the top panes of glass in the front windows behind the block instruments to reduce the effect of the evening sun which would otherwise shine straight in. Rather than the usual wooden clock, either round or drop case, the Warren sported a neat little brass clock of the variety manufactured for the Great Western Railway by Kay's of Paris. I always thought this association rather uncharacteristic of the GWR. When Dawlish box was switched out the signalman at the Warren had to remember to operate a plunger that rang the platform bell on the station at Dawlish to inform staff of approaching trains.

Although it was just a few minutes walk from home and therefore very handy, Teignmouth was a fairly straightforward box to work. With the through siding from Old Quay and all the other sidings now abolished only a crossover remained. Normal working was therefore "straight up and down" but traffic was steady, the box being absolutely essential as a block post in order to keep trains moving, especially with the extended times for those which called at Dawlish and Teignmouth stations.

Positioned right on the ramp of the down platform, at the west end of the station and in the shadow of Shute Hill bridge, the box always rekindled my original thoughts of Teignmouth as being a grey, uninteresting place. Watching the activity on the station and in the car park behind the box brought distraction at times of mental laziness. Down stopping trains halted with the locomotive just at the top of the platform ramp, a few feet short of the box. The track had a slight cant through the station which produced an amusing phenomenon whenever a stopping train arrived. On finally coming to rest there would be a short moment of time after which, the locomotive, seemingly in need of a rest, would relax on to its springs, its body tipping a few degrees further towards the platform. This was something I always noticed, the movement being more pronounced with certain classes of locomotive.

The low height of Teignmouth box, along with its tight proximity to the down line meant that if a down train was passing, or departing the station, at the same time as an up train ran through then only the roofs of the vehicles on the up train could be seen. To assist the signalman to catch sight of the tail lamp of an up train in this situation a mirror had been installed. This purpose built apparatus was placed on the up side of the line diagonally opposite the box, the mirror being positioned at an appropriate angle for the signalman to see the rear of the train as it receded away. The mirror was bracketed to a signal post that was topped with a finial.

The tail lamp, for the signalman, signifies safety even though it displays a red light. This light, at the tail end of each train, marks an obstruction to a following train but to the signalman proves that the train is complete and therefore it is safe to allow another to approach through the section from the signal box in rear. Looking out for the tail lamp perched on a bracket on the last vehicle is an instinctive action for a signalman, as is watching for any sign of danger along the length of a train such as a door open, or on the catch, or a hot axle box.

Whilst the tail lamp might normally signify that the train had arrived or passed safely and so left a clear section behind, additional care was needed at the large station boxes like Newton Abbot East and West over and above the simple observance of the tail lamp to ensure this was in fact the case. With trains dividing and detaching, or indeed attaching, vehicles in the station it was often the case that carriages, vans or a shunt engine would still be sitting in the section when the affected train passed the box complete with tail lamp to continue its journey. Such moves were normally known about, either from the working timetable, advice from the shunters, or by conference between the signalmen. Occasionally they were not! It was always imperative therefore to assume the habit of checking the track circuit indications on the signal box diagram or glancing towards the station for a visual check before deciding or not to send the "Train out of Section" signal. To complicate the issue at Newton Abbot was the existence of the mid-station signals which meant that, dependent on where the remaining vehicles were standing they could either be in the section or safely within "station limits" of the box in rear. In the latter instance the section would be clear enabling the "Train out of Section" signal to be sent.

At Torre it was necessary for the signalman to go to the window and look down for the tail lamp, so high was the operating floor from the track. Not only did the box sit on the up platform but it was unusually tall, being three storeys high, its all round windows giving a panoramic view over the station footbridge to the rooftops of Torre and to the old yard behind. This yard was now closed to rail traffic but, like many similar yards, still provided home to the local coal merchant - in this case Western Fuels. In its heyday, Torre yard had served the whole of the Torquay area, there having been no separate freight facilities at Torquay itself. The cavernous lower floor of the box, which went down to track level inside the platform, housed the cranks and wheels that connected the levers from the floor above to the outside world. On the middle floor was the lower part of the lever frame with its mechanical interlocking, electric locks and contact boxes. An inside staircase served the three storeys punctuated by a landing at the middle level.

The driver's view of Torquay box, situated at the Paignton end of the down platform. It was constructed from stone in keeping with the station buildings. (Author)

Largely being add-on features, the toilet facilities at each box varied in terms of size and location. They might be outside in a hut, under the stairs, downstairs in the locking room, in a converted porch cupboard or in a specially constructed cubicle at one end of the operating floor. The variety could form the subject of a book in its own right. At Torre the toilet was at the far end of the middle floor. The throne was enormous, the largest I ever encountered, with a massive, heavy wooden seat that you didn't sit on - you climbed on! In fact it was so large and heavy that when down it rested on specially provided wooden supports each side of the bowl, rather than on the porcelain itself. A cast iron cistern with operating chain and handle completed the facility. The view from this draughty toilet was of the wooden locking room floor, the covered locking itself and the coal yard through large glazed windows to the rear of the box.

The gradient through Torre station, at 1 in 55, was particularly steep as the line dropped towards Torquay eventually reaching almost sea level at Paignton. Up trains would growl around the reverse curves through the station on their way towards Kingskerswell. Down trains would coast cautiously by, wheel flanges squealing on the inside of the rails. Not all trains called at Torre. Most of the locals stopped together with just a couple of the long distance class 1s. The first train down in the morning in fact called for 12 minutes. This was the 04.25 from Newton Abbot that comprised a brake compartment coach and a van off the second portion of the papers. The extended stop was to allow for unloading of newspapers into the station building which was now used by the wholesaler as a sorting room.

Being a two-shift job (from 06.30 to 21.05), Torre was rarely open at the unearthly hour that this train called but the first job for the early turn signalman after opening up was to drop across to the station to collect an assortment of papers, not just for Torre but Aller Junction too. A stock of elastic bands were kept in the train register desk for securing the rolled up papers for Aller. These were given to the guard on the first up stopper to be hurled out as the train rattled through the junction. It was essential of course to ensure the guard of the unit and his driver received a tabloid each too.

My last shift as a Newton Abbot reliefman was on an August Saturday at Torquay, manning the box from 07.00 to 17.30 for the holiday traffic. It was another rest day worked too. My old colleague, Adrian Vaughan, who was on holiday in the area paid me a visit that day, which was rather fitting as I would be learning in Oxford Panel on the Monday, a place he chose not to go to when the mechanical boxes he knew and loved in the area were superseded by it.

EPILOGUE

This tale of signal box life must end here as, after what was a most enjoyable period on the relief at Newton Abbot, I moved on to Oxford to work in the panel box there - a totally new experience. Then, following a spell in signal engineering, I returned to enjoy further Western boxes in Somerset and Cornwall and, after a time working in Australia, had a stint in a number of mechanical boxes in central Scotland. But these experiences will have to be saved for a whole new "Entry in the Train Register".

So in conclusion, besides being a place of work the signal box is a way of life and a place from where you have time to look at the world, whether it be watching the variety of trains passing with their cargoes, both human and freight, or spying the silver outline of a jet airliner trailed by its exhaust stream as it cuts its way through a clear blue sky like a wire through cheese. It is a place where you can enjoy the bird song at first light and at dusk, and brew a cup of tea just when you fancy. On a clear night you can contemplate the stars, attempting to fathom the mystery of time and how it is that you are actually seeing something millions of years ago or gaze upon the moon and then view the earth's landscape from its mellow light.

At each end of the day you can marvel from the window at how the sky produces tints and patterns and sometimes shares the red hues of the shepherd's delight or, in the morning, the shepherd's warning. At the end of a rain storm you can be treated to the grandstand view of a rainbow. On frosty mornings you can be amazed by the white fur that hangs on every tree as if someone in heaven had sprinkled sugar icing during the night and by every cobweb revealed, draped like discarded lace across a fence or impaled between branches on a bush or between a roof edge and fascia board. You can step outside the box when the snow is falling and hear no sound and experience a feeling as if being enveloped in cotton wool. And when the snow stops falling you can marvel at a white landscape which, just for a short while, remains undisturbed from human violation.

There's a feeling of relaxed contentment in settling in for a night shift looking forward to the small hours with the warmth from the fire, some supper and a procession of various trains to come; the Papers, the Sleepers, the "Owl" and the "Waker", the milk empties, the blue spot, the parcels, the Postal and the loose coupled freights. Perhaps an hour or two of mellow music, easy listening from the radio before the descent of silence from man. A silence you can really hear.

This tail end of the story I am writing more than 33 years since the first time I was alone at Whiteball and these concluding paragraphs are being drawn up sitting at the table in Bewdley South signal box on the Severn Valley Railway. This is the nearest to the real thing as I remember it: there is a GWR lever frame with brass leads; 1947 style block instruments on the shelf; but West Country expresses do not thunder past. There are no loose coupled freights in the night, no Sleepers, no Postal and no Papers but there is the occasional Western Hydraulic.

Outside on the track a squirrel makes its way along the line, leaping from sleeper end to sleeper end, stopping occasionally to stand upright on the rail to check for predators. The afternoon sun shines through the windows onto the levers, picking out their bright colours and casting their parallel shadows across the brown linoleum floor. The block bell rings out two beats for "Train Entering Section"……

APPENDICES

APPENDIX A

Classes of Train

Class	Description	Code
1	Express passenger train, postal train, newspaper train, or breakdown van train or snow plough going to clear the line, or light locomotive going to assist disabled train. Officers' Special train not requiring to stop in section.	4
1	Royal Train.	4-4-4
2	Ordinary passenger train, mixed train, or breakdown train or snow plough NOT going to clear the line.	3-1
3	Express parcels train composed of vehicles permitted to run at 90 mph or over.	1-3-1
4	Freightliner train.	3-2-5
4	Parcels train, Company or express freight train composed of vehicles permitted to run at 75 mph or over.	3-1-1
5	Empty coaching stock train (not specially authorised to carry class 1 headcode).	2-2-1
6	(a) Fully-fitted Company or block train, parcels train or milk train.	5
6	(b) Ordinary fully-fitted express freight train.	4-1
7	Express freight train, not fully-fitted, but with brake force not less than that shown in Section E of the Working Manual for Rail Staff.	1-2-2
8	Freight train, not fully-fitted, but with brake force not less than that shown in Section E of the Working Manual for Rail Staff.	3-2

Class	Description	Code
9	Unfitted freight train (where specially authorised).	1-4
9	Freight train, Officers' Special train or Engineer's train requiring to stop in section.	2-2-3
0	Light locomotive, light locomotives coupled or locomotive with brake tender(s).	2-3
0	Locomotive with not more than two brake vans.	1-1-3
-	Trolley requiring to go into or pass through tunnel.	2-1-2
-	Train which can pass an out-of-gauge or exceptional load similarly signalled on the opposite or an adjoining line.	2-6-1
-	Train which cannot be allowed to pass an out-of-gauge load of any description on the opposite or an adjoining line between specified points.	2-6-2
-	Train which requires the opposite or an adjoining line to be blocked between specified points.	2-6-3
-	Opposite line, or an adjoining line used in the same or opposite direction, to be blocked for passage of train conveying out-of-gauge load.	1-2-6
-	Out-of-gauge load requiring to pass in wrong direction.	1-6-2

APPENDIX B

Other standard bell codes

Description of other bell codes	code
Call attention.	1
Train entering section.	2
Train approaching (where authorised).	1-2-1
Cancelling.	3-5
Last train signalled incorrectly described.	5-3
Warning Acceptance.	3-5-5
Line now clear in accordance with Regulation 4 for train to approach.	3-3-5
Train out of section, or obstruction removed.	2-1
Blocking back inside home signal.	2-4
Blocking back outside home signal.	3-3
Train or vehicles at a stand.	3-3-4
Locomotive assisting in rear of train.	2-2
Locomotive with one or two brake vans assisting in rear of train.	2-3-1
Locomotive arrived.	2-1-3
Train drawn back clear of section.	3-2-3
Obstruction Danger.	6
Train an unusually long time in section.	6-2
Stop and examine train.	7
Train passed without tail lamp. To box in advance.	9
" " " " " To box in rear.	4-5
Train divided.	5-5
Shunt train for following train to pass.	1-5-5
Train or vehicles running away in wrong direction.	2-5-5
Train or vehicles running away in right direction.	4-5-5
Opening of signal box.	5-5-5
Closing of signal box.	7-5-5
Closing of signal box where section signal is locked by the block.	5-5-7
Testing block indicators and bells.	16
Shunting into forward section.	3-3-2
Shunt withdrawn.	8
Working in wrong direction.	2-3-3
Train clear of section.	5-2
Train withdrawn.	2-5
Distant signal defective.	8-2
Home signal defective.	2-8
Automatic Half Barrier crossing defective.	8-4

APPENDIX C

Four Character Train Identification System

The first figure indicates the classification of the train (as in Appendix A).
The second character indicates the destination area or Region.
The third and fourth figures represent the individual number of the train or a route number.

The second character destination indications:

Letter	Denotes destination for trains originating and terminating within the Western Region
A	London Division
B	West of England Division
C	Cardiff Division
	Denotes destination Region for Inter-Regional trains leaving the Western Region
E	Eastern Region
M	London Midland Region
O	Southern Region
S	Scottish Region
V	Denotes Inter-Regional trains arriving from outside of the Western Region
F	Light Locomotive movements between depots and divisions
X	Royal Trains and trains conveying out-of-gauge and other exceptional loads
Z	Inter-Regional and Western Region excursion, military and special trains

Destination descriptions for Light Locomotives to main running and maintenance depots:

0F70	Old Oak Common	0F77	Plymouth (Laira)	0F82	Severn Tunnel Jc
0F71	Reading	0F78	St. Blazey	0F83	Newport (Ebbw Jc)
0F72	Oxford	0F79	Penzance	0F84	Cardiff (Canton)
0F73	Swindon	0F80	Gloucester	0F85	Margam
0F74	Bristol (Bath Road)	0F81	Worcester	0F86	Swansea (Landore)
0F76	Newton Abbot				

Destination descriptions for Inter-Divisional Light Locomotives other than those to main running and maintenance depots:

0F90	London Division	0F91	West of England Division
0F92	Cardiff Division		

Destination descriptions for Light Locomotives travelling Inter-Regionally:

0V00 To W.R.	0O00 To S.R.	0M00 To M.R.
0E00 To E.R.		

GLOSSARY

Every walk of life has created a language for its specific purpose. Throughout this book I have used jargon and terminology specific to railways and especially to signalling in order to bring realism and to capture everyday language from the railway of the time. Some of the words and phraseology are explained in the text but many require a separate explanation in order to assist the reader's comprehension. In some instances multiple phrases share the same derivation. Railway vocabulary varied throughout the length and breadth of British Railways, some terminology was common whilst some was specific to an area or even line. In this book everyday words and phrases common to the Western Region are used.

Backboard	A semaphore distant signal arm (but also used to refer to a colour light distant).
Backroad	A line avoiding or bypassing a town or station such as at Frome and Westbury.
Bang Road	A movement in the direction against the normal flow of traffic.
Block Block Section	Section of line between two signal boxes.
Block Indicator Block Instrument	Instrument which indicates the state of the block section between two signal boxes.
Blocking Back	The action of setting a train or vehicles back towards the block section approaching the signal box.
Block Shelf	The shelf fitted above the levers inside a signal box upon which the electrical instruments are placed.
Board	A semaphore signal arm (although used to describe a colour light signal also).

Booking Boy	A person, usually a school leaver, employed to maintain entries in the train register book, answer telephones and assist with chores and errands in the larger or busier signal boxes.
Call Attention	A single beat sent on the block bell to call the attention of the signalman in the adjacent box prior to exchanging another message by bell.
Check Checked	The action of a train being slowed but not stopped by virtue of the distant having to be kept at caution and perhaps one or more stop signals at danger.
Clearing Point	The point to which the line must be clear and locked before a train can be accepted from the signal box in rear. Usually 440 yards but sometimes less.
Detonators Dets	Audible signals comprising small metal caps containing an explosive charge that can be clamped to the rail by lead straps. These are compressed by the wheels of a passing train to cause them to be exploded and so create a loud noise to attract the attention of the driver.
Disc Dummy Dummies	A shunt signal in the form of a disc with a coloured stripe which is rotated to show a proceed indication.
Fitted Head	The first portion of a goods train where the wagons are fitted with the vacuum brake controlled from the locomotive in order to provide additional brake force for an otherwise loose coupled/unfitted train.
Footnotes	Local signal box instructions specific to the individual box which supplement or modify the general rules and regulations.
Fully Fitted	A goods train conveying vehicles all of which are fitted with the automatic brake controlled from the locomotive.
Ganger	A member of the permanent way department responsible for a gang of men and in some instances the maintenance of a section of line.

General Purpose Relief	A signalman who could be called upon to undertake any signalling duties in a given district.
Groundman Handsignalman	A competent person (usually a signalman) undertaking special duties such as the clipping of points and the hand signalling of trains during planned or emergency work.
Home Station	The location at which a railway employee was based.
Interrupter Track circuit interrupter	Device fitted to the rail of trap points which, when ruptured by the flange of a wheel permanently interrupts the operation of the track circuit, signifying that a train has been derailed.
Is Line Clear? Ask on Ask out Ask the road Asked Clear	The action of asking the next signal box to accept a train.
Light Engine	A locomotive travelling on its own with no vehicles attached.
Line Clear	The action of accepting a train. Position of the block indicator once a train has been accepted.
Missing the distant	Action of a train passing a distant signal showing caution and so braking, prepared to stop at the home signal. Phrase usually used in the context when the distant should have been cleared in time to give the train a clear run.
Off	A signal showing a proceed or clear indication.
On	A signal showing its most restrictive state (stop for a stop signal, caution for a distant signal).
On Line Train on Line Train Entering Section	The action of informing the next signal box that a train has entered the block section. Position of the block indicator.
Partially Fitted	A goods train conveying vehicles of which only a proportion, marshalled next to the locomotive, are fitted with the automatic brake (see Fitted Head).

Passing out Taking on	Achieving competence to be allowed to work a signal box without supervision.
Peg Peg Up Peg Over	Action of moving the block indicator to "Line Clear" or "Train on Line" positions (e.g. Peg Line Clear).
Pilotman	A competent person (usually a senior signalman) acting as a human staff for the safe passage of trains in either direction over a line during failure of equipment or when an adjacent line is out of use.
Pull Off	Action of pulling levers to clear signals to proceed.
Rest Day Relief	A signalman whose normal duties were to rotate on a roster providing individual weekdays off to a set number of signalmen in support of the normal working week.
Right Away	A handsignal given by raising one arm above the head to denote the instruction to depart.
Runner	An express passenger train not booked to call at a major station such as Newton Abbot.
Running Shunt	A shunt signal in a running line facing to the normal direction of traffic which has to be cleared to the proceed position before the main signal can be cleared to show proceed.
Sectional Appendix	A publication detailing the lines, signalling and special rules applicable to an area or division of the railway.
Six-foot	Space between up and down lines.
Slack Working	A simplified method of working reducing the actions required by the signalman.
Station Limits	The stretch of line between the outermost home signal and the most advanced starting signal controlled by the same signal box. In many instances no station, as such, existed within this area.
Stick Circuit	An electrical circuit driving a relay which, once energised, holds this state over a contact of the relay until such time as another condition disengages it.

Table C.2 of Sectional Appendix	A table in the Sectional Appendix which listed single lines worked under the control of a responsible person only.
Through the Road	Action of shunting or crossing a train from one running line to another either for regulating purposes or single line working.
Tickle Tickled	A minimal check (see checked).
Train Approaching bell signal	A special bell signal used where signal boxes are spaced close together and where a train needs to be offered forward before it enters the section in rear. The code is 1-2-1.
Train out of Section Clear Back Knock out Knocked out	The action of informing the signalman in rear that a train has arrived safely through the block section and is complete.
Train Register	A book provided in each signal box into which signalmen record the exchange of bell signals and train movements.
Unpeg Drop the Block	Action of moving or restoring the block indicator to "Normal".

Born and brought up in Kent, John Francis attended Maidstone Grammar School before joining the Southern Region of British Railways as a trainee signal engineer. An early boyhood interest in railways developed into a specific interest in signalling. This encompassed both the operational and engineering aspects of what is a vast railway subject in its own right. John's career has therefore seen him employed both as a signal engineer and as a signalman. He migrated to the West Country at the age of 19 to fulfil an ambition to work Western Region signal boxes but has since undertaken many roles in the signalling profession including returns to the signalling grades.

Back Cover:
Dainton Tunnel Signal Box in the small hours. (Author)